Proactive Strategies for Protecting Species

Proactive Strategies for Protecting Species

Pre-Listing Conservation and the Endangered Species Act

EDITED BY

C. Josh Donlan

UNIVERSITY OF CALIFORNIA PRESS

University of California Press, one of the most distinguished university presses in the United States, enriches lives around the world by advancing scholarship in the humanities, social sciences, and natural sciences. Its activities are supported by the UC Press Foundation and by philanthropic contributions from individuals and institutions. For more information, visit www.ucpress.edu.

University of California Press
Oakland, California

Library of Congress Cataloging-in-Publication Data

Proactive strategies for protecting species : pre-listing conservation and the Endangered Species Act / [edited by] C. Josh Donlan. — First edition.
pages cm
Includes bibliographical references and index.
ISBN 978-0-520-27688-8 (cloth : alk. paper) — ISBN 0-520-27688-4 (cloth : alk. paper)—ISBN 978-0-520-96049-7 (ebook)—ISBN 0-520-96049-1 (ebook)
1. United States. Endangered Species Act of 1973.
2. Conservation of natural resources—United States.
I. Donlan, C. Josh, 1972- author.
S930.P76 2015
639.9—dc23
2014039739

Manufactured in the United States of America

24 23 22 21 20 19 18 17 16 15
10 9 8 7 6 5 4 3 2 1

The paper used in this publication meets the minimum requirements of ANSI/NISO Z39.48–1992 (R 2002) (*Permanence of Paper*).

Contents

Contributors *ix*

Foreword *xiii*

Michael J. Bean

Preface *xvii*

PART ONE: INTRODUCTION AND PERSPECTIVES *1*

1. An Introduction to Pre-Listing Conservation *3*
   C. Josh Donlan and Catherine Rothacker
2. A Primer on Species Avoidance, Minimization, and Compensatory Mitigation under the US Endangered Species Act *14*
   Becca Madsen
3. Perspective: Endangered Species, the Desert Tortoise, and Job Creation *26*
   Myles Traphagen
4. Perspective: Renewable Energy and Endangered Species *36*
   Sean Kiernan

5. Perspective: The Challenges and Benefits of Pre-Listing Conservation Approaches to Military Readiness 43
Ryan Orndoff

6. Perspective: Stewardship over Regulation and Harnessing the Agricultural Sector for Species Conservation 52
Terry R. Fankhauser

7. Perspective: Forest Conservation and Private Landowners 61
Rhett Johnson and Mary Sniekus

PART TWO: DESIGNING PRE-LISTING CONSERVATION PROGRAMS 71

8. Pre-Listing Conservation: Law, Policy, and Pilot Projects 73
Ya-Wei Li and Timothy Male

9. A Primer on Biodiversity Measurement Systems 94
Bobby Cochran and Nicole Maness

10. A Landowner-Centered Approach to Incentivizing Participation in Pre-Listing Conservation Programs 105
Michael G. Sorice and Troy Abel

11. Market Models and Finance for Upstream Species Conservation 115
C. Josh Donlan, Abhishek Jain, and Barbara Müller

12. Tools to Promote Transparent and Efficient Markets for Species Conservation 131
Joanna Silver

13. The Role of Electronic Marketplaces in Scaling Environmental Markets 141
Michael Van Patten and Aaron Martin

PART THREE: CASE STUDIES 147

14. Prospects for Pre-Listing Conservation in Freshwater Ecosystems 149
Daniel A. Auerbach and Todd K. BenDor

15. The Greater Sage-Grouse, Energy Development, and Pre-Listing Conservation 167
Shauna Ginger, Sara Vickerman, and Bruce Taylor

16. The Gopher Tortoise, Military Readiness, and Pre-Listing Conservation 188
Todd Gartner, C. Josh Donlan, Michael G. Sorice, James Mulligan, Mary Snieckus, and Rhett Johnson

17. The Future of Pre-Listing Conservation Programs for Wildlife Conservation 219
Timothy Male and C. Josh Donlan

References 231
Index 257

Contributors

TROY D. ABEL
School of Visual Arts
Virginia Tech
Blacksburg, VA, 24061
tabel@vt.edu

DANIEL A. AUERBACH
Department of Ecology and Evolutionary Biology
Cornell University
Ithaca, NY 14853
auerbach.dan@gmail.com

MICHAEL J. BEAN
3821 Legation Street NW
Washington, DC 20015
michaeljbean@gmail.com

TODD K. BENDOR
Department of City and Regional Planning and UNC Institute for the Environment
University of North Carolina at Chapel Hill
New East Building, Campus Box #3140
Chapel Hill, NC 27599
bendor@unc.edu

BOBBY COCHRAN
Willamette Partnership
4640 SW Macadam Avenue, #50
Portland, OR 97239
cochran@willamettepartnership.org

C. JOSH DONLAN
Advanced Conservation Strategies
PO Box 1201
Midway, UT 84049
and
Department of Ecology & Evolutionary Biology
Cornell University
Corson Hall
Ithaca, NY 14853
jdonlan@advancedconservation.org

TERRY R. FANKHAUSER
Colorado Cattlemen's Association
8833 Ralston Road
Arvada, CO 80002
terry@coloradocattle.org

TODD GARTNER
World Resources Institute
10 G Street NE, Suite 800
Washington, DC 20002
tgartner@wri.org

SHAUNA GINGER
U.S. Fish and Wildlife Service
2600 SE 98th Avenue, Suite 100
Portland, OR 97266
shauna_ginger@fws.gov

ABHISHEK JAIN
Robert H. Smith School of Business
University of Maryland
College Park, MD 20742
jabhishek.in@gmail.com

RHETT JOHNSON
The Longleaf Alliance
12130 Dixon Center Road
Andalusia, AL 36420
rhett@longleafalliance.org

SEAN KIERNAN
SunEdison
600 Clipper Drive
Belmont, CA 94002
skiernan@sunedison.com

YA-WEI LI
Defenders of Wildlife
1130 17th Street NW
Washington, DC 20036
yli@defenders.org

BECCA MADSEN
Madsen Environmental
215 E. University Drive
Denton, TX 76209
bmadsen@madsenenvironmental.com

TIMOTHY MALE
Mission:Wildlife
7003 Woodland Avenue
Takoma Park, MD 20912
timothymale@gmail.com

NICOLE MANESS
Willamette Partnership
4640 SW Macadam Avenue, #50
Portland, OR 97239
manessn@willamettepartnership.org

AARON MARTIN
Mission Markets Inc.
394 Broadway, 6th Floor
New York, NY 10013
amartin@missionmarkets.com

BARBARA MÜLLER
Höflingerstrasse 10
Finkenstein, Austria 9584
babs_mueller@gmx.at

JAMES MULLIGAN
Green Community Ventures
P.O. Box 1401
Lamoille, NV 89828
james@greencommunityventures.org

RYAN ORNDORFF
Headquarters US Marine Corps
Marine Corps Installations Command
3000 Marine Corps, Pentagon
Washington, DC 20350
ryan.orndorff@usmc.mil

CATHERINE ROTHACKER
Advanced Conservation Strategies
2800 Quebec Street NW
Washington, DC 20008
catherine.rothacker@gmail.com

JOANNA SILVER
Markit Environmental
620 8th Avenue, 35th Floor
New York, NY 10018
joanna.silver@stitchbirdconsulting.com

MARY SNIECKUS
American Forest Foundation
1111 19th Street NW, Suite 780
Washington, DC 20036
msnieckus@gmail.com

MICHAEL G. SORICE
Virginia Tech
Blacksburg, VA 24061
msorice@vt.edu

BRUCE TAYLOR
Defenders of Wildlife
1880 Willamette Falls Drive, #200
West Linn, OR 97068
btaylor@defenders.org

MYLES B. TRAPHAGEN
Solar Biology LLC
2242 E. Copper Street
Tucson, AZ 85719
mbtrap@gmail.com

MICHAEL VAN PATTEN
Mission Markets Inc.
394 Broadway, 6th Floor
New York, NY 10013
mvp@missionmarkets.com

SARA VICKERMAN
Defenders of Wildlife
1880 Willamette Falls Drive, #200
West Linn, OR 97068
svickerman@defenders.org

Foreword

The US Endangered Species Act is a final backstop in the effort to prevent the extinction of wild plants and animals. If it fails, then our loss is permanent and irreversible. As the American naturalist Charles William Beebe memorably observed, "The beauty and genius of a work of art may be reconceived, though its first material expression be destroyed, a vanished harmony may yet again inspire the composer; but when the last individual of a race of living beings breathes no more, another heaven and another earth must pass before such a one can be again."

Beebe wrote those words in 1906, less than a decade before the last passenger pigeon took its last breath. Just under thirty years earlier, when Beebe was born in 1877, the passenger pigeon was still one of the most abundant vertebrates in North America. Before Beebe reached the midpoint in his life, it was gone. By the time Beebe died in 1962, the passenger pigeon had been joined in oblivion by the Carolina Parakeet and the Heath Hen, two other once common North American birds. Still others appeared headed toward the same fate, including the California Condor, the Whooping Crane, and—at least throughout much of its range—the nation's symbol, the Bald Eagle. Early in his life, Beebe had written that "to be a Naturalist is better than to be a King." Perhaps by the end of his life he may have felt that to be a naturalist was to be afflicted with a profound sense of loss.

Beebe did not live long enough to see the extraordinary recovery of the Bald Eagle, the successful breeding in captivity and reintroduction to the wild of the California Condor, or the steady rebuilding of the continent's tiny population of Whooping Cranes. He did not live long enough to see the enactment of the Endangered Species Act or the many conservation successes it made possible. Those many successes have instilled hope in those who came after Beebe and who share Beebe's passion for nature and his fascination with its creatures.

Hope and passion, however, are unlikely to be sufficient to arrest the continuing loss of biological diversity that the Endangered Species Act seeks to halt. For many species, the protections of the Endangered Species Act come very late in the game, when the odds are heavily stacked against success. If there is one clear lesson from the experience with the Endangered Species Act over the past four decades, it is that conservation efforts need to get started earlier, before plant and animal species reach the point at which they are at a high risk of extinction. In the language of this book, conservation efforts need to be started upstream of the Endangered Species Act.

The contributors to this volume explore a variety of ideas to incentivize upstream conservation efforts for species that are likely candidates for future Endangered Species Act protection. The focus on incentives is entirely appropriate. Nothing in the Endangered Species Act compels landowners—or anyone else for that matter—to refrain from activities that are detrimental to such species or to undertake activities that are beneficial to such species. That is, no regulatory or other legal protections attach to such species by virtue of the fact that they may someday become endangered. Unless and until they are formally designated as endangered or threatened, no duty of care is owed to them.

That no legal duty is owed to such species, however, only means that other conservation strategies must be employed to secure their well-being. Among the most promising of these are strategies that seek to align the objectives of conservation with the economic and other objectives that property owners have in owning and managing land or water resources. With that alignment, conservation efforts are more likely to be embraced and less likely to be resisted.

The contributors to this volume have diverse backgrounds, experiences, and perspectives. What they have in common is a recognition that more effective approaches to species conservation are needed and a willingness to be creative in searching for those more effective approaches. To the extent that they succeed in identifying workable new strategies upstream of the Endangered Species Act, we can look forward to continuing to enjoy our nation's natural heritage without the need to await the passing of another heaven and another earth.

Michael J. Bean, author with Melanie J. Rowland of
The Evolution of National Wildlife Law

Preface

Like many fun adventures, this book started with a new friendship. An introduction led to a few phone conversations, which led to a chat over a few beers, which led to a successful grant proposal, which led to an ambitious project focused on improving how the US Endangered Species Act works. This book is the result, and it would not have happened if Todd Gartner and I had not crossed paths back in 2010. I am grateful we did. I am even more grateful we had fun along the way.

Incentivizing biodiversity conservation prior to regulatory triggers is starting to receive more attention both in the United States and abroad. In 2012, the US Fish and Wildlife Service published an Advance Notice of Rulemaking in the Federal Register "inviting public comment to help us identify potential changes to our regulations that would create incentives for landowners and others to take voluntary conservation actions to benefit species that may be likely to become threatened or endangered species." Doing so in a responsible way would provide value to all parties: individuals whose actions have impacts on species, individuals who seek opportunities to create benefits for species, and the government agencies charged with managing species. Doing so in a responsible way would also result in conservation benefits for many species. Acting early, more often than not, is cheaper, more effective, and less contentious. This volume is the first of its kind that attempts to provide insights and guidance on creating voluntary programs that incentivize conservation actions "upstream" of regulation like the Endangered Species Act.

Many deserve thanks for supporting the efforts that made this book possible. First, I would like to thank everyone who contributed chapters; it is their efforts that make this volume what it is. Second, I would like to thank the funders: Wildlife Conservation Society through the Wildlife Action Opportunities Fund (established by support from the Doris Duke Charitable Foundation), Robert and Patricia Switzer Foundation, American Forest Foundation, US Department of Agriculture Natural Resources Conservation Service, Toyota Foundation, and Cornell University. Third, I would like to thank supporters and colleagues of my organization, Advanced Conservation Strategies. Our foundation is science, yet we work and collaborate outside of science to innovate and implement new solutions and ventures for environmental and sustainability challenges. We integrate behavioral economics, finance, human-centered design, markets, science, and technology to solve problems in novel ways. It is in this spirit that I took on this book project. Fourth, I would like to thank the many people who reviewed chapters or the entire book: P. Adams, D. Auerbach, M. Bailey, M. Bean, C. Braun, B. Cochran, T. Cutsinger, J. Goldstein, K. Hamilton, R. Johnson, S. Knick, J. Knott, B. Lee, R. Lave, J. Li, J. M. Scott, T. Montgomery, K. Norman, J. Serfis, R. Simmons, L. Smith, N. Thitt, D. Tulchin, M. Trap-hagen, and R. Victurine. I would also like to thank the many colleagues who have been stimulating "partners in crime" on thinking about new approaches to biodiversity conservation, in particular, Richard Cudney, Stefan Gelcich, Harry Greene, Kurt Holle, Jamie Mandel, Barbara Saavedra, Alfredo Sfeir, Mike Sorice, and Chris Wilcox. I also thank Gloria Luque for putting up with my mediocre Spanish and French, her friendship, and for being herself. Last, I would like to thank my editors, Blake Edgar, Merrik Bush, and Sheila Berg. All were a pleasure to work with, and their efforts improved the quality of this book.

I hope that this volume provides value to those interested in creating new solutions for biodiversity conservation. It attempts to provide insights from science, policy, and finance on the design of pre-listing conservation programs for at-risk species. This volume is also about people—people whose lives are touched by the Endangered Species Act and the species that it strives to protect. The diversity of perspectives and opinions of these stakeholders must be taken into account if biodiversity conservation incentive programs are going to succeed at the necessary scale. Whether you are in a classroom, boardroom, break room, or coffee shop, I hope you find value in *Proactive Strategies for Protecting Species.*

C. Josh Donlan
June 2014
Paris, France

PART ONE

Introduction and Perspectives

CHAPTER 1

An Introduction to Pre-Listing Conservation

C. JOSH DONLAN AND CATHERINE ROTHACKER

ABSTRACT

The US Endangered Species Act has been successful in preventing extinction. From other perspectives, however, it has underperformed, is fraught with challenges, and is in need of reform. At the forefront of challenges is a reactive framework that sometimes leads to perverse incentives and legal battles that strain support and resources. Given the challenges of species recovery, programs focused on conserving species before they require Endangered Species Act listing have the potential to provide conservation and economic benefits, including aligning the interests of project developers, private landowners, conservation advocates, and government agencies. Pre-listing conservation programs can complement and improve the performance of existing ESA programs by encouraging actions that achieve net conservation benefits for at-risk species upstream of costly regulation. However, strong incentives will be needed in order to do so at the scale needed. *Proactive Strategies for Protecting Species* explores the perspectives, opportunities, and challenges surrounding design and implementation of pre-listing conservation approaches to species conservation. The volume brings together diverse stakeholder perspectives across different sectors on at-risk species conservation and provides a legal, biological, sociological, financial, and technological foundation for designing solutions for incentivizing species conservation upstream of regulation. Last, it explores case studies of at-risk species that could benefit from pre-listing conservation approaches and discusses both the opportunities and challenges ahead. Properly designed and implemented, pre-listing conservation programs have the potential to deliver more funding for species conservation and stronger incentives for environmental stewardship on private lands.

INTRODUCTION

From the perspective of species extinction, the US Endangered Species Act (ESA) has been a success (Male and Bean 2005). Of the over two thousand species protected by the ESA, only ten have gone extinct after listing (Langpap and Kerkvliet 2010; USFWS 2014). Yet the ESA it is not without challenges and failures. For example, only thirty delistings have occurred (covering twenty-five species) declaring a species or population recovered (USFWS 2014a). At the forefront of the challenges facing the ESA is a reactive framework that often leads to perverse incentives and legal battles that strain support and take resources from programs that are already underfunded (Brook et al. 2003; Stokstad 2005). Between 2008 and 2012, the federal government defended more than 570 ESA-related lawsuits, which cost taxpayers more than $15 million in attorney fees alone (Hastings 2012). This spending is significant given that annual recovery plan implementation budgets for the US Fish and Wildlife Service (USFWS) are around $65 million (GAO 2005).[1] While citizen involvement and litigation play an important role in species protection (Brosi and Biber 2012), we suspect most people would welcome seeing fewer dollars spent in the courtroom and more on species recovery.

In September 2011, following an agreement with plaintiffs, the USFWS announced a six-year plan to review and address the more than 250 species listed as candidate species under the ESA (Environment News Service 2011). In addition to candidate species, the USFWS agreed to make ninety-day findings on more than six hundred citizen petitions for the protection of at-risk species over the next two years. Pursuant to

1. The National Marine Fisheries Service (NMFS) and the USFWS share the responsibility of implementing the ESA. The NMFS manages marine and anadromous species, while the USFWS manages land and freshwater species. Although this volume focuses on terrestrial and freshwater species, and subsequently the USFWS, much of its information is applicable to NMFS and the species it manages. For simplicity, we refer only to the USFWS in this volume. In most cases, however, the USFWS and the NMFS could be used interchangeably.

section 50 CFR 424.02 of the ESA, "candidate" means any species being considered by the Secretary of Interior or the Secretary of Commerce "for listing as an endangered or a threatened species, but not yet the subject of a proposed rule" (USFWS 2004). Candidate species are not subject to ESA legal protections. Many environmental proponents view the candidate status as a loophole that denies species the legal protection they deserve; some species have been on the candidate list for decades. Yet the USFWS commonly faces an overwhelming workload with an underfunded budget, due in part to a steady stream of petitions and legal challenges. The USFWS states the new plan for candidate species will make ESA implementation "less complex, less contentious, and more effective" (USFWS 2011d).

A strategic step toward making the ESA less complex, less contentious, and more effective is to create scalable incentive structures for conservation actions that benefit at-risk species prior to the regulatory triggers of the ESA. Doing so will create value for those species before they become threatened or endangered under the ESA, and may help preclude listing altogether. Prior to becoming ESA-listed, a species can be perceived as a low priority and thus have little influence on development and other land use decision making. Yet once a species is listed, it may be protected at great expense (figure 1.1). The result can be large sums spent on lawsuits, significant drains on agency capacity, and perverse incentives. Concern over potential land use prohibitions under the ESA can create incentives for private landowners to manage their land in ways that may harm species (Lueck and Michael 2003). Yet the majority of declining species in the United States reside largely on private lands (Groves et al. 2000). Incentive programs are needed that shift management for declining species on private lands from a perceived liability to an asset. Doing so "upstream" of costly regulation is the focus of this volume.

THE NEED FOR UPSTREAM SPECIES CONSERVATION

Programs focused on upstream conservation actions could provide the needed incentives to achieve net conservation benefits for candidate and other at-risk species. Such programs, which we refer to as pre-listing conservation (PLC), would provide at least five broad benefits. First, it would incentivize early conservation actions, which generally reduce the cost and difficulty of species recovery. Second, it would incentivize proactive habitat management, which is particularly important for the

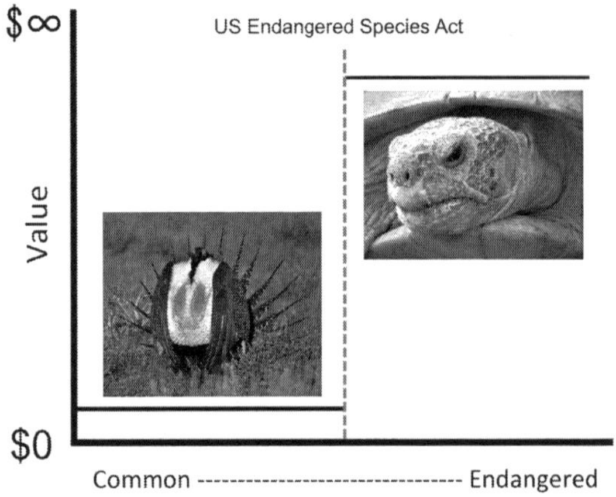

FIGURE 1.1. A simplified framework on how species are valued in the United States. Species have little influence on development and land use decision making until they become listed under the Endangered Species Act. Once listed, a species must be protected even, if it comes at great expense to individuals and society. This often results in conflict and perverse incentives. Increasing the value of species prior to becoming listed and creating incentives to preclude species from being listed would improve the value "landscape" of species conservation. See chapters 3 and 15 for perspectives on a candidate species, the Greater Sage-Grouse (*Centrocercus urophasianus*), and an ESA-listed species, the desert tortoise (*Gopherus agassizii*). © J. Stafford–USFWS and S. Dobrott.

majority of at-risk species that require active management to maintain viable populations (i.e., conservation-reliant species) (Scott et al. 2010). Third, it would facilitate more outcome-based programs compared to current ESA programs, since project developers could explicitly offset impacts *tomorrow* by funding PLC activities *today*. PLC outcomes could be evaluated and verified prior to impacts occurring. Fourth, successful PLC programs could reduce and possibly prevent the need to list some species. And fifth, PLC programs could mobilize new conservation funding and provide much-needed financial incentives for conservation on private lands.

Unlike many species conservation programs "downstream" of the ESA, PLC programs could provide value to all stakeholders involved. For those stakeholders that are having species impacts related to certain activities, participation in a PLC program provides a means of managing the risk of future regulation if a species becomes listed under the ESA. This form of insurance could provide regulatory predictability, saving time and resources if listing occurs. This case is applicable to many individuals and collectives across the US landscape today: the Department of Defense and its need to maintain military readiness, companies installing solar and wind energy infrastructure on public and private lands, oil and gas companies operating on public lands, and private and public agencies upgrading our nation's infrastructure. For those in the position to create additional benefits for at-risk species, PLC programs could provide a form of additional revenue in exchange for environmental stewardship. For private landowners, conservation nongovernmental organizations (NGOs), or for-profit enterprises, PLC programs could mobilize new funding for species conservation. And finally, for government agencies whose mandate it is to protect species and their habitats, PLC programs would provide an overarching framework to engage stakeholders and incentivize proactive management prior to species becoming officially protected under the ESA. If properly designed and executed, PLC programs could be a win-win for the species and all stakeholders.

While the ESA already provides a few tools that promote conservation action before listing, they often lack the financial support and regulatory predictability needed to sufficiently incentivize such voluntary actions. Candidate Conservation Agreements do not contain regulatory assurances or offer participants any guarantees about ESA obligations if species listing occurs. Habitat Conservation Plans do not legally require participants to recover species or achieve a net benefit standard, and they have not been implemented for nonlisted species alone (USFWS and NMFS 1996). Candidate Conservation Agreements with Assurances (CCAAs), the tool most relevant to PLC programs, encourage nonfederal landowners to conserve candidate species in exchange for a permit that authorizes certain adverse impacts to the species if it is listed (Li and Male this volume). By issuing a permit, the USFWS is in effect recognizing the benefits of voluntary conservation measures initiated before listing and allowing those benefits to offset certain post-listing adverse impacts. The use of CCAAs has been limited, however, with a total of twenty-five finalized since 1999. A number of factors have contributed to low CCAA participation, including a lengthy approval process and a lack of financial incentives (Bean 2005; Womack 2008). Further, the USFWS may require detailed information about future impacts in order to adequately evaluate the effects on the species within a CCAA.

Many individuals and institutions, however, cannot provide this information because of uncertainty regarding future actions. Thus new tools are needed that provide strong incentives and regulatory certainty for conservation actions taken for at-risk species before they become protected under the ESA.

In March 2012, the USFWS issued an Advance Notice of Proposed Rulemaking stating that it intends to "propose a rule to encourage landowners and other potentially regulated interests to fund or carry out voluntary conservation actions beneficial to candidate and other at-risk species by providing a new type of assurance that, in the event the species is listed, the benefits of appropriate voluntary conservation actions will be recognized as offsetting the adverse effects of activities carried out by that landowner or others after listing" (USFWS 2012). Public input across sectors has been positive to this approach. The purpose of this volume is to provide information and guidance in the process of designing, piloting, and scaling PLC programs. We hope this book provides value to the diverse set of people that are working toward second-generation approaches and solutions to species conservation. While the focus of the volume is species conservation in the United States, many of the chapters are applicable to species conservation outside of the United States.

ORGANIZATIONAL STRUCTURE

This volume strives to be pragmatic and solutions oriented. It builds on previous volumes that have examined incentives and endangered species conservation (Shogren 2005; Scott et al. 2006; Adler 2011). It does not embrace extremes: nowhere will you find calls to abolish the ESA, nor will you find the naive perspective that the ESA has no problems and needs no reform. Rather, we offer a diversity of perspectives on a fresh approach to species conservation. We have striven to provide insights on the tools needed to design successful PLC programs, tools from a variety of disciplines, including law, policy, biology, sociology, technology, and finance.

Proactive Strategies for Protecting Species takes a market perspective, for three important reasons (figure 1.2). First, the majority of stakeholders who would be involved in PLC programs operate in markets: the buying and selling of products or services. Thus it is a preferred and familiar mode of making transactions. Second, conservation incentive agreements that include direct payments are becoming increasingly com-

FIGURE 1.2. A pre-listing conservation (PLC) marketplace, where project developers proactively manage their environmental risk for at-risk species by purchasing credits generated through conservation measures by private landowners. In exchange for financing a net conservation benefit for an at-risk species, the project developer receives predictability on regulatory requirements if and when the species is ESA listed. The additional conservation dollars generated from the PLC marketplace serve as financial incentives for environmental stewardship on private lands. The gopher tortoise (*Gopherus polyphemus*), Lesser Prairie-Chicken (*Tympanuchus pallidicinctus*), and Greater Sage-Grouse (*Centrocercus urophasianus*) are three examples where a PLC marketplace could potentially provide net conservation benefits for at-risk species upstream of regulation. The Lesser Prairie-Chicken, however, was listed as threatened under the ESA in April 2014 (USFWS 2014b; see Male and Donlan this volume). © J. Womack and S. A. Cuomo–USAF, S. Fairbairn–USFWS, L. Lamsa, USFWS–Southeast.

mon due to a suite of potential advantages, including their voluntary nature and goal of efficiently compensating individuals for providing a public good (Jack et al. 2008; Milne and Niestan 2009). Programs that involve some value transfer mechanism (e.g., direct payments, technical assistance, or regulatory predictability) require some type of market structure. Third, placing PLC in a market perspective forces stakeholders to think about three programmatic aspects that are necessary for success at scale: supply, transactional infrastructure, and demand. One must understand the perspectives and incentives of the target stakeholders that are asked to supply benefits for at-risk species. Demand must be present for upstream conservation benefits for at-risk species to be produced, and the infrastructure must be present to quantify and verify those benefits. While some aspects of this volume focus on what many readers likely envision when they hear the word *market,* some sections do not. A market can take on a variety of different structures—an important point that should be kept in mind throughout this volume.

Proactive Strategies for Protecting Species is divided into three parts. This first part provides policy background and important perspectives on species conservation from different stakeholders. Part 2 provides insights on designing PLC programs. Part 3 presents three case studies and a forward-looking conclusion.

Part 1 begins with Becca Madsen's primer on species conservation under the ESA, setting the stage for designing and implementing PLC programs. Madsen explains how the ESA is triggered, what protections it affords, and the mitigation hierarchy that determines when PLC actions might be applicable. The remainder of part 1 is devoted to essays on sector-specific perspectives and the potential value of pre-listing conservation. With over a decade of on-the-ground experience, Myles Traphagen describes desert tortoise (*Gopherus agassizii*) conservation in the Mojave Desert under the ESA. Despite the massive resources being invested in desert tortoise conservation, the business as usual situation can be summarized like this: great for jobs, not so great for the desert tortoise. Traphagen provides unique insight into the complexities and daunting challenges of endangered species recovery. The next two chapters focus on the potential demand for PLC programs and markets: the renewable energy sector and the military. Renewable energy (e.g., solar and wind) companies are investing billions in the United States, in some locations where at-risk species are present; and the Department of Defense is striving to balance base consolidation and military readiness with environmental sustainability, including species conservation. Sean Kiernan of SunEdison and Ryan Orndoff of the US Marine Corps provide perspectives on the challenges they face with regard to endangered species protection and the potential value of PLC approaches. The final two chapters in this part offer perspectives from potential suppliers of PLC markets: private forest landowners and ranchers. Terry Fankhauser of the Colorado Cattlemen's Association discusses the potential role of ranchers in providing species benefits and the approaches needed to realize those benefits. Rhett Johnson and Mary Snieckus discuss the importance of their perspectives on aspects of PLC programs before design is undertaken of initiatives to incentivize species conservation on private lands. All these perspectives are important, especially since much evidence suggests that successful program design relies heavily on empathy: designing programs that take into account the perspectives of its stakeholders (Brown 2009).

Part 2 focuses on program design, discussing the legal, biological, sociological, financial, and technological aspects of PLC programs. In chapter 8, Ya-Wei Li and Timothy Male of Defenders of Wildlife provide the legal and policy foundation for PLC programs. Importantly, they demonstrate how the USFWS can use existing authority under the ESA to approve PLC projects and how agreements and conferences could be structured during the approval process. They provide a clear policy road map for establishing pilot projects. In chapter 9, Bobby Cochran and Nicole Maness of the Willamette Partnership offer a primer on biodiversity measurement systems. They discuss the common components and requisites that are involved in designing the tools needed to quantify biodiversity benefits within incentive and market-based conservation programs. In chapter 10, building on human-centered design approaches (Brown 2008), Michael Sorice and Troy Abel of Virginia Tech advocate a landowner-centered approach to designing incentive programs. They make a convincing argument that PLC programs in which program administrators directly involve private landowners in the design process will better recognize the social and ecological complexity of recovering at-risk species and result in greater participation. In chapter 11, Josh Donlan and colleagues examine potential market structures and finance for PLC programs. Using the gopher tortoise (*Gopherus polyphemus*) as an example, the authors provide a financial analysis of PLC credits that suggests that the approach can be more cost-effective than mitigation downstream of the ESA. In the last chapters in this part, Joanna Silver (Markit) and Michael Van Pattern (Mission Markets) discuss the role of technology in providing efficient and transparent transactional infrastructure in environmental markets. Silver discusses the important role of registries in markets, as well as alternative transaction platforms such as auctions and introductory platforms. Van Patten provides a complementary perspective by discussing how the use of transaction platforms and exchange technology can help increase visibility and access for businesses wishing to engage in actions to reduce their net environmental impact. Van Patten makes the argument that without mechanisms like exchanges and centralized marketplaces, most environmental markets will remain opaque and underutilized by major stakeholders.

Part 3 presents three case studies in the context of PLC programs that capture both the barriers these initiatives have encountered and the successes they have achieved thus far. Daniel Auerbach and Todd BenDor discuss how proactive conservation approaches and mitigation are being applied in freshwater ecosystems. They draw on the challenges and successes of several freshwater case studies to provide recommendations for maximizing PLC's full potential in aquatic ecosystems. Shauna Ginger (USFWS) and colleagues (Defenders of Wildlife) explore the challenges and opportunities surrounding the Greater Sage-Grouse (*Centrocercus urophasianus*) and PLC approaches. As energy development continues to expand in the western United States, market and mitigation approaches are likely to play a larger role in conservation strategies for sagebrush ecosystems. Integrating PLC approaches with a landscape-scale conservation strategy that functions across states with different regulations and policies will be both challenging and critical. Ginger and colleagues provide a preliminary road map for doing so. Todd Gartner (World Resources Institute) and colleagues provide a detailed PLC case study on the gopher tortoise. The authors discuss the lesson learned from their efforts to design and implement the first market-based PLC program: a candidate conservation banking pilot program focused on the gopher tortoise in the southeastern United States. Last, Timothy Male and Josh Donlan look forward to the immediate and future opportunities for PLC programs in the United States and abroad.

PROACTIVE STRATEGIES FOR PROTECTING SPECIES

With no major revisions to the ESA in over twenty-five years, the law is in desperate need of reform (Male 2014a). Science-based tools should be used to guide listing decisions; instead, private, citizen-driven lawsuits are currently playing that role. Similarly, politics are heavily influencing how funding is allocated to species listed under the ESA: a few species, like salmon and steelhead trout, receive the overwhelming majority of dollars while hundreds of species receive little to no money for recovery efforts. Other countries, like New Zealand and Australia, are taking a more apolitical and transparent approach that focuses on saving as many species per dollar invested as possible (Joseph et al. 2009; Male 2014b). Clear, science-based criteria are needed to consistently define the terms *threatened, endangered,* and *recovered* (Harris et al. 2011). More effort needs to be devoted to accelerating recovery as opposed to preventing declines; a "net benefit" standard should be adopted when appropriate (Male 2014a; see Li and Male this volume).

PLC programs can contribute to these needed reforms. They can provide a science-based framework for species conservation action prior to lawsuits. They can create new revenue streams that are species-specific and nonfungible with respect to special interests (e.g., PLC dollars for the Greater Sage-Grouse could not be spent on the gopher tortoise). PLC's outcome-based framework would encourage science-based, consistent definitions of ESA terminology, mentioned above, and conservation actions could be assessed for impact (e.g., "net conservation benefit") before a transaction is fully executed (e.g., delivery of payment or regulatory predictability). PLC can facilitate and contribute to all of these ESA improvements, and it would do so upstream of regulatory triggers.

Incentivizing conservation of at-risk species is quickly becoming a priority in the United States and elsewhere. Doing so on private lands is particularly important since the majority of the habitat of at-risk species is found there. Properly designed and implemented, PLC programs can deliver net conservation benefits and align stakeholder interests. We hope that this volume provides a solid foundation and road map for implementing PLC programs for the many at-risk species that could benefit from upstream conservation approaches. PLC programs would at minimum provide uplift for candidate and at-risk species not yet listed. At best they would preclude the need for listing altogether. They could also help shift the current conservation models to more proactive frameworks that provide flexibility to developers while rewarding private landowners for conservation actions. Species protection needs more funding and stronger incentives for environmental stewardship on private lands. PLC programs can deliver both. The time for proactive strategies for protecting species is now.

CHAPTER 2

A Primer on Species Avoidance, Minimization, and Compensatory Mitigation under the US Endangered Species Act

BECCA MADSEN

ABSTRACT

Passed by Congress in 1973, the US Endangered Species Act outlines a formal process for granting a species federal protection. A 1982 revision provided for a permitting process to allow judicious incidental take under certain conditions. The US Fish and Wildlife Services and National Marine Fisheries Service regulate incidental take under section 7 of the Endangered Species Act for federal agencies or those whose activities coincide with those of federal agencies. When a federal nexus and federal agencies are not involved, incidental take permits are regulated under section 10 of the Endangered Species Act. Like many natural resource laws, the Endangered Species Act draws from a theoretical framework, often referred to as the mitigation hierarchy, to inform the permitting of exemptions to actions that would normally be prohibited. Once an incidental take permit is granted, minimization and mitigation activities are still required. Avoidance, minimization, and mitigation measures are considered appropriate when they are based on the needs of the species. In general, minimization and mitigation activities are conducted by (1) the permit applicant or a consultant hired by the applicant, (2) a local or regional entity connected to a Habitat Conservation Plan, or (3) an operator of a species conservation bank.

INTRODUCTION

Green energy has arrived on the island of Maui. In August 2012, more than sixty wide-load trucks traversed the Mokulele Highway with bits and pieces of eight turbines for the Auwahi Wind Farm. This 21-megawatt wind energy project, however, is not without environmental impacts (Stephens 2012). The project site is home to a number of endangered species: the Hawaiian Petrel (*Pterodroma sandwichensis*), the Hawaiian Goose (*Branta sandvicensis*), the Hawaiian hoary bat (*Lasiurus cinereus semotus*), and the Blackburn's sphinx moth (*Manduca blackburni*). The development of the wind farm will result in the degradation of the moth's habitat and create the potential for bird and bat collisions with wind turbines. Before construction could begin, the project developer had to apply for an incidental take permit to the US Fish and Wildlife Service (USFWS) under the requirements of the US Endangered Species Act (ESA). A permit requires an on-site study of the endangered species present and potential project impacts, as well as the drafting of a Habitat Conservation Plan that outlines measures to avoid, minimize, and mitigate impacts on the species (Auwahi Wind Energy 2011). The wind energy company will spend over $150,000 on species conservation, including non-native predator management, habitat restoration, a conservation easement, and research. It will also contribute funds to Haleakala National Park's Hawaiian Goose and Hawaiian Petrel recovery programs (Sempra 2012). These events illustrate some of the fundamental aspects of endangered species conservation and mitigation driven by the ESA. Here, I provide a brief primer on the ESA and its regulatory requirements. My goal is to provide a foundation for understanding and exploring opportunities in the context of pre-listing conservation programs that strive to incentivize conservation actions upstream of the ESA.

Two agencies are responsible for implementing and enforcing the ESA: the USFWS, which has jurisdiction over terrestrial species, and the National Marine Fisheries Service, which has jurisdiction over marine species and anadromous fish (e.g., salmon). For convenience, I use "USFWS" to refer to both.

Passed by Congress in 1973, the ESA outlines a formal process for granting a species federal protection (USFWS 2004) (box 2.1). The ESA prohibits the take of endangered or threatened species, which are defined respectively as "any species which is in danger of extinction throughout all or a significant portion of its range" and "any species which is likely to become an endangered species within the foreseeable future throughout all or a significant portion of its range" (USFWS 2004). The term *take* refers to any action that would harass, harm, pursue, hunt, shoot, wound, kill, trap, capture, or collect a listed species. Even without lethal intent, common actions like construction and agricultural activities can result in what is termed an incidental take of a species. Originally, the ESA absolutely prohibited take. A 1982 revision provided for a permitting process to allow judicious incidental take under certain conditions (Wilhere 2009). The USFWS regulates incidental take under section 7 for federal agencies or those whose activities coincide with those of federal agencies, which is referred to as a federal nexus. A federal nexus extends to applicants who are using federal funds or applying for a permit from another federal agency. For example, development projects that impact wetlands and require a permit from the US Army Corps of Engineers would then also require an incidental take authorization under section 7 of the ESA if endangered species were present at the site. When a federal nexus or federal agencies are not involved, incidental take permits are regulated under section 10 of the ESA.

Like many natural resource laws, the ESA draws from a theoretical framework often referred to as the mitigation hierarchy to inform the permitting of exemptions to actions that would normally be prohibited. The mitigation hierarchy can be summarized as avoidance, minimization, rehabilitation (or restoration), and compensatory mitigation (i.e., biodiversity offsets). The mitigation hierarchy seeks to prevent or minimize negative impacts by allowing offset activities only as a last resort for unavoidable impacts after other activities in the hierarchy have been undertaken (Madsen et al. 2010). Before allowing compensatory mitigation, project developers must demonstrate that they have taken steps to avoid, minimize, and rehabilitate impacts to a natural resource. Under the ESA, a permit may be granted only if doing so does not "appreciably reduce the likelihood of the survival and recovery of the species in the wild" (USFWS and NMFS 1996).

INCIDENTAL TAKE PERMITS: TRIGGERS AND REGULATORY REQUIREMENTS

One important difference between sections 7 and 10 permits is that under section 7 federal agencies (and those with a federal nexus) are technically allowed to avoid and minimize impacts only with respect to

Box 2.1. Listing under the US Endangered Species Act (ESA)

"Listing" refers to the process of a species being put on the Endangered and Threatened Species list (USFWS 2013a). Listing and its associated activities are complex.

- The US Fish and Wildlife Service (USFWS) formally reviews whether or not a species should be listed under the ESA after (1) it decides to undertake its own review, (2) it receives a citizen petition, or (3) it declares a limited-time emergency designation.
- Whatever the instigation, the USFWS has to decide within 90 days whether there should be a full review. After full review, which is officially less than one year, the USFWS is supposed to decide whether or not to list the species. There are currently over 2,000 plant and animal species on the ESA list.
- Another ~200 species are candidate species, that is, "plants and animals for which the USFWS has sufficient information on their biological status and threats to propose them as endangered or threatened under the ESA, but for which development of a proposed listing regulation is precluded by other higher priority listing activities" (USFWS 2011a).
- The ESA requires that the USFWS designate geographic areas "essential to the conservation" of listed species. However, less than half of listed species have critical habitat designated (USFWS 2011b, 2013a).
- The USFWS is responsible for writing and implementing species recovery plans, which detail the steps needed to recover an endangered species to a state where it can be removed from the ESA. Over 1,000 species recovery plans have been written.

the mitigation hierarchy. While section 7 guidance states "it is not appropriate to require mitigation for the impacts of incidental take," in practice compensatory mitigation is implemented as *conservation measures* (USFWS and NMFS 1998). Under section 7, the USFWS may propose *reasonable and prudent alternatives* to a proposed federal agency action if the USFWS deems that the project may jeopardize an endangered species. These alternatives amount to activities that avoid and minimize impacts to the species. Some examples are moving a planned road away from an endangered species' breeding location, postponing construction activities until after an endangered species' breeding season, and modifying the operation of hydroelectric dams that block

Box 2.2. The US Fish and Wildlife Services Index of Federal Register notices reveals the inner workings of incidental take permits by archiving notices of availability, receipts of permit application, requests for comments, and permit authorizations (USFWS 2013d)

All of these documents demonstrate development impacts on endangered species. Typical activities include utility projects, transportation development, forestry, agriculture, and residential and commercial development. Below are some example activities that could trigger a consultation under the US Endangered Species Act.

- A Texas electric utility company that will impact multiple species across the state during construction, operation, and maintenance of various facilities (e.g., electric transmission and distribution lines).
- Timber harvesting on several hundred acres in South Carolina that could impact the Red-cockaded Woodpecker.
- A Missouri wind energy project that could impact the endangered Indiana bat.
- A Texas county government applying for an incidental take permit for multiple species and various impacts due to construction and maintenance in their jurisdiction.
- Construction of five miles of a potable water pipeline by a regional water district in California that could impact the coastal California gnatcatcher.

endangered fish migration. In contrast, section 10 requires that those with permits must "to the maximum extent practicable, minimize and mitigate the impacts" (USFWS 2004). For example, a section 10 incidental take permit might highlight measures to minimize take but then allow conservation activities that mitigate (i.e., offset) take within a Habitat Conservation Plan.

A variety of activities can trigger a section 7 or section 10 consultation (box 2.2). The first step in determining whether the ESA is triggered is to study whether an action may have the potential to impact endangered species. Under section 7, a federal agency consults with USFWS to determine whether their actions are likely to adversely affect an endangered species. The section 7 consultation process is conducted to ensure that the activity does not jeopardize the continued existence or recovery

TABLE 2.1 EXAMPLES OF TYPICAL MINIMIZATION MEASURES UNDER SECTION 7 AND TYPICAL MITIGATION MEASURES UNDER SECTION 10 OF THE US ENDANGERED SPECIES ACT

Section 7 Minimization Measures	Section 10 Mitigation Measures
• To minimize effects of grazing on listed aquatic species, monitoring and potentially implementing livestock exclusions on a stream in Tonto National Forest, Arizona. • Monitoring and implementing various avoidance and protection measures for the Indiana bat (*Myotis sodalis*) during forest harvesting and prescribed burns in Monongahela National Forest, West Virginia. • Enhancing species viability, improving in-stream flow, and improving water quality for impacts of a hydroelectric dam in the Klamath River.	• Purchasing mitigation bank credits for habitat impacts and funding activities to divert potential migratory bird impacts to mitigate an electric utility's impacts on multiple species in 100 counties in Texas. • Establishing a new breeding group of Red-Cockaded Woodpeckers (*Picoides borealis*) to offset impacts from timber harvesting in South Carolina. • Establishing a 200+ acre conservation easement on breeding habitat and implementing restoration activities for wind project impacts on the Indiana bat in Ohio.

of a listed species and does not result in the destruction or adverse modification of a species' critical habitat. If the consultation concludes with a biological opinion finding of *no jeopardy* and *no adverse modification,* then the action can proceed provided the permittee complies with the terms and conditions of the incidental take statement (USFWS and NMFS 1998). If the proposed action is likely to adversely affect a species and hence requires formal consultation, then the action agency "must comply with the reasonable and prudent measures and implementing terms and conditions in the Services' incidental take statement to avoid potential liability for any incidental take" (USFWS and NMFS 1998). For federal agencies conducting activities that may impact endangered species, the incidental take statement details nondiscretionary *reasonable and prudent measures* to minimize impact (table 2.1).

For nonfederal actors, a section 10 consultation is triggered when a listed species inhabits or has known habitat in the area where a planned development may involve take. If the development will not involve species take or impact habitat, then no permitting is required. If habitat is unoccupied, there is no penalty for impacting the habitat, but the landowner must prove to the USFWS that the land is unoccupied. In addition, there is no take of species and therefore no permitting needed if land uses do not alter or disturb habitat. Nonpermitted take can result in civil and criminal penalties, including a fine of up to $50,000 per violation (Gilliland and Mays 2003; USFWS and NMFS 1996).

Section 10 of the ESA provides an exemption to the no-take rule via an incidental take permit for landowners who want to develop property with endangered species present. Section 10 exemptions are allowed if the following conditions are met:

- The taking of federally listed species is incidental to otherwise lawful activities.
- The taking is minimized and mitigated to the maximum extent practicable.
- Adequate funding for a conservation plan is ensured.
- The taking will not appreciably reduce the likelihood of the survival and recovery of the species in the wild.
- Other measures required by the USFWS deemed necessary and appropriate for the purposes of the conservation plan are met. (USFWS 2004)

To receive a section 10 incidental take permit, the applicant must develop a Habitat Conservation Plan (HCP) that describes (1) the likely impacts of the development, (2) the steps taken to avoid and minimize species impacts, (3) alternative actions considered, and (4) the compensatory mitigation activities planned and the funding available to implement those activities. The other components of the permit application are an Implementation Agreement and a draft National Environmental Policy Act (NEPA) analysis. The Implementation Agreement legally obligates both the permittee and the USFWS to fulfill the terms of the HCP. The draft NEPA analysis outlines alternative actions considered. The result of the NEPA analysis may indicate that no further NEPA review is required, referred to as a categorical exclusion if land uses have no significant environmental effect. Alternatively, the analysis may indicate the need for further research and analysis via an Environmental Assessment or an Environmental Impact Statement.

HCPs and associated NEPA documents go through a formal review process by the USFWS that includes open public comment periods. After all steps are completed, the USFWS may authorize an incidental take permit. With this permit, the developer or landowner is granted exemption for any incidental take that may arise so long as practices outlined in the HCP are followed. HCPs can last from five to fifty years. Along with the assurance of no penalty for take incidental to approved activities, a benefit of the incidental take permit is the *no surprises* assurance, which was added to the ESA during a 1994 rulemaking. This essentially provides long-term regulatory certainty by stipulating the maximum amounts of management and conservation activities, as well as financial commitment, in exchange for the incidental take permit (USFWS 2004; USFWS and NMFS 1996).

AVOIDANCE, MINIMIZATION, AND COMPENSATORY MITIGATION UNDER THE ESA

Once an incidental take permit is granted, minimization and mitigation activities are still required. Section 7 of the ESA explicitly emphasizes the minimization of take. The incidental take statement associated with a section 7 permit includes an account of "those reasonable and prudent measures that the Secretary considers necessary or appropriate to minimize such impact" (USFWS and NMFS 1998). The many activities associated with section 7 impacts are technically minimization measures, even off-site habitat conservation or purchase of credits from a conservation bank (see figure 2.1). Examples of minimization activities under section 7 are education of employees about the species, reduction of predation pressure, translocation or avoidance of the species, and monitoring (USFWS and NMFS 1998).

The term *mitigation* is not explicitly defined in the ESA; however, examples are given for "mitigation and enhancement measures . . . including, but not limited to, live propagation, transplantation, and habitat acquisition and improvement, as are necessary and appropriate to minimize the adverse effects of the agency action upon the endangered species, threatened species, or critical habitat concerned" (USFWS 2004). The USFWS defines mitigation as "actions that reduce or address potential adverse effects of a proposed activity on species included in [a Habitat Conservation Plan]" (USFWS and NMFS 1996).

In addition to requiring minimization measures, section 10 allows for mitigation activities (table 2.1). A section 10 application requires an HCP, which includes "steps the applicant will take to minimize and mitigate such impacts" (USFWS 2004). Mitigation measures can be developed to address permanent habitat loss or other types of species disturbances. Some examples of mitigation follow.

- Payment into an established conservation fund or bank.
- Preservation (via acquisition or conservation easement) of existing habitat.
- Enhancement or restoration of degraded habitat.
- Establishment of buffer areas around existing habitat.
- Modifications of land use practices.
- Restrictions on land access.

Avoidance, minimization, and mitigation measures are considered appropriate by the USFWS when they are based on the needs of the species (USFWS and NMFS 1996). If available, species recovery plans provide a basis for determining those needs; they provide a prescription for preserving and restoring habitat and addressing species threats in order to facilitate recovery. When impacts to endangered species are allowed under section 7 or section 10 permits, these are the actions that developers are asked to do as minimization or mitigation. In general, minimization and mitigation activities are conducted by (1) the permit applicant or a consultant hired by the applicant, (2) a local or regional entity connected to an HCP, or (3) an operator of a species conservation bank (EDF 1999; Fox and Nino-Murcia 2005) (see figure 2.1). These actors mirror the actors involved with wetland and stream mitigation under the US Clean Water Act (e.g., permittee-responsible mitigation, in-lieu fee programs, and wetland banking) (Auerbach and Bendor this volume; Madsen et al. 2010).

Minimization and mitigation measures conducted by the permitee can be timely and costly (Kiernan this volume). Under section 10, applicants must create an HCP, which includes a mitigation plan. The development of an HCP can take up to two years and usually entails hiring a team of experts (Gilliland and Mays 2003). HCPs also require a financial plan and dedicated funds for mitigation and monitoring. Costs can range from thousands of dollars for HCPs mitigating take from residential construction to hundreds of millions of dollars for regional HCPs covering hundreds of thousands of acres (Riverside County 2004; East Contra Costa County 2006). Under section 7, applicants may conduct minimization measures themselves or request that the USFWS carry out the activities so long as the action agency covers the costs. Section 10 applicants also may have the option to contribute payments to government agencies or organizations like the US National Fish and Wildlife Fund to mitigate the effects of habitat destruction. This payment option may be a convenient means to fulfill mitigation requirements, but applicants are still required to undergo the lengthy and costly process of developing an HCP.

A popular mitigation pathway under section 10 is the use of programmatic HCPs, which are similar to in-lieu fee programs that are common in wetland mitigation. Under an in-lieu fee program, a permittee pays a fee to a government or nonprofit entity that is responsible for the program. In return for this contribution, the permittee is absolved of the regulatory requirements. The administrator of the in-lieu fee program creates a landscape-scale plan for mitigation and uses funds collected to undertake mitigation activities. For wetlands mitigation, in-lieu fee programs are often preferred over permittee-responsible mitigation because of the potential for larger-scale restoration with landscape connectivity (DOD and EPA 2008). In addition to the biological benefits, programmatic HCPs can provide a more efficient process for landowners. For example, a regional HCP can be developed to replace multiple individual HCPs for development projects within a county. Developers can operate under the regional HCP by agreeing to follow certain land management practices and paying a mitigation fee. Those fees are used for acquisition of habitat, management, and other conservation activities. Cities, counties, coalitions of government agencies, and citizen groups can establish programmatic HCPs for a defined geographic region.

Species conservation banking is the third option for fulfilling regulatory obligations for endangered species mitigation under section 10 (figure 2.1). A conservation bank is a site where endangered species habitat has been restored, enhanced, and preserved for the purpose of providing credits that can be purchased as a form of compensatory mitigation (Fox and Nino-Murcia 2005; Carroll et al. 2008). Like wetland banking, species conservation banking strives to provide conservation in perpetuity with a required nonwasting endowment fund (Madsen et al. 2010). Credit purchase absolves the section 10 permit applicant from further maintenance or monitoring requirements. Unlike wetland mitigation banking, however, regulations for species conservation banking have not been codified; they currently exist only as policy guidance (USFWS 2003b). There are currently over one hundred species conservation banks in the United States (Madsen et al. 2011). The USFWS has promoted conservation banks as a mitigation strategy, stating "[conservation banking] has considerable promise as a mitigation strategy because 1) it allows owners of endangered species habitat to derive

Definition: Species conservation banking is in-kind, off-site mitigation in which multiple projects with like impacts are mitigated for at the same location—a conservation bank. Conservation banking is based on the idea that conserving large tracts of high quality habitat provides greater conservation benefits that multiple single mitigation projects that are smaller in scope.

Pros: All species conservation bank credits are created in advance of impacts. Conservation banks are permanently protected and include a non-wasting endowment fund for management activities to maintain the species.

Cons: Conservation banking does not have a stated "no net loss" principle, but rather a species recovery goal. There are not yet official regulations for conservation banking, only agency guidance.

Species conservation bank credits: Credits are primarily created through preservation and management of habitat. The unit of credit is most often an acre of habitat. Occasionally, due to specific-specific biology, the unit may be a breeding pair or combination of habitat and species. In the case of aquatic species, the unit may be a liner foot of riparian habitat.

Acreage under conservation: As of 2011, species conservation banks made up a total of 74,807 acres.

Volume of annual credit sales: $200 million.

Species conservation bank credit pricing:
National Range: $2,500 - $300,000
Median: $15,000
Average: $31,683

Status of US Conservation Banks, 2011

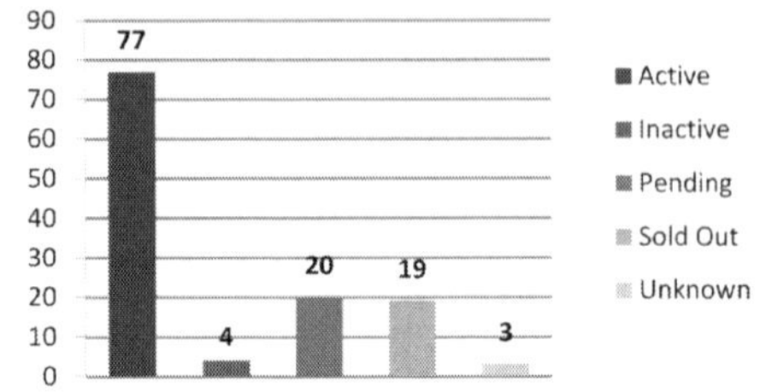

Location of US Conservation Banks, 2011

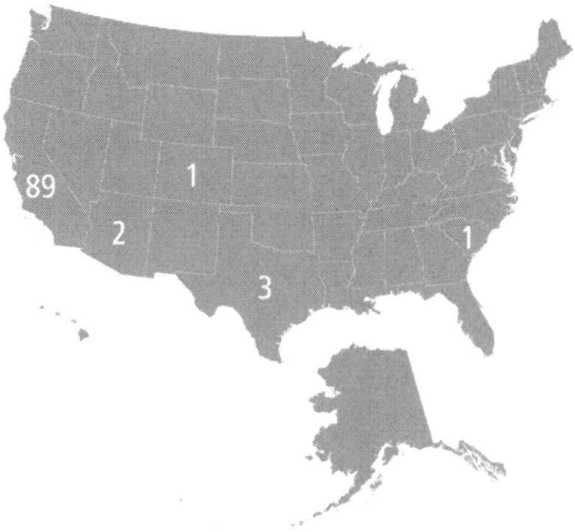

Species	Credit Price Range
California red legged frog (*Rana draytonii*)	$15,000–$90,000
Fairy shrimp (*Branchinecta lynchi*)	$150,000–$300,000
Golden-cheeked warbler (*Dendroica chrysoparia*)	$2,750–$7,000
Gopher tortoise (*Gopherus polyphemus*) -credit -relocation	 $12,000–$20,000 $1,500–$3,000
Salmonids (*Salmonidae*)	$80,000–$120,000
San Joaquin kit fox (*Vulpes macrotis mutica*)	$2,500–$15,000
Utah prairie dog (*Cynomys parvidens*)	$1,836

FIGURE 2.1. Summary of species conservation banking in the United States. Reproduced with permission from Forest Trends' Ecosystem Marketplace.
SOURCE: Madsen et al. 2010, 2011.

economic value from their land as habitat, 2) it allows parties with mitigation obligations to meet their obligations rapidly (mitigation lands are simply purchased as credits), and 3) the mitigation lands are provided prior to the impact (eliminating uncertainty about whether a permittee might fail to fulfill the HCP's obligations after the impact has occurred)" (USFWS and NMFS 1996). California has by far the greatest number of conservation banks (see figure 2.1). This is due, in part, to stringent state endangered species regulations and a large number of federally listed endangered species. Conservation banks have historically been focused on terrestrial endangered species; however, banks focused on aquatic species have emerged in recent years (Madsen et al. 2010; Auerbach and Bendor this volume).

CHAPTER 3

Perspective: Endangered Species, the Desert Tortoise, and Job Creation

MYLES B. TRAPHAGEN

ABSTRACT

The Mojave population of the desert tortoise (*Gopherus agassizii*) is a threatened species that was listed in 1989 as a Distinct Population Segment under the US Endangered Species Act. Since 1980, over one thousand publications have been produced on the desert tortoise, and a minimum of $300 million has been spent by federal, state, and municipal government agencies on desert tortoise conservation. Despite this body of scientific knowledge and monetary effort, experts believe the population is still declining. No accurate estimate of the population exists, and confidence in existing methods for surveying the desert tortoise is low. With the advent of renewable energy projects on public land in the southwestern United States, desert tortoise conservation and recovery will become even more daunting in the coming decade. Mitigation strategies and efforts to date have underperformed. Without significant changes, it is likely that the millions of dollars that will be spent on the desert tortoise in the name of renewable energy projects in the coming decade will not result in any conservation uplift or benefit for the species.

INTRODUCTION

During the height of fiscal political discussions, Vice President Joe Biden led an effort to identify and eliminate wasteful federal spending. In doing so, he took a shot at the desert tortoise (*Gopherus agassizii*). In a June 2011 message on the White House website titled "There's a New Sheriff in Town," Biden stated, "And I bet you didn't know that your tax dollars pay for a website dedicated to the desert tortoise. I'm sure it's a wonderful species, but we can't afford to have a standalone site devoted to every member of the animal kingdom" (Danelski and Goad 2011). Unbeknownst to the vice president, the desert tortoise was, in fact, the only species to enjoy its own government website (www.desertortoise.gov), and it even has its own iPhone application. Not even our country's flagship species—the bald eagle—has such a technological presence. While shutting down a website dedicated to an endangered species will do little to reduce federal spending, the desert tortoise serves as perhaps our best example of the challenges and complexities of endangered species recovery in the United States.

THE DESERT TORTOISE INDUSTRY

Since 2004, the US Fish and Wildlife Service (USFWS) has maintained a dedicated Desert Tortoise Recovery Office that employs four full-time biologists charged with "focusing exclusively on research, monitoring, recovery plan implementation, and associated recovery permitting, rather than on regulation." The Recovery Office strives to facilitate increased scientific understanding and improved recovery progress by increasing research activities outlined in the 2011 Revised Recovery Plan for the Mojave population of the desert tortoise (USFWS 2011e). In addition to government programs, numerous nongovernmental organizations have contributed to the recovery effort. For the past thirty-eight years, the Desert Tortoise Council has produced an annual symposium attended by two hundred to three hundred people. These symposiums provide a forum for the latest scientific research and public policy. Documentaries have been made on the tortoise, and mascots have been born, like Mojave Max, the "spokestortoise" for the Clark County Desert Conservation Program. Max is based on an actual desert tortoise who lives at the Desert Tortoise Conservation Center near Las Vegas, Nevada, and whose spring emergence is celebrated as the desert counterpart of Groundhog Day.

The 6.5 million acres of desert tortoise critical habitat have created an industry: a boom of seasonal commercial activity from which thousands of people make their livelihoods (figure 3.1). An army of biologists spends their days in the field conducting desert tortoise surveys and monitoring. That army is supported by an unseen crew of administrative personnel tasked with overseeing permitting, reporting, and archiving of data. The industry has employed thousands of people in numerous government agencies, nonprofit organizations, consulting firms, and self-employed "bio-gypsies" who migrate to the desert Southwest to perform seasonal work, not unlike commercial fishermen pursuing the annual run of salmon. Many people are making a good living off the desert tortoise, with annual wages commonly exceeding that of a US senator. The industry has built careers, produced hundreds of advanced degrees, and resulted in over 360 peer-reviewed publications (Lovich and Ennen 2013). The industry that it is charged with recovering the desert tortoise, however, appears to be reliant on its continued endangered status. The desert tortoise has proved to be an excellent job creator.

Perhaps no other endangered species has enjoyed more resources, attention, and funding than the desert tortoise. Despite this multimillion-dollar industry, arguably few conservation benefits have been realized (Lovich and Ennen 2013). While this monumental effort has possibly averted extinction, desert tortoise populations in the Mojave Desert appear to have declined precipitously over the past three decades.

A COSTLY ENDEAVOR

The first desert tortoise listing action occurred in 1980 when the Beaver Dam Slope population was listed as Threatened under the US Endangered Species Act (ESA) (USFWS 1980b). Nine years later the Mojave population was classified as Threatened, and the following year it was listed as a Distinct Population Segment (USFWS 1989; USFWS 1990). At that point, the desert tortoise industry was launched. A decade later, the US General Accountability Office (GAO) reported that expenditures on desert tortoise recovery in the period 1990–2001 had exceeded $100 million, the exact investment unknown because Congress did not require species-level expenditure reports prior to 1989 (GAO 2002).

To update the figure, I compiled federal and state desert tortoise expenditure reports from 2002 to 2011. From 1990 to 2011, I estimate, the federal and state governments have spent a minimum of $260 million on desert tortoise conservation. This analysis does not include municipal and local expenditures from such entities as Clark County (Nevada), which has spent $32.7 million dollars on its Multiple Species Habitat Conservation Plan that is largely focused on the desert tortoise (RECON Environmental 1995; Clark County and USFWS 2000). The

FIGURE 3.1. A morning meeting of biologists at Ivanpah Solar Electric Generating Station in San Bernardino County, California. Biologists performing desert tortoise surveys at the Ivanpah Solar Electric Generating Station. © L. LePre-USBLM.

actual figure spent on desert tortoise conservation far surpasses $300 million when expenditures incurred by private developers are included. These largely untraceable expenditures, such as preconstruction surveys, monitoring during construction activities (e.g., fiber optic cables), and tortoise-proof fencing for highways, cost tens of millions of dollars. Ravens, whose numbers are inflated due to anthropogenic food subsidies and who prey on young tortoises, are culled in many locations across the Mojave Desert (Boarman and Berry 1995; USFWS et al. 2008). These monitoring and mitigation activities have become part of the daily routine within the 47 million acres of potential desert tortoise habitat (Nussear et al. 2009). All of these operations require constant on-the-ground monitoring by biologists, yet their associated costs are privately funded and rarely disclosed by private industry.

HOW MANY DESERT TORTOISES EXIST TODAY?

Spotting a desert tortoise is not difficult when wandering the Mojave Desert, but surveying and monitoring tortoises is challenging. The main challenge is estimating the ratio of the number of tortoises spotted to the number that are missed in a survey—a figure needed to estimate the true population. An impressive amount of science has been dedicated to the goal of monitoring desert tortoises, from survey methods to surveyor bias to mathematical modeling approaches (e.g., Anderson et al. 2000; Doak et al. 2005; Freilich et al. 2005; Inman et al. 2009; Reed et al. 2009; Zylstra et al. 2010). But the difficult, yet fundamentally critical, question, how many desert tortoises exist today?, remains unanswered. This is in part due to the challenges of monitoring a cryptic species that spends approximately 98 percent of its time underground (Zimmerman et al. 1994), which is further complicated by the lack of good historical data on desert tortoise populations (Berry et al. 1986). In my view, the knowledge base and number of studies conducted on counting desert tortoises has become saturated. Despite this, there is not one peer-reviewed publication that provides a population estimate for the animal. A number of recent reviews on the desert tortoise share a similar take-home message.

> The methods that have been employed by the USFWS to estimate population density of desert tortoises are inadequate for detecting modest trends in population density. (Inman et al. 2009, 1)

> No existing data or analyses are adequate to estimate long term status or trends in (a) desert tortoise populations, (b) habitat for desert tortoises in any

> recovery unit, and/or (c) threats to tortoise populations regionally. . . . [S]tatus and trends of populations/metapopulations within Distinct Population Segments are potentially impossible based only upon assessment of tortoise density because assessing density of populations for rare and cryptic species is exceedingly difficult (and potentially impossible). (Tracy et al. 2004, 46)

Despite the shortcomings in methodology and analysis, the preponderance of evidence seems to suggest that the population is more than likely to be decreasing.

LOOKING BACK

If a pre-listing conservation program were in place for the desert tortoise five to ten years before it became listed under the ESA, would the desert tortoise be better off today? Although no such experiment has occurred with the desert tortoise, the example of the Multiple Species Habitat Conservation Plan (MSHCP) of Clark County may be the best example thus far of predevelopment mitigation. With Las Vegas and surrounding cities inside its borders, Clark County has experienced explosive growth in the past few decades that has surpassed the rate of growth of most other areas in the United States. In 1950, the population of the Las Vegas area was less than 50,000; today over two million live in Clark County. The county, however, planned for growth, and in 1995 Clark County established an MSHCP that addressed seventy-nine species of plants and animals. The MSHCP is intended under section 10(a) of the ESA to support the issuance, by the USFWS, of thirty-year permits that would

- allow the "take" of threatened or endangered species resulting from otherwise lawful activities on nonfederal properties within the county; and
- allow the "take" of threatened or endangered species that are currently unlisted but may become listed in the future.

While by definition the MSHCP addresses multiple species, the impetus for the plan was the desert tortoise. A $550 per acre developer fee was established for disturbing land covered by the MSHCP. Portions of the fee were used to build the Desert Tortoise Conservation Center in 1990, a facility located on US Bureau of Land Management (BLM) land that was set up to receive tortoises from land development activities in Clark County. By 2006 the Center had received over 14,000 desert tortoises

(Tracy 2006). As the first of several thousand tortoises began to crowd the center, a second site was established: the 26,000-acre Large Scale Translocation Study Site located west of Las Vegas. Over 6,000 tortoises were translocated to the new location. However, the success of the translocations and the potential species benefits are unknown and remain controversial (Dodd and Siegel 1991; Heaton et al. 2008). Only four studies have explicitly studied desert tortoise translocation (Tracy et al. 2004; Field et al. 2007; Esque et al. 2010; Nussear et al. 2012). Three of the studies used a combined total of 794 telemetered animals, and all found that mortality rates on translocated tortoises were not significantly higher than those of control populations. However, no long-term studies of translocation have been conducted. Thus the conservation benefits of the thousands of desert tortoise translocations that have taken place within Clark Country remain largely unknown. This example highlights the critical need to document the outcomes of conservation activities, preferably prior to impacts, if they are to serve as advance mitigation for development (Auerbach and Bendor this volume).

LOOKING FORWARD

It would be foolish to argue that job creation around species conservation is bad. Yet it is the outcomes that are debatable—outcomes that have (or have not) resulted from those jobs, resources, and efforts. The desert tortoise provides an opportunity to pause and take a retrospective view, as well as a view forward. Some researchers have recently done the latter, calling for a new approach that incorporates broad stakeholder contribution (Averill-Murray et al. 2012). I provide a personal perspective on some aspects of desert tortoise conservation in the coming decade.

With the advent of renewable energy projects on public land in the southwestern United States, desert tortoise conservation and recovery will become even more daunting in the coming decade (Kiernan this volume). Yet these projects will bring increased funding and regulatory oversight and the potential to infuse public lands with renewed attention and resources. But will these resources be used strategically and wisely, incorporating the lessons of the past? A recent example yields a dismal outlook.

Brightsource Energy's Ivanpah Solar Electric Generating Station (ISEGS), located in southeastern California 40 miles west of Las Vegas, gives us insight into the future challenges of desert tortoise conservation (figure 3.2). In October 2010 Brightsource Energy launched the first

FIGURE 3.2. Located in California's Mojave Desert on federal land, the Ivanpah Solar Electric Generating System is one of the world's largest solar thermal power projects. The facility formally opened in February 2014. The $2.2 billion project will produce enough electricity to power 140,000 homes. © M. Traphagen.

large-scale solar project in California; it proceeded to hire one hundred biologists the following year. At a cost of $22 million, the biologists located, translocated, and stood guard over the 166 desert tortoises known to be present on the 3,500-acre solar site located on public land (Brightsource Energy 2012). While the biologists protected tortoises from harm (e.g., from bulldozers), it is much less clear whether their activities contributed to species recovery. So far three tortoises have died during Brightsource activities. As of May 2012, Brightsource Energy had spent a total of $56 million on the desert tortoise (Cart 2012). Yet the population of desert tortoises is three fewer than when the project began. From any perspective, that is a staggering sum of money to minimize local mortality at a single location (i.e., roughly $340,000 per tortoise).

The ISEGS was under regulatory review for several years prior to its construction. The initial permit application to the BLM and the California Energy Commission was submitted in August 2007. Preconstruction tortoise surveys, using the USFWS-approved methodologies, were performed that same year, nearly four years before construction began. Those surveys estimated there were a total of twenty-five desert tortoises on the site. No additional surveys were conducted until October 2010, when construction began. But by 2011, following additional surveys, over three hundred tortoises were detected: some were placed in holding pens, while others were translocated adjacent to the site. Brightsource Energy's original tortoise estimate was off by an order of magnitude (CEC 2011).

This discrepancy in desert tortoise estimates serves as a test case for the USFWS survey protocol. Despite the vast underestimation of desert tortoises in the Ivanpah Valley, biologists appear to have an unflagging faith in the survey methodology. An example of this faith can be seen in a statement made by a biologist ten months before the project broke ground at the evidentiary hearing before the California Energy Resources Conservation and Development Commission: "I mean as every biologist here knows, I mean that 25 number, and that's pretty accurate, the protocol surveys. I mean there could be, you know, 30 or something like that" (CEC 2011). The USFWS made a similar statement at the hearing supporting the methodology and the initial survey results.

The reality, however, was clearly different. From the first "clearance surveys" of Unit 1 at ISEGS (there are three main power units), 35 tortoises were detected, 20 adults and 15 juveniles. This represents a density estimate of 10.8 adult tortoises km^{-2}. According to the USFWS, the average density for the northeastern Mojave Recovery Unit is 1.7 adult tortoises km^{-2}. The ISEGS is not located on land that is considered Critical Habitat for the desert tortoise; rather it is located on federal land that was classified as Category 3, or "least important" for desert tortoise habitat. Clearly, at a minimum, the system underperformed in assessing desert tortoises and habitat importance at the ISEGS site. Yet I argue that many desert tortoise experts would have predicted the final survey results: there are lots of tortoises in the Ivanpah Valley. If biannual spring and fall surveys were conducted at ISEGS during the initial project application, perhaps Brightsource Energy, the USFWS, and the BLM would have reconsidered their choice of the Ivanpah Valley to site the solar plant.

In my view, there are four lessons to be drawn from the desert tortoise situation at ISEGS:

1. Preconstruction protocol surveys are unreliable. Changes in protocols (and training) are needed.
2. There are likely more tortoises in the Mojave Desert than are thought to occur.
3. Poor-quality work by consultants hired to perform surveys is problematic.
4. The desert tortoise continues to be a difficult species to detect and accurately survey.

Biologists, land managers, and agency personnel need to critically address the shortcomings of the current survey methods. If we are unable to accurately estimate populations of desert tortoises, how can we make land designations such as Critical Habitat or "least important" habitat with any degree of validity?

CONCLUSION

If what the literature suggests is true, then the status of the desert tortoise will continue to decline toward a fragmented and unhealthy population exposed to a suite of increasing threats. Over 300,000 acres of the Mojave Desert are currently being developed for solar energy (BLM and DOE 2012). The outcomes to date from the ISEGS are not optimistic for the desert tortoise. Without significant changes to mitigation strategies and activities, it is likely that the millions of dollars that will be spent on the desert tortoise in the name of renewable energy projects in the coming decade will not result in any conservation uplift or benefit for the species. The end result may be our nation's most expensive conservation failure. If so, it will be a failure of the collective: government, academia, developers, and private consulting and special interest groups.

CHAPTER 4

Perspective: Renewable Energy and Endangered Species

SEAN KIERNAN

ABSTRACT

The recent emergence of large-scale solar energy projects in the southwestern United States has provided a unique opportunity to help shift the nation's electricity generation toward low-carbon sources. The Southwest is also home to a significant number of threatened, endangered, and at-risk species. The geographic intersection of prime solar resources and endangered species habitat has led to challenges, tensions, and even lawsuits. Environmental compliance—in particular, permits related to endangered species—heavily influences many aspects of solar project development. Environmental permitting is commonly viewed as a high-risk factor, particularly in terms of uncertain time requirements. Improving the process of endangered species protection would help reach the necessary balance between species protection and clean energy. Short-term improvements could be achieved in two areas: increasing information access and increasing the level of responsibility of the development community. Additional improvements will be more likely achieved by working within the current parameters of the US Endangered Species Act. Pre-listing conservation exemplifies one such approach that could be feasibly implemented immediately without major regulatory changes. The solar industry would likely support pre-listing conservation programs, but they would do so only if the proper incentives were in place.

INTRODUCTION

The recent emergence of large-scale solar energy projects in the southwestern United States has provided a unique opportunity to help shift the nation's electricity generation toward low-carbon sources. Today, over 4,000 megawatts of solar photovoltaic capacity is in operation in the United States, with over 500 megawatts installed in the first quarter of 2012 alone (SEIA 2012a). That is enough electricity to power approximately 350 homes for an entire year. This output does not include concentrated solar thermal power, which will surpass 1,300 megawatts in the coming years (SEIA 2012b). The prospect of generating tens of thousands of megawatts of electricity by means of low-cost solar technology is no longer the stuff of science fiction (Jacobson and Delucchi 2011).

The growing use of solar technology for utility-scale projects has been spurred by progressive state-level renewable portfolio standards and financially attractive federal tax credit mechanisms. Currently, thirty-seven states have adopted some form of renewable portfolio standard (Anonymous 2012b). These policies vary in their design and adoption: each state can favor one form of renewable energy over another. In the southwestern United States, however, utilities have strongly favored solar technology in order to meet renewable portfolio standards. The majority of the proposed generation involves solar photovoltaics (PV), and large installations are typically referred to as utility-scale PV. These projects consist of PV panels mounted on purpose-built, ground-level structures (as opposed to rooftops) and connect directly to the electricity grid. Utility-scale PV projects are usually located in areas with significant insolation like the southwestern United States.

The Southwest is also home to a significant number of threatened and endangered species listed under the US Endangered Species Act (ESA). For example, almost a quarter of ESA-listed species are found in California (USFWS 2012c). The geographic intersection of prime solar resources and endangered species habitat has led to challenges, tensions, and even lawsuits seeking to strike a balance between renewable energy development and species protection (Associated Press 2010; Clarke 2012; Woody 2012).

Utility-scale PV projects have an impact on the natural environment largely via land modification (Lovich and Ennen 2011). Both the location and the size of a PV project influence its potential impacts on endangered species. For example, a typical utility-scale PV project of 20 megawatts can require between 160 and 200 acres of land. Several larger projects (~100s megawatts) are currently under way and will require thousands of acres (BLM and DOE 2012). The construction of utility-scale PV projects entails land grading, which typically removes significant amounts of vegetation across a site location. Grading clears and levels the site location, which is necessary to safely and efficiently install PV structures. Given the impacts of grading and other construction activities, utility-scale PV projects must routinely assess their potential negative impacts on endangered species. As the deployment of PV continues to grow, there is increasing pressure on the industry to maintain a necessary balance between the benefits of solar power and the protection of at-risk species (Clarke 2012).

PROJECT DEVELOPMENT AND RISKS

Utility-scale PV project development involves several critical factors, including

- Project site: Where will the installation occur?
- Revenue contract: Does a utility commit to pay for the power generated, and at what prices?
- Secured interconnection: How does the installation link into the existing power grid?
- Financing: How do creditors view the investment risk of the project?
- Regulatory approval: What permits are needed to allow construction and operation?

Not securing any of these factors, or delays in doing so, can threaten a project's overall viability. Permitting is commonly viewed as a high-risk factor, particularly in terms of the uncertain time requirements to complete environmental compliance prior to construction (Ardour Capital Investments 2010). In addition, permitting interacts with each of the other development factors. For example, access to transmission interconnection can outweigh the potential risks of siting a project where endangered species are present. Similarly, project developers usually sign a power purchase agreement (PPA) with a utility prior to beginning the permitting process. The PPA typically specifies a guaranteed date by which the project must be built, operating, and producing power. Permitting delays that cause a project to miss this deadline can result in termination of the PPA and the collapse of the project. Thus environmental compliance—especially permits regarding endangered species—heavily influences many aspects of PV project development. If there is risk that a PV project could impact an endangered species, which triggers a number of regulatory requirements, it can become difficult to secure project financing.

ENDANGERED SPECIES: WHY AVOIDANCE AND MITIGATION IS CHALLENGING

While many factors that influence utility-scale PV projects are beyond the control of the developers, careful site selection would seem to be an obvious means to avoid the added burden of dealing with ESA compliance. If a project can be sited in an area where there is no risk of impacting endangered species, then it will have a higher probability of success. The reality, however, is that the necessary conditions of solar insolation and transmission interconnection tend to result in the siting of projects where endangered species are present. Thus siting constraints mean that a utility-scale PV project commonly requires additional permitting. Ultimately such projects must address potential impacts to endangered species through mitigation, such as habitat acquisition, to offset losses caused by the project. Permitting delays can take a number of different forms; however, the processes required by the ESA are often the most time consuming. A utility-scale PV project can comply with the ESA through two avenues: section 10 and section 7 (Madsen this volume).

Section 10 of the ESA enables the US Fish and Wildlife Service (USFWS) to issue permits for impacts to an ESA-listed species, including individual mortality, or "take." Incidental take permits require project developers to engage with the USFWS in the creation of a Habitat Conservation Plan (USFWS and NMFS 1996; Madsen this volume). This costly and time-consuming process involves expert consultation in order to draft and review a Habitat Conservation Plan, which is then subject to a series of public comment periods. The duration of this process generally conflicts with a typical PV project development schedule of two to three years. From a practical standpoint, a utility-scale PV project that demands section 10 permitting will have a very low likelihood of being built. The risk is simply too great that the length of the permitting process will result in the termination of a project's PPA.

Section 7 of the ESA provides a more effective solution for utility-scale PV projects to comply with endangered species requirements.

Section 7 obligates federal agencies to consult with the USFWS to ensure that any action authorized by other agencies will not jeopardize the continued existence of an endangered species (USFWS and NMFS 1996; Madsen this volume). Utility-scale PV projects must work with federal agencies for various reasons. The section 7 process is commonly used if a project is sited on federal land (e.g., land being leased from the US Bureau of Land Management) or if the project is located on private land but requires a permit from a federal agency (e.g., US Army Corps of Engineers). In both circumstances, project developers can request that the Bureau of Land Management or Army Corps of Engineers consult with the USFWS as a means to secure the necessary permits under the ESA. The timing of section 7 compliance is more attractive compared to section 10; however, the former can take years to navigate. Timing depends heavily on the capacity and resources of the local USFWS offices.

Project developers strive to complete the mitigation process as quickly as possible while also minimizing costs. In many cases, an incidental take permit requires that project developers secure an area equal to or greater than the impact site. That area is purchased explicitly for the management of the endangered species in perpetuity. Mitigation ratios are a common requirement: usually, for every acre of impact, project developers are required to protect three acres. A 3:1 mitigation ratio can drive up compliance costs, particularly for large PV projects. In addition, opportunities to secure land that is deemed valuable to an endangered species can be limiting, particularly for larger solar projects that threaten species with small ranges. In many instances, solar project developers may feel as if they are playing a game of "bring me a rock" with agencies, as the latter often have not identified mitigation opportunities a priori, resulting in a dynamic and chaotic mitigation process. This can add millions of dollars in additional cost to the project. In the end, the utility's ratepayers absorb these extra costs.

ROOM FOR IMPROVING THE PROCESS?

A balance must be struck. In order for the United States to more effectively address the effects of greenhouse gas emissions and climate change, it needs to continue to foster the success of utility-scale PV projects. However, the many benefits of these projects should not come at the expense of at-risk species. Improving the process of endangered species protection would help us reach the necessary balance between species protection and clean energy. Given the urgency of endangered species/renewable energy conflicts, I believe it is prudent to pursue improvements in both the short and long term.

In my view, short-term improvements could be achieved in two areas: increasing information access and increasing the level of responsibility of the development community. All too frequently developers are isolated from important information. For example, developers would benefit from having better access to information and resources regarding the potential location of protected species. Lack of this information leads to poor decision making, often at significant expense to the developer. While sensitive information (e.g., species location data) needs to be handled carefully, arming developers with better information about the potential for an endangered species to be present in locations where they are considering projects will lead to better decision making.

Providing developers with better access to information, however, should come with the expectation that the development community will take greater responsibility in accounting for their potential to impact endangered species, for example, by selecting project sites that are not located in sensitive areas. While this may seem obvious, too often projects have been proposed in areas where significant impacts on protected species are certain. This is often the result of ignorance about or indifference to the protection of specific species. For the utility-scale PV industry to continue to thrive, however, it will need to continually demonstrate that the protected species and their risks are appreciated and can be managed effectively. This needs to happen if for no other reason than that failing to account for the risk of protected species' impacts erodes project viability and increases the chances of project delays.

Long-term solutions require more substantive policy changes. While some in the development community may favor wholesale changes to the ESA, most would agree that these changes would take significant time to be implemented and will likely provide no benefit to the solar industry over the next decade. Therefore, improvements are more likely to be achieved by working within the current parameters of the ESA. Pre-listing conservation (PLC) approaches, the focus of this volume, exemplifies one such approach that could be feasibly implemented immediately without major changes to the ESA (Li and Male this volume). The solar industry would likely support PLC programs, but they would do so only if the proper incentives were in place (e.g., streamlined compliance and regulatory certainty in exchange for preemptive and voluntary conservation actions for at-risk species).

Another area for improvement is revising the current rules that prohibit federal lands to be utilized for compensatory mitigation. For example, if a utility-scale PV project is required to mitigate for loss of habitat as a result of site construction, it is prohibited in conducting activities on federal lands even it would result in large conservation benefits for the target species. Given that nearly 15 million acres in the Mojave Desert are controlled by the Bureau of Land Management and that nearly 30,000 megawatts on over 300,000 acres are currently being developed for solar in that area (BLM and DOE 2012), the inability to permanently preserve or restore federal land for species mitigation purposes creates additional limitations for species protection and reduces the long-term outlook for several protected species. Simply put, utility-scale PV projects are facing the prospect of not having access to a sufficient amount of land for mitigation. While land controlled by the BLM cannot be used for mitigation, there are virtually few to no restrictions on the same land to prevent its development.

Utility-scale PV will continue to play a more prominent role in the US energy infrastructure. The prospect of a substantive effort to address global climate change combined with the improving economic competitiveness of solar energy makes this role certain. The potential for utility-scale PV projects to impact endangered species appears to be inevitable. Thus the goal must be to develop more efficient and cost-effective means to address and mitigate these potential impacts. Endangered species compliance processes can and should be improved, since they are currently acting as a barrier to the continued growth of solar and its positive benefits for the environment. This can be done immediately by providing better access to information and incentivizing innovative mitigation strategies. The solar industry will need to continue to take strides to improve its level of responsibility when managing its interaction with endangered species. A greater level of awareness and expertise in siting projects in a manner that avoids impacts on endangered species is required and should be expected as the industry matures. Innovative mitigation strategies, such as the PLC approach, can help ensure that solar energy will flourish and the indirect environmental benefits that it provides will endure.

CHAPTER 5

Perspective: The Challenges and Benefits of Pre-Listing Conservation Approaches to Military Readiness

RYAN ORNDORFF

ABSTRACT

The 2.3 million acres of US Marine Corps installations constitute irreplaceable assets required for military training. They are also home to many endangered and at-risk species. The measures to avoid and minimize the adverse impacts on protected species from military training activities are increasingly imposing significant restrictions on the use of critical ranges and training areas, which ultimately degrades the ability to support overall combat readiness. As habitat loss and degradation continue and the number of species listed under the US Endangered Species Act grows, the range of potential solutions to maintain a balance between military readiness and species protection must broaden. There is increasing interest within the US Department of Defense in fostering effective partnerships, strategies, and tools that can preclude the need to list species, including pre-listing conservation approaches. While policy tools exist to support mechanisms to implement pre-listing conservation actions, the complementary regulatory connection and incentives do not currently exist. Without clear, regulatory predictability, incentives for voluntary, upstream conservation actions for candidate species on military lands will remain weak to nonexistent.

INTRODUCTION

The US Marine Corps (USMC) is "America's Expeditionary Force in Readiness" and has a statutory responsibility to be ready to respond to any crisis, at any time, in any place—from humanitarian assistance missions to major combat operations. As such, USMC installations are critical, irreplaceable assets for ensuring military readiness. These installations encompass over 2.3 million acres of land and near-shore areas, which include coastal, freshwater, and terrestrial ecosystems, that provide the critical infrastructure to support continuous training, from developing individual skills to executing large-scale, live-fire exercises. In addition to providing training and readiness infrastructure, installations provide support to Marines and their families through services such as housing, schools, and medical facilities. Sustaining these land uses on our installations has become increasingly complex over time with new training needs and modernization requirements.

Land use decisions and development outside the fence line directly and indirectly affect land use and operations on and around USMC installations. While often originally established in remote or rural locations, military installations are now confronting new challenges posed by regional growth and development. Common examples of conflict are noise-sensitive land developments like residential communities or schools near USMC installations. As landscapes surrounding USMC installations transform from rural to suburban and urban settings, there has also been an impact on the natural environment. Formerly abundant natural resources have become increasingly degraded or scarce and now commonly require protection through federal, state, and local regulations. In some cases, development outside the fence line has resulted in military installations becoming islands of relatively undisturbed habitat that support significant numbers of rare and at-risk species, including many that are protected under the US Endangered Species Act (ESA). Currently, sixty-two threatened and endangered species reside on USMC installations (four hundred listed species reside on all Department of Defense lands). In accordance with the federal regulations to protect species listed under the ESA, the military must include species protection in its land use planning processes and decisions by working in cooperation with the US Fish and Wildlife Service and the National Marine Fisheries Service (USFWS and NMFS 1998).

The measures taken to avoid and minimize the adverse impacts on protected species from military training activities are increasingly imposing significant restrictions on the use of critical ranges and training areas, which ultimately degrades the ability to support overall combat readiness (DOD 2013). In 2002 the Government Accountability Office published a report identifying primary encroachment issues to military training, which included endangered species habitat and protected marine resources, along with unexploded ordnance, competition for radio frequencies, competition for airspace, air and noise pollution, and urban growth around military installations (GAO 2002).

DOWNSTREAM SPECIES CONSERVATION ON MILITARY LANDS

Many examples exist of species conservation programs on military lands driven by ESA regulation (Benton et al. 2008; Stein et al. 2008; Wolfe et al. 2012). Perhaps one of the most long-standing case studies involves the Red-Cockaded Woodpecker (RCW; *Picoides borealis*), which occurs on numerous military installations in the southeastern United States. The RCW has been federally protected since the passage of the ESA in 1973. The primary causes for its decline have been loss of nesting habitat combined with degradation of remaining habitat due to fire suppression and hardwood encroachment into mature pine forests (Conner et al. 2010). While the historic range of the RCW once extended from Virginia to Texas, it is now limited to several core populations that are relatively small and fragmented. Recovery goals rely primarily on conserving and restoring habitat on a variety of federal and state lands, including military lands. Of the thirteen identified primary core populations, ten rely on military lands, three of them exclusively. The coastal North Carolina primary core population resides largely on the Marine Corps Base Camp Lejeune and the nearby Croatan National Forest and the Holly Shelter State Lands.

Camp Lejeune consists of a variety of ranges and training areas necessary to support amphibious, ground, and aviation activities. The base also supports large expanses of relatively mature pine forest with a growing population of RCWs largely due to proactive planning and ecosystem-based forest management. While military training and endangered woodpeckers have been coexisting at Camp Lejeune, the overlap of high-use ranges and training areas with RCW populations significantly restricts when and how these lands can be used. In some ways, however, managing for land conditions beneficial to the RCW can directly support military activities. For example, forest management and prescribed burning to promote beneficial habitat conditions improves training conditions by reducing fuel loads for potential wildfires, improving line of sight conditions, providing open maneuver corridors, and reducing potential interference of communications equipment. However, the protective measures required to avoid adverse impacts on the species restrict certain critical training activities, such as off-road vehicle maneuvering, digging to establish fighting and communications positions, and conducting live-fire training. As training demands on Camp Lejeune have increased and the RCW population has grown, balancing species protection and mission readiness has become increasingly challenging.

On the opposite coast of the country, Marine Corp Base Camp Pendleton in northern San Diego County bears a striking resemblance to Camp Lejeune in its importance for training and species conservation. Over 125,000 acres, the base contains some the last remaining undeveloped coastal habitats in Southern California and supports seventeen listed species and numerous other species of concern. The overlap of training space and species habitat presents significant restrictions to training activities (figure 5.1). To help address this challenge, Camp Pendleton conducted a study in 2003 to specifically identify the scope of species protection requirements and the extent to which they impact military readiness. In particular, the study evaluated the capability of the base to support the 739 essential training requirements—termed the Marine Essential Task List—that are necessary to maintain combat readiness. The assessment determined that up to 30 percent of the tasks critical for tactical training scenarios could not be completed in a manner that met Marine Corps standards; this was primarily due to measures required to avoid impacts to threatened and endangered species.

While the USMC recognizes that its installations play an important role in species conservation, the unintentional reliance on military installations as refuges for declining species is unsustainable—from the perspective of both biodiversity conservation and national security. The predicament is not unique to the USMC; rather it extends to all branches of the Department of Defense (DOD) (Benton et al. 2008). As habitat loss and degradation continue and the number of species listed under the ESA grows, the range of potential solutions to maintain a balance between military readiness and species protection must broaden. We need alternatives to the traditional approach of managing our responsibilities solely within our fence lines and reactively responding to regulatory triggers.

FIGURE 5.1. At military bases like Camp Lejune, North Carolina, the Department of Defense must find solutions to balance the need to maintain military readiness with endangered species protection. © J.F. Metzger-USNavy.

ESA regulations that apply to federal agencies are largely dedicated to consultation related to adverse effects of federal actions. A 2004 ESA amendment regarding the designation of critical habitat shifted this focus slightly for listed species, providing an incentive for actions that relieve rather impose regulatory restrictions. The amendment states:

> The Secretary [of Interior or Commerce] shall not designate as critical habitat any lands or other geographical areas owned or controlled by the Department of Defense, or designated for its use, that are subject to an Integrated Natural Resources Management Plan prepared under section 101 of the Sikes Act (16 U.S.C. 670a), if the Secretary determines in writing that such plan provides a benefit to the species for which critical habitat is proposed for designation. (16 U.S.C 1533 §(a)(3)(B)(i))

The Sikes Act of 1960 calls on the military services to carry out programs for the conservation and rehabilitation of natural resources on military installations and facilitates cooperative planning between the Department of Defense, Department of the Interior, and state agencies.

The 2001 Sikes Improvement Act not only facilitated this cooperative planning but also required all military installations with significant natural resources to develop and implement an Integrated Natural Resource Management Plan. The primary goal of such a plan is to outline programs that manage natural resources for the benefit of endangered species on an installation while also ensuring "no net loss" of training capability and military access. Current DOD policy requires Integrated Natural Resource Management Plans to embrace an ecosystem-based approach for managing natural resources with a specific emphasis on listed and at-risk species and their habitats (DOD 2013). Integrated Natural Resource Management Plans allow the military flexibility in a nonregulatory context to maximize the use of training assets as well as to provide benefits to endangered species that are equivalent to or greater than the benefits provided through critical habitat designation.

Designation of military lands as critical habitat would pose additional restrictions on training capabilities beyond those related to ESA-listed species. The 2004 ESA amendent specifically gives the military the incentive to go beyond species protection and toward more proactive ecosystem management. While the amendment retains the consultation requirements for specific actions that may affect a species, it facilitates proactive natural resource management to act as a mechanism to relieve, rather than impose, potential regulatory restrictions arising from designation of military lands as critical habitat. Past proposals for critical habitat for endangered species on Camp Pendleton, for example, would have affected over 60 percent of the training areas, further impacting military readiness. In response, the USMC more than doubled the annual investment in species monitoring, management, and habitat restoration between 2005 and 2011. However, this incentive is only applicable and effective when species populations have already declined to the point that they require ESA protection and designation of critical habitat.

MOVING SPECIES CONSERVATION UPSTREAM OF REGULATION

How do the challenges and approaches to maintaining ESA compliance and military readiness relate to pre-listing conservation (PLC)? First and foremost, the examples of Camp Pendleton and Camp Lejeune illustrate the specific impacts that ESA-driven species protection requirements can have on military training and why this issue is of primary concern to the USMC. As such, there is increasing interest within the DOD in fostering effective partnerships, strategies, and tools that can preclude the need to list species, especially given the increasing numbers of listing petitions and pending determinations. An ounce of prevention is preferable to a pound of cure.

But what actions, where, and how many are needed? Managing for listed species with detailed recovery plans is itself a daunting and time-consuming challenge. Species recovery plans include detailed discussions of species threats, necessary conservation actions, and responsible parties for implementing actions and conservation targets. Targeting conservation actions for nonlisted species (e.g., candidate species) with less information will be, perhaps, even more challenging. Certain at-risk species, however, have general or location-specific conservation strategies (e.g., Candidate Conservation Agreements) or are focus species in State Wildlife Action Plans. Thus a first step in incentivizing PLC initiatives is to develop or refine a conservation strategy that focuses actions on specific outcomes.

A second important step is to define a clear relationship between PLC actions and potential future regulations. This will be particularly important if PLC actions occur on military ranges or training areas. While programs with assurances are available to nonfederal landowners (i.e., Candidate Conservation Agreements with Assurances), explicit connections between voluntary conservation actions for candidate species on military lands and regulatory certainty of potential implications if the species is ESA-listed do not exist. Developing mechanisms that do so would provide strong incentives for increasing management of candidate species on military lands, as well as with neighboring partners (Li and Male this volume). The least desirable long-term outcome for a candidate species is one similar to the RCW: the survival of a species is imperiled and military readiness is at risk for the foreseeable future. Looking beyond the fence line of military installations and working in partnership with other federal and nonfederal landowners provides an opportunity to proactively prevent population declines that result in regulatory triggers while also minimizing risk to military missions (Gartner et al. this volume). Yet to do so, the USMC needs stronger signals and incentives. Regulatory certainty for PLC approaches and partnerships would increase the incentive to direct resources to support upstream conservation actions that promote species recovery and prevent species declines.

In my view, PLC approaches focused on private lands near and adjacent to military installations hold great potential for achieving species protection and maintaining military readiness. The 2011 amendments to the Sikes Act (16 U.S.C. § 670c-1) authorize military services to enter into agreements to provide not only for the maintenance and improvement of natural resources on military installations but also for the maintenance and improvement of natural resources located off military installations. These agreements, with states and local governments, nongovernmental organizations (NGOs), individuals, or other federal agencies, must also serve to relieve current or anticipated challenges that could restrict, impede, or otherwise interfere with current or anticipated military activities. PLC programs can deliver on both of these objectives. Relatedly, the DOD has the authority to partner with eligible entities (e.g., NGOs, land trusts, and state agencies) to acquire real estate interests in private lands (e.g., conservation easements) and provide funding for natural resource conservation where such actions would alleviate either current or anticipated future restrictions to military training. Lands protected or managed outside the fence line as partnerships could serve to both benefit at-risk species upstream of regulation and restrict incompatible development that would interfere with military operations. The level of investment of time and resources to implement and sustain these types of partnerships and agreements is substantial, and thus the return on the investment needs to be clearly defined, especially in a climate where resources are increasingly constrained. While the policy tools above provide the potential mechanisms to implement PLC actions, the complementary regulatory connection and incentives do not currently exist.

New and improved approaches to balancing species conservation and military readiness are needed; they should embrace a "carrot and stick" model with respect to incentives. Today the only incentive is the avoidance of "sticks": the potential for military training restrictions driven by the ESA. Upstream approaches, such as PLC, could provide the necessary positive incentives for creating a more effective and efficient balance, both in terms of costs and in terms of conservation benefits. PLC programs can deliver substantial conservation benefits to the hundreds of candidate species, including those that reside on and adjacent to military installations. For the USMC, the only current incentive for implementing voluntary PLC actions is the hope that our actions result in conservation outcomes that preclude the need to list a candidate species. This is a weak incentive. In fact, the incentive for inaction is much stronger. Without regulatory predictability, voluntary, proactive management of candidate species on military lands comes with a great deal of risk. In the event that a candidate species is listed, areas where conservation measures were implemented for species benefits could be subject to training restrictions to avoid and minimize adverse impacts under the ESA. What was compatible prior to regulatory protections would thus become incompatible, as a direct result of voluntary conservation measures upstream of regulation. Without clear, regulatory predictability (Li and Male this volume), incentives for voluntary, upstream conservation actions on military lands for candidate species will remain weak to nonexistent.

As our national security needs evolve, it is imperative that the military maintain the flexibility to adapt training to emerging threats. As landscapes continue to change, so must the strategies for conservation of species and the ecosystems on which they depend. The development of PLC incentives that promote proactive actions for species conservation upstream of costly regulatory triggers is a necessary evolution that will serve to increase regulatory efficiency, build effective partnerships, promote broader ecological sustainability, and sustain our military readiness into the future. In order to be effective, the incentives and assurances for PLC approaches must be firmly put into place.

CHAPTER 6

Perspective: Stewardship over Regulation and Harnessing the Agricultural Sector for Species Conservation

TERRY R. FANKHAUSER

ABSTRACT

Ranchers and farmers rely on the health of their land and are committed to natural resource stewardship to ensure it will continue to sustain future generations. These groups are and can become partners in prelisting conservation initiatives rather than adversaries locked in litigation over the US Endangered Species Act. Rich with at-risk species habitat, private lands are essential to protecting wildlife. Market-based initiatives, such as the upcoming Partners for Western Conservation program organized by the Colorado Cattlemen's Association, provide a key opportunity to work with farmers and ranchers to protect species and avoid the complexities of the Endangered Species Act. If incentive-based programs harness the best available science, focus on measurable conservation benefits, and are equitable, flexible, and transparent, progress can be made in protecting vulnerable habitats and species. Proactive market-based initiatives will promote goodwill between landowners and environmentalists, landscape-level conservation, environmental risk management, and partnerships among diverse stakeholders.

INTRODUCTION

Over the years, ranchers and their practices have evolved with the natural environment because they understand that adaptability equals

FIGURE 6.1. Ranchers rely on the land for their livelihoods, and thus environmental stewardship is central to their existence. © Colorado Cattlemen's Association.

survivability. Many ranchers know that often it is not themselves but Mother Nature that is in control (figure 6.1). Ranchers have come to embrace the view that when properly cared for the earth's natural assets will deliver thriving and varied rewards. These rewards can be abundant livestock and crops but also healthy habitats for at-risk species.

I have the great opportunity to work for some of the most progressive ranchers in the world on initiatives to ensure the health of the land for generations to come. The ranching families of the Colorado Cattlemen's Association (CCA) are leaders in developing conservation easement approaches that mesh with multigenerational working ranches (Wright and Anella 2007; Anonymous 2012a). These ranchers are not solely focused on their cattle but also on their land, water, and wildlife resources. Their conservation ethic is uniformly tied to their driving need to produce food and fiber for a hungry world. They desire to deliver those services with excellence. Recently, the members of CCA created the nonprofit organization Partners for Western Conservation (PWC), whose goal is to develop a broad marketplace for conservation practices. PWC believes that enhancing Colorado's natural assets through incentive-based conservation programs will allow ranchers' livelihoods and lifestyles to flourish now and in the future. We also believe that species conservation measures should take place upstream of costly and often controversial regulation.

Providing incentives for environmental stewardship to private landowners and regulated industries upstream of regulatory triggers can be more efficient and cost-effective than managing natural resources to meet regulatory laws like the US Endangered Species Act (ESA). In a time of diminishing financial resources and increasing expectations, we see private lands as a huge, untapped reservoir for at-risk species conservation. For instance, the majority of prime wildlife habitat in Colorado exists on private lands.

In PWC's efforts to support conservation incentive programs, we are often faced with concerns about paying landowners for conservation actions. These concerns range from ethical opposition to preference for regulatory approaches. In my view, decoupling conservation actions by private landowners from economics only delays implementation and decreases the quality of the desired outcome. I believe proactive, meaningful investments in a public good such as at-risk species conservation will always be more efficient than reactive, prescriptive measures. My experiences suggest that the greater agriculture community believes that reactive measures, such as the ESA, often discourage species conservation. When landowners must comply with environmental regulations, they often incur significant costs resulting from land use limitations and other restrictions. Well-intended environmental laws can thereby turn landowners into adversaries rather than partners in land and species stewardship.

The CCA's vision is to render the ESA unnecessary. This law is riddled with obstacles, including litigious off-ramps that clog the courts and delay meaningful conservation action (Hastings 2012). While I appreciate the spirit of the law, the complexities and barriers inherent in the ESA can stymie alternative approaches to species conservation that strive to be effective and efficient. The ESA is a classic regulatory approach that has extensive inputs but yields few results. If the dollars invested in listing species under the ESA were invested instead in prelisting conservation programs focused on incentives and markets, I believe the federal government would save millions. Ranchers and agriculture landowners know such programs would work. Given the incentive and the market, US farmers and ranchers have consistently overproduced our commodities, even at the risk of driving prices downward. The same will hold true with species conservation markets. The supply of ranchers and farmers who are willing to participate in conservation markets already outweighs the current demand.

The cost of not acting is great, not only for at-risk species, but also for the livelihoods and businesses involved. There is growing consensus that the current reactive, regulatory approach to at-risk species conservation is failing (Stokstad 2005). As a former president of the CCA noted, "If meetings recovered the grouse, we would be eating them for Sunday dinner." Innovative action in partnership with farmers and ranchers is essential to advancing species conservation.

WHY FARMERS AND RANCHERS?

Farmers and ranchers are our nation's largest group of land stewards. In Colorado, for example, farmers and ranchers are the caretakers of more natural resources than any other entity, including the federal government. It is important for them to be major players in species conservation markets.

As farmers and ranchers produce food and fiber from natural resources, they can harm natural resources through misuse. The preponderance of these negative impacts to natural resources comes from management decisions fostered by a lack of knowledge. My personal experience has led me to believe that the vast majority of farmers and ranchers understand the correlation between proper stewardship of natural resources and increased production yields of their agricultural commodities. The question then becomes, what more can agriculturists do for our natural resources, and why hasn't this been done?

Doing more comes at a cost. This cost may be manifested in decreased production of agriculture commodities, an out-of-sync production system, or direct expenses to the landowner. While best intentions exist, the farmer and rancher cannot afford to implement greater conservation practices than necessary due to the variety of costs these practices impose. In my view, there is no more efficient way to deal with the implementation of conservation practices than to establish a rich resource reserve managed by individuals who have intimate, multigenerational knowledge of their natural resources. The larger agriculture community and a growing group of conservation practitioners believe that a promising strategy to create a reserve of conservation practices is a market-based credit system that makes species protection financially viable. This credit system could focus on the conservation of at-risk species but operate upstream of the ESA.

Marketplaces function by bringing together buyers, sellers, verifiers, and possibly aggregators. From agricultural producers' perspective, this is how their marketplaces function today. The buyers and sellers are self-explanatory. The verifiers come in many forms, including veterinarians, ownership inspectors, genetic documentation, and other certifications and procedures. The aggregators are, more often than not, where we will sell our products. To ranchers and farmers, this market structure is both familiar and efficient. The CCA believes certain criteria will be useful in engaging the agricultural sector in at-risk species conservation markets (table 6.1).

With intergenerational agricultural land transitions and subsequent nonagricultural conversions on the rise, there is a sense of urgency in the opportunity of ranchers and farmers to play a significant role in emerging species conservation markets. Conserving working landscapes that host biodiversity and ecosystem services provides benefits to all stakeholders. Agricultural producers have a tendency to engage in actions that are relevant and tangible. They are far less likely to engage in a species conservation marketplace that does not have measurable and meaningful outcomes. There is a suite of potential benefits from species conservation markets that would encourage agricultural producers to play a major role in these programs (see table 6.1).

There are real challenges to creating a comprehensive conservation marketplace that would allow for the integration of a variety of objectives and metrics rather than a focus on individual projects. While agricultural producers will agree to engage in a piecemeal approach, all stakeholders should realize that only a comprehensive approach is likely to curb the negative implications of an approach driven by regulatory triggers. In short, if candidate species are to avoid ESA listing or listed species are to be de-listed, a comprehensive, structured, and transparent decision-making framework must be put in motion. Furthermore, efficiencies will be found in a comprehensive species marketplace through diminished administrative costs to the regulator and the regulated entities. These potential savings could then be reinvested in the marketplace, yielding even greater returns.

Farmers and ranchers are at a crossroads in their relationship with the ESA. Beyond the ESA not providing the conservation outcomes needed, it is extremely difficult for ranchers and farmers to understand the law's implementation. In my experience, questions always arise with regard to keeping a species off the ESA list: How much habitat is needed? What are the population objectives for the species? What assurances will I have if I engage in species or habitat protection? Invariably the answers are ambiguous—"It depends"—or otherwise unhelpful, acting to dissuade engagement by the very landowners needed for the successful conservation and recovery of at-risk species. These are some

TABLE 6.1 DESIRABLE CRITERIA AND POTENTIAL BENEFITS OF A SPECIES CONSERVATION MARKET THAT ENGAGES THE AGRICULTURAL SECTOR

Desirable Criteria

- Be market-based so that it maximizes the amount of species conservation achieved per dollar invested.
- Be science-based such that it relies on the best available science, including expert opinion, to determine the most appropriate conservation actions.
- Be applicable across a broad geography.
- Achieve measurable conservation benefits.
- Provide practical benefits to project developers.
- Be transparent and fair to all stakeholders.
- Focus on achieving priority conservation goals while also complementing other conservation approaches.
- Meet the standards and approval of key regulating entities if necessary (e.g., US Fish and Wildlife Service).
- Be flexible so that it may be adapted to changing social, political, economic, and environmental conditions.
- Appeal to a broad spectrum of private landowners by being structured so that it is straightforward and provides powerful financial incentives.
- Appeal to a broad range of regulated and nonregulated investors in environmental services, including federal, state, and private entities.

Potential Benefits

- The ability to aggregate outcomes that would result in greater landscape-level benefits, which are often impossible with isolated projects and piecemeal approaches.
- Provision of a practical tool to project developers for managing environmental risks and liabilities.
- Reduction in the cost and complexity of environmental compliance with state and federal regulations.
- Increased assurances from regulators (e.g., recognition of effective conservation actions).
- Increased financial incentives for land stewardship activities through new environmental markets.
- Improved financial sustainability for landowners through diversification of income sources.
- Job creation for local communities.
- Increased participation in conservation activities.
- Provision of a framework to encourage project developers to invest more in conservation activities without additional regulation and to integrate conservation activities into a larger planning process.

of the reasons agricultural producers are hungry for a comprehensive approach to species conservation.

ROAD MAP FOR SUCCESS, COMMITMENTS, AND CHALLENGES

In Colorado, ranchers, conservation organizations, businesses, and agencies have recently come together to design an ambitious species conservation program based on credit trading. Using a systemwide approach, the Colorado Habitat Exchange is based on a number of aspects and activities (table 6.2). I am optimistic that the Exchange will demonstrate that a well-designed credit trading system can achieve measurable conservation objectives.

In life, we all have commitments; some are callings, others are engrained in our being. One consistent commitment among farmers and ranchers is that to the land. Throughout the past decades, I have witnessed this commitment. Once, I watched a rancher voluntarily pull his cattle from an area where he held a federal land permit because of a dry summer; he did so in the hope of leaving plenty of winter forage for elk. On another occasion, a farmer planted a less productive crop because it provided better soil cover that would minimize erosion and sedimentation into a nearby stream. In my experience, these examples are commonplace in the agriculture community, and this commitment to the land represents an opportunity for species conservation with landscape-level benefits.

I learned years ago that Maslow was right: at the base of people's hierarchy of needs are food, water, and shelter. What I didn't consider at the time was that these basic requirements aren't only for human beings, but for all nature. This understanding led me to question whether agriculture was as uniquely positioned to provide animals with the same needs as humans. The answer is, absolutely.

Food producers face significant challenges over the coming decades. The UN Food and Agricultural Organization (FAO) estimates there will be 9.1 billion people to feed by 2050, which will require a 70 percent increase in food production (FAO 2009). At the same time urbanization will continue, with about 70 percent of the world's population in urban settings by 2050 and less than 1 percent involved in food production. The FAO concludes that while production will necessarily increase, other services that are provided by agriculture, such as climate change mitigation, endangered species protection, and ecosystem services, will

TABLE 6.2 CHARACTERISTICS THAT FORM THE FOUNDATION OF THE COLORADO HABITAT EXCHANGE, A SPECIES CONSERVATION PROGRAM BASED ON CREDIT TRADING

1. Identify species habitat projects, standards, and metrics.
   - Identify priority habitats and species.
   - Develop and set standards for practices and land uses that lead to measurable habitat improvement based on existing standards of the Colorado Division of Wildlife and others.
   - Develop metrics for habitat evaluation that draw from existing Colorado Division of Parks and Wildlife standards, as well as other agencies and non-governmental organizations.
2. Develop transactional infrastructure.
   - Identify stakeholder roles and responsibilities, including buyers, sellers, aggregators, certifiers, and verifiers.
   - Develop frameworks for registries, trading, monitoring, and marketing.
   - Outline step-by-step processes for buyers and sellers and points of engagement among collaborators.
   - Estimate financial costs of transactional infrastructure.
3. Assess market potential, along with institutional and technical capacity to implement.
   - Determine potential (1) supply of species habitat improvement projects, (2) landowner participation, and (3) demand for the purchase of conservation credits resulting from projects.
   - Identify specific potential buyers and sellers.
   - Assess legal, policy, and landowner context.
   - Examine existing rules for environmental markets and mitigation.
4. Structure agreements between buyers and sellers and among other collaborators.
   - Design standardized templates for management and protection agreements.
   - Review options for payment types.
   - Establish equity and fairness criteria for evaluation of payment options.
   - Select a contract type.

challenge traditional food production. Further, agriculture will continue to compete with other human uses of land and water. Ultimately, agricultural producers and society at large will have to do more with less—less land, less water, and less labor to deliver the growing demand for food and other natural resource–based expectations.

Given this forecast, what is agriculture's future in protecting our environment? This is a question that needs an answer. The FAO report speaks of the need to reduce the negative impacts of agricultural production in order to increase food security (FAO 2009). The same could be said for securing the future of our environment. I believe that food and fiber production can be synergistic with the protection of our natural assets. In fact, I am sure that the conservation of land, water, and species can be enhanced, alongside ranching and farming activities. Ranchers and farmers have consistently demonstrated innovation in response to agricultural markets. Today, ranchers are producing more beef than in the 1970s when cattle numbers were at their peak. They are doing so with fewer inputs and less land. In order for farmers and ranchers to produce conservation benefits, they must be able to diversify their land's producing capabilities by diversifying their income streams. In order to accomplish this, I believe regulatory approaches must be replaced by creative market approaches. Doing so will unleash innovation in species conservation on agricultural lands.

At the end of a long day on the land, ranchers have one line that sticks with them on the drive home. The one that comes to mind for me has to do with ethics and integrity. It is often delivered in various forms, but the meaning is the same. It goes something like this: It's not about what you do in life, it's about how you do it. To properly address the conservation of imperiled habitats and species, the time has come for proactive, results-oriented conservation initiatives. The correct way to implement those initiatives is upstream of regulation, not in courtrooms thousands of miles away. Give ranchers and farmers a species conservation market, and you will see species conservation activities explode on private lands.

CHAPTER 7

Perspective: Forest Conservation and Private Landowners

RHETT JOHNSON AND MARY SNIECKUS

ABSTRACT

The right of private individuals to own and manage land is a core value in the United States, and our common law legal system has evolved to favor land development and economic extraction, as opposed to managing land for environmental benefits. Incentivizing environmental stewardship and rewarding private forestland owners (accounting for 264 million acres) for providing environmental public goods is critical to the conservation of biodiversity and ecosystem services. Conservation easements and US Farm Bill programs have been the premier approaches to private forest conservation. While family forestland owners value their property for many environmental reasons, they are aging, and many are selling their property for economic reasons. New programs are needed that strongly incentivize environmental stewardship while helping to cover the economic costs of doing so. Pre-listing conservation programs could help achieve this goal. Pre-listing conservation approaches will be most successful if they incorporate landowner needs and perspectives into project design and focus on offering private forestland owners more choices on how to conserve their forests for future generations.

INTRODUCTION

The right of private individuals to own and manage land is a core value in the United States. Private property was considered a cornerstone of the US Constitution by its authors for two reasons (Adams 1851). First, stable property rights are a powerful incentive for wealth creation and prosperity, both prerequisites for successful self-government. Second, property rights have long been linked with individual liberty. By helping to preserve the economic independence of individuals, secure private property encourages participation in the political process and willingness to challenge government policy. Viewed in this light, the ownership of property represents personal empowerment (Ely 2008).

The US common law legal system has evolved to favor land development and economic extraction, as opposed to managing land for environmental benefits (Sprankling 1996). To help counter these market forces, government programs have been in place for decades to incentivize landowners to manage their land in ways that provide some environmental services to society. For example, the US Soil Conservation Service was formed in 1933 to provide technical and financial assistance to landowners so that best farming practices were adopted to preserve soil health and prevent erosion. Today under the US Farm Bill (H.R. 2642; Pub. L. 113–79), cost-share and other voluntary programs continue to provide technical assistance and financial incentives to forestland owners to plan and implement conservation practices on their land (Cain and Lovejoy 2006).

Over the past decades, the economic and environmental pressures on private, working forests has increased dramatically (Stein et al. 2009). Incentivizing environmental stewardship and rewarding private forestland owners for providing environmental public goods is critical to the conservation of biodiversity and ecosystem services. Private forestlands occur across the United States but are concentrated in the East, in the prairie-forest border in Texas and Oklahoma, and within riparian areas or isolated forests in the Midwest, Northeast, and interior basins of the West (Robles et al. 2008).

Private landowners own 56 percent of the 751 million acres of forest in the United States; families and individuals own 264 million acres (Butler 2008; USDA 2008). Private forestlands filter an estimated 25 percent of all Americans' drinking water and provide critical habitat for 60 percent of all plants and animals that the US Endangered Species Act classifies as at risk of decline or extinction in forty-eight states (Stein et al. 2009; Stein et al. 2010). In some places in the United States, at-risk species occur only in private forests (Stein et al. 2010).

While some technical assistance and incentive programs are in place, forestland owners are rarely fully compensated for the environmental public goods they provide. While investments in private forestlands are inherently long-term, costs are annual, liquidity is low, and risks can be high. If Americans are to continue to enjoy all the benefits they receive from private forestlands, then reasonable returns from forestland investments are needed. Despite the clear environmental and economic benefits of private forests, US landowners today have few incentives or opportunities to manage their land for biodiversity or ecosystem services (Ruhl et al. 2007). Here we provide a landowner perspective on environmental stewardship. In particular, we share some insights about family forestland owners that can improve the design of conservation programs that aim to incentivize environmental benefits on private lands. We provide personal perspectives on forest conservation on private lands from two landowners with whom we have been collaborating (see boxes 7.1 and 7. 2) and offer a brief summary of family forestland owners and conservation based on our experience working with them in the southeastern United States over the past decade.

FACTS ABOUT FAMILY FORESTLAND OWNERS

The average forestland owner in the United States is aging, not active on the land, and considering selling the land in the near future. While the average family forest owner owns 25 acres of forests, the majority own fewer than 10 acres (Butler 2008). Excluding these small forest parcels (<10 acres), the average family owns 58 acres. Average forest holdings tend to be smaller in the northern United States and larger in the Intermountain West. Seventy percent of family forestland owners are fifty-five or older and own approximately 75 percent of all private forestland (Butler 2008). One in five acres of US private forestland is owned by someone who is seventy-five or older. Most family owners have little or no activity planned on their forestland in the next five years, and one in five acres of private forests in the United States is owned by an individual who plans to sell or transfer all or some of his or her land in the next five years.

Despite these demographic challenges, family forestland owners around the country express a strong desire to be forest stewards and to leave a healthy forest legacy to future generations. Specifically, they give five main reasons for owning their forestland: beauty and scenery, family heritage, privacy, protection of nature, and a connection to their home (Butler 2008). When forest owners are asked about their major concerns, environmental and economic issues are at the top and include

Box 7.1. A Landowner Perspective: Longleaf Pine Steward Faces Challenges to Lasting Conservation

Tom Smith, a retired military officer, owns 1,100 acres of pine forests in the Florida panhandle near the Alabama border. Much of the land had been used to grow timber plantations of loblolly (*Pinus taeda*) and slash pine (*Pinus elliottii*). However, the soils are sandy and loamy, perfectly suited for native longleaf pine (Pinus palustris).

A portion of Tom's property already supports a mature longleaf pine stand with a healthy, intact understory community of plants and animals, including the gopher tortoise (*Gopherus polyphemus*), a candidate species under the US Endangered Species Act. Over the past fifteen years, Tom has planted longleaf pine and wiregrass, an important understory plant and food source for gopher tortoises, on his property (figure 7.1). Fire is a natural and critical component of longleaf pine ecosystems, and Tom uses regular prescribed burning to maintain ecosystem health. A reproducing gopher tortoise population now inhabits his longleaf pine stands. Tom recently cleared a loblolly pine stand and replaced it with longleaf seedlings. As Tom thins and burns his slash pine stands, they are quickly becoming marginal habitat for gopher tortoises. Tortoises are present there along forest edges, road shoulders, and power line right-of-ways. As the slash pine stands become economically mature, Tom intends to harvest the timber and convert the stands to longleaf pine. Although Tom's primary interest is the ecological restoration of the endangered longleaf pine ecosystem, he hopes to generate sufficient income from his property to support his management and restoration goals.

Tom is seventy-five years old, and none of his heirs share his commitment to longleaf pine conservation. He fears that an intergenerational transfer of his property will ultimately result in the loss of the environmental benefits he has achieved over the past fifteen years. Tom has struggled to secure a land easement agreement because of the upfront and financial endowment costs required to guarantee land management in perpetuity. On multiple occasions, Tom has offered to donate his land to the Longleaf Alliance, a local nonprofit organization whose mission is the restoration and conservation of longleaf forest ecosystems. The Longleaf Alliance has assisted Tom in land management activities on his property, including prescribed fire and other practices intended to improve gopher tortoise habitat. While it is interested in owning the property as a demonstration forest, the Longleaf Alliance does not hold land easements, has no means to assist Tom financially, and has no legally binding mandate to receive Tom's property and honor his desire to maintain longleaf pine restoration as the priority.

Tom welcomes any opportunity to create and sell credits tied to gopher tortoise habitat under a pre-listing conservation program. He is optimistic that proceeds from a pre-listing conservation program could be used to finance his restoration and management goals, as well as perhaps help him secure a conservation easement.

FIGURE 7.1. The conversion from loblolly pine (*Pinus taeda*), a species poorly suited to sandy soils, to longleaf pine (*P. palustris*) greatly increases a landowner's ability to profitably manage timber. It also provides quality habitat for wildlife and plant communities. The use of fire, via prescribed burns, throughout the life of a longleaf pine stand and the enhanced transmission of light through the canopy to the forest floor encourage a diversity of grasses and forbs that are important for many species, including the gopher tortoise.

insects or tree diseases, keeping land intact for future generations, wildfires, trespassing, and high property taxes (Butler 2008). All this suggests that new programs that strongly incentivize environmental stewardship while helping to cover the economic costs of doing so could maintain and improve biodiversity and ecosystem services on private forests.

WHAT FAMILY FORESTLAND OWNERS THINK ABOUT CONSERVATION PROGRAMS

A recent study asked family forestland owners in the southern United States their thoughts on conservation easements, which is the premier strategy for biodiversity conservation on private lands (GfK 2009; Rissman et al. 2007). While conservation practitioners have been successful in implementing land easements on more than 19.5 million acres throughout the United States (Henefin 2013), survey results suggest that property rights are a major concern of forestland owners. These landowners expressed serious concerns about programs that (1) limit control over their land, (2) involve permanence (i.e., conservation easements held in perpetuity), and (3) limit options for future generations. Landowners also expressed a lack of trust in program administrators, the government in particular (GfK 2009).

Conservation programs under the Farm Bill provide technical assistance, cost-sharing payments, and term easements to private landowners (Cain and Lovejoy 2006). Forestland owners more commonly participate in programs under the Farm Bill compared to conservation easements. In 2006, 6 percent (660,000) of US family forestland owners participated in Farm Bill cost-share programs designed to improve forest health. This represents approximately 20 percent of all family-owned forestland and over 55 million acres (Butler 2008). The Farm Bill is popular with private forest owners for a number of reasons, among them, flexibility, term limits, and a portfolio of programmatic options. While landowners prefer programs that include financial and technical assistance, they are also partial to programs that provide flexibility in the level of participation and the practices in which they choose to engage. Contracts under Farm Bill programs are for specific periods, and reenrollment is common. Because of this flexibility, landowners have the opportunity to directly experience how certain programs will affect them without making an initial, long-term commitment to land conservation practices. Consequently, landowners can become familiar

Box 7.2. A Landowner Perspective: A Family Tradition of Protecting Wildlife through Wise Management

William Brown, a certified public accountant, and his wife own 360 acres of forest in southern Mississippi. Their forest is a short 15-mile commute from their main residence, and they maintain a small home on the property for weekend stays and social gatherings. The forestland has been passed down through multiple generations and provides the couple and their adult children with much pleasure, along with some income. A private professional forestry consultant helps manages the timber on the property. The management practices are designed to enhance the overall value of the property, including timber stand improvement through harvests, prescribed fire, invasive species control, wildlife food plots, watershed protection, and longleaf pine restoration. Wildlife is a priority for the Browns, and the family has been recognized for more than a decade for their environmental stewardship. They are particularly fond of the gopher tortoise, which is present on their property. With technical assistance, the family marks tortoise dens and monitors individuals. The appearance of new juveniles is an event celebrated with the grandchildren.

The Brown's overall management goal is to make the property financially self-sustaining, as well as provide some additional income. A hurricane negatively impacted the property several years ago. The salvage operations left open but manageable stands of slash pine on sandy sites. Rather than clear-cut and sell the timber in a depressed market, the family opted to retain the stands. They planted longleaf pine seedlings within the damaged stands and began an aggressive prescribed fire regime to minimize woody underbrush and promote grasses and forbs that serve as fuels for future fires. The new management regime will provide improved wildlife habitat, particularly for Bobwhite Quail (*Colinus virginianus*) and gopher tortoises.

Periodic timber harvests continue to provide income to the family. However, the necessary interval between harvests and the small size of their timber stands limit the ability of the property to provide the continuous income stream needed to meet recurring management costs. The family has enjoyed significant technical assistance from the state forestry and wildlife agencies, federal programs, and the nonprofit organization Longleaf Alliance. A number of federal cost-share programs have reduced the out-of-pocket costs of their management and restoration activities. The US Department of Agriculture Natural Resources Conservation Service's Environmental Quality Incentives Program and the Wildlife Habitat Incentives Program have provided funding to plant trees, perform prescribed burns, and control invasive plants. The Browns often speak at landowner forums. Their most prominent message is that management inputs are necessary in order to derive the conservation benefits that forests can provide. Like many private landowners, the Browns derive far more value from the intangible returns of their forest than from the sale of timber products. Yet they need to produce sufficient income to afford the land and to continue to manage it in a manner consistent with their land ethic. While favorable tax policies provide some relief in terms of the Browns' ability to maintain and manage their property, the family would welcome a pre-listing conservation program focused on species like the gopher tortoise. A program that provides explicit financial incentives for managing private property for species habitat would help families like the Browns maintain their property. The Browns are already committed to private forest conservation, and they view a pre-listing conservation program as an opportunity to achieve their long-term goal. As William Brown told us, "What was once viewed as a source of income has become a passion and love to preserve the land, forest, wildlife, and habitat to be enjoyed now and hopefully for future generations."

and comfortable with conservation programs, practices, and technical assistance providers over time and build relationships that lead to greater engagement in land stewardship.

LESSONS LEARNED

As pre-listing conservation (PLC) approaches gain interest, the perspectives and needs of family forest owners should be carefully considered to ensure success and productive collaborations (Sorice and Abel this volume). First, many family forestland owners share the goal of conserving and stewarding healthy forests over the long term. By keeping in mind that these landowners want to leave a forest legacy to their families, PLC advocates can approach them as true partners. Second, financial incentives are an important factor for ensuring that forest owners are able to participate in a proposed program. Well-managed forests can produce income to help defray management costs and cover property taxes, an important consideration for many families. Third, in order to increase program participation, the "conservation toolbox" must be diversified. Conservation easements, especially those that support continued forest management, are a smart tool for some forestland owners. So are Farm Bill programs that provide technical assistance, cost-sharing payments, and term easements; these programs have achieved higher rates of enrollment by providing more flexibility to landowners on the length of their commitment. Other incentive-based programs, like PLC programs, should be added to the toolbox. Fourth, private forestland owners appreciate both predictability and choice. PLC advocates should be candid about the terms of agreement, the availability and source of technical assistance, and the timing and source of payments if any. PLC programs can improve conservation outcomes by better incorporating landowner needs and perspectives into project design and focusing on offering private forestland owners more choices on how to conserve their forests for future generations.

PART TWO

Designing Pre-Listing Conservation Programs

CHAPTER 8

Pre-Listing Conservation

Law, Policy, and Pilot Projects

YA-WEI LI AND TIMOTHY MALE

ABSTRACT

The US Fish and Wildlife Service can use its existing authority under the US Endangered Species Act to create pre-listing conservation pilot projects. Through these projects, the US Fish and Wildlife Service can recognize the benefits of conservation measures taken before a species is protected under the Endangered Species Act, which can offset future adverse impacts to the species if the project is expected to generate an overall benefit. The method of establishing projects and the amount of regulatory predictability offered to participants will depend on several factors. Two important factors are whether the project occurs on federal lands or requires federal agency approval and whether participants know what adverse impacts will be offset by pre-listing conservation pilot activities. All projects should be anchored in a pre-listing agreement. These agreements can take several forms, depending partly on whether the adverse impacts will require authorization under Section 7 or Section 10 of the Endangered Species Act. All approaches should include a Section 7 "conference" on the agreement. To increase regulatory certainty for project participants, the conference must analyze both the beneficial effects of the pre-listing conservation pilot measures and, if known, the future adverse effects to be offset under the project. The US Fish and Wildlife Service must also address at least three policy issues when establishing pilot projects. The lessons learned from pilot projects will establish the foundation for an expanded and improved pre-listing conservation program.

INTRODUCTION

Wildlife conservation is generally less expensive and more effective when deployed before species populations reach crisis levels. Yet the US Endangered Species Act (ESA) does not always encourage early conservation. For example, if a land developer finds a rare plant that might become listed under the ESA, he receives no regulatory benefit for protecting the plant now and may even be tempted to remove it to avoid future development restrictions.

To seek public input on this issue, the US Fish and Wildlife Service (USFWS) issued an Advance Notice of Proposed Rulemaking on March 15, 2012 (USFWS 2012a). The Advance Notice states that the USFWS intends to "propose a rule to encourage landowners and other potentially regulated interests to fund or carry out voluntary conservation actions beneficial to candidate and other at-risk species by providing a new type of assurance that, in the event the species is listed, the benefits of appropriate voluntary conservation actions will be recognized as offsetting the adverse effects of activities carried out by that landowner or others after listing." This volume is dedicated to this approach: prelisting conservation (PLC).

The USFWS can begin demonstrating the concept of PLC through a limited number of carefully selected pilot projects. Pilots will enable the USFWS to identify strengths and gaps in how it implements PLC. The lessons learned will be invaluable to creating an improved and expanded PLC program in the future. Pilots will also allow the USFWS to implement the PLC concept immediately rather than wait for new rules to be drafted and issued, a process that can span several years. We describe how the USFWS can create pilot projects using its existing rules and policies under the ESA.

PLC can offer at least four key benefits to conservation. First, it incentivizes early conservation, which generally reduces the costs and difficulty of species recovery. Second, it incentivizes habitat management and improvements beyond only preservation, which is needed to conserve and recover many conservation-reliant species (Scott et al. 2010). Third, agencies and landowners who use PLC to offset impacts that occur after listing could also offset impacts that occur before listing. This would represent a significant gain for candidate species, as the ESA affords them no statutory protection. And fourth, PLC can reduce and possibly eliminate the need to list a candidate species. Even if listing is required, early conservation may allow the USFWS to list a species as threatened rather than endangered. For these reasons, suitable pilot projects are worth pursuing from the perspective of wildlife conservation.

While the ESA already provides several tools to achieve these conservation goals, some of them lack the regulatory predictability needed to incentivize voluntary conservation of unlisted species. Habitat Conservation Plans (HCPs), for example, have never been used to cover only unlisted species and, according to the USFWS and the courts, are not legally required to recover species or result in a "net benefit" for conservation (USFWS and NMFS 1996; Center for Biological Diversity vs. US Fish and Wildlife Service 2002). Candidate Conservation Agreements (CCAs) do cover only unlisted species but do not offer federal agencies and other participants assurances or guarantees about their ESA obligations if a species is listed.

Candidate Conservation Agreements with Assurances (CCAAs) are the tool most similar to PLC, because they encourage nonfederal landowners to conserve candidate species in exchange for an enhancement of survival permit that would authorize certain incidental take if the species were listed. By issuing the permit, the USFWS is recognizing the benefits of the voluntary conservation measures initiated before listing and often allowing those benefits to offset post-listing incidental take that occurs on the property. As described in this chapter, we regard CCAAs as one component of the PLC framework. Because CCAAs apply only to nonfederal entities, however, they do not encourage federal agencies to conserve candidate species. Further, when issuing an enhancement of survival permit under a CCAA, the USFWS must have some information about the adverse impacts to be offset by the conservation actions under that CCAA. Not all landowners, however, can provide this information at the time they enter into a CCAA. For those landowners, the USFWS needs a tool to incentivize PLC actions, even if it does not know exactly how those actions may be used to offset future adverse impacts.

FIVE STEPS OF PILOT PROJECTS

PLC pilot projects can be structured in many ways, depending on factors such as the number of project participants, the type and life history characteristics of species, the size and nature of impacts to species, and whether the project involves an activity that requires the approval of a federal agency. Despite these variables, most pilot projects will involve the five steps outlined below. Because the purpose of this section is to provide an overview of pilot projects, it refers to certain concepts that we explain further in later sections.

Step 1: Define project and draft agreement

There are several possible ways to set up a pilot project. For example, a landowner interested in generating credits from conservation measures on his property can ask the USFWS to assess the potential for creating a successful project. A developer could also pay landowners to take conservation measures on their own land, with the goal of generating enough credits to more than offset future impacts from the developer's projects. In all cases, participants work closely with the USFWS to initiate projects. For PLC projects, consultations and partnerships between the USFWS and the appropriate state wildlife agency will be important. A state connection is important because states have primary authority to regulate unlisted species that are not in the federal trust, including most candidate species. The USFWS, acting on its own, has limited authority over those species under federal law.

All key aspects of a PLC project should be reflected in an agreement signed by project participants and the USFWS. At a minimum, each agreement should include the following.

Background information:

- Project participants and their individual roles and obligations under the project.
- Brief summary of status of affected species, including discussion of potential directions for recovery, relevant data gaps, and uncertainties. This information may also be placed in appendixes, particularly if it is not directly relevant to implementing the agreement.

"Overall benefit" approval standard:

- Beneficial PLC actions to be taken under the project.
- If known, a description of the specific proposed activities that will adversely impact the species and will be offset by the PLC actions. If this information is unavailable, a description of the general types of activities that may be offset by the PLC actions.

- How the project will meet the PLC approval standard of an overall benefit to the species, after accounting for the beneficial and any known adverse impacts resulting from the activities covered by the PLC project. An overall benefit is achieved when the long-term benefits to the species resulting from a project exceed the adverse impacts to the species resulting from the activities offset under the project (see "Key Legal and Policy Issues" below).

Crediting-debiting process:

- When and how the USFWS will formally recognize the benefits from the PLC actions, a process called "crediting."
- How the USFWS will allow project participants to use credits to offset future incidental take, a process called "debiting." As explained later, the ESA already provides three methods of crediting and debiting PLC actions: conservation banking, section 7 conferencing, and CCAA policy. Each PLC project will use one of these methods, depending on the nature of the project.
- Any arrangements to trade or bank credits.

Additional required provisions:

- Any regulatory assurances or predictability provided to project participants, including provisions on changed and unforeseen circumstances.
- Duration of agreement, including any ongoing obligations to continue with the conservation actions if the species is listed and conditions for terminating agreement.
- Biological monitoring, reporting, and adaptive management requirements.
- Funding requirements for PLC actions, including where the funding will come from and who is responsible for providing it.

Step 2: Complete section 7(a)(4) conference on approval of draft agreement

Before a federal agency takes an action that may impact a candidate species, it can enter into discussions with the USFWS to assess the likely impacts of the action on the species and adopt conservation measures to avoid, minimize, or offset those impacts (USFWS and NMFS 1998). This process is called a "conference" and occurs under section 7(a)(4) of the ESA. The USFWS's policy is to conduct a conference on any natural resource decision it makes that affects a candidate species (USFWS and NMFS 1998). This policy applies to the approval of any PLC agreement. The main purpose of conferences is to determine whether a proposed activity is "likely to jeopardize" a candidate species. We believe conferences can serve another important purpose. Without a conference, a PLC agreement has no direct recognition under the ESA: it is simply an agreement between the USFWS and project participants. A conference fills this gap by linking the agreement to the ESA's framework.

There are at least two options for structuring conferences based on the types of activities they cover. Under option 1, a conference covers only the beneficial impacts of the PLC actions and not the adverse impacts of the activities to be offset by those actions. This option is most suitable if, at the time of the conference, project participants lack a clear understanding of future adverse activities. Because these conferences do not cover adverse impacts of any type, they can be structured as "informal conferences" (USFWS and NMFS 1998).

Option 2 is to confer on both the beneficial PLC actions and the future adverse impacts and to issue a draft section 7 incidental take statement or a final section 10(a)(1)(A) "enhancement of survival" permit after evaluating the overall impacts. The final permit would have a delayed effective date tied to the date of any future listing of the covered species, as under current CCAA policy (USFWS and NMFS 1999). The main advantage of conferencing on both the beneficial and the future adverse impacts is to front load any ESA effects determination that may be triggered if the species is listed, including determinations arising from section 7(a)(2) consultations for federal agency actions. By issuing effects determinations far earlier than is usually the case, project participants will receive greater regulatory predictability about the ESA requirements that may apply after listing. The USFWS, of course, cannot evaluate the impacts of adverse activities unless those activities are described at the time of the conference. Because this information is not always available at such an early stage, option 2 may not be feasible in many situations.

Step 3: Performing PLC actions and monitoring results

Project participants begin performing the conservation actions described in a PLC agreement and monitoring the implementation and effectiveness of those actions, which are periodically reported to the USFWS. The USFWS evaluates the results to ensure that the project is producing the desired outcomes for the species and either recommends or requires additional conservation measures to compensate for any unexpected shortfalls, depending on whether such contingencies were agreed to in advance and reflected in the agreement.

Step 4: If a species is listed, finalize any draft incidental take authorizations

If a species is listed despite all prior conservation measures, three scenarios are possible. First, if the earlier conference included a final section 10(a)(1)(A) permit, that permit should automatically take effect upon listing, just as it does under CCAA policy. Second, if instead of a section 10(a)(1)(A) permit, the USFWS had issued a draft section 7 incidental take statement, the USFWS could finalize that statement without much difficulty, assuming certain conditions are met. As part of the conference, the USFWS would have also issued a final "conference report," which could convert into a final "biological opinion" after listing. Third, if the earlier conference covered only the beneficial PLC actions, the USFWS would need to determine how those actions could offset any future adverse impacts under the project. Project participants can assist with this determination by providing information to the USFWS on any such impacts.

Step 5: Continue implementing PLC actions to achieve specified conservation goals

The duration of the conservation actions is specified in the PLC agreement. As a general principle, we believe permanent impacts must be permanently offset, first by avoidance and minimization and then by compensatory mitigation of unavoidable impacts. If necessary, a PLC agreement should provide for funding or other assurances to hold participants responsible for continuing to implement agreed upon conservation measures. Step 5 also involves implementation of adaptive management measures and review of the successes and challenges of the project.

THREE CATEGORIES OF PILOT PROJECTS

Pilot projects may have many similarities, but they also differ in important ways. One key difference is how the USFWS recognizes the benefits

TABLE 8.1 RELATION BETWEEN THE THREE CATEGORIES OF PROJECTS AND THE THREE CREDITING-DEBITING METHODS

Crediting-Debiting Method	Category 1	Category 2	Category 3
Conservation Banking or Recovery Credit System	X		
Candidate Conservation Agreement with Assurances	X	X	X
Section 7(a)(4) conference			X

of PLC actions (i.e., crediting) and allows those benefits to offset adverse impacts (i.e., debiting). Under the ESA, the appropriate method will typically depend on (1) whether participants are federal agencies or nonfederal entities and (2) whether the participants have provided enough information about the activities to be offset by the PLC measures such that the USFWS can evaluate, at the time the PLC agreement is drafted, the adverse impacts of those activities on the species.

We have identified three existing methods to credit and debit PLC actions: conservation banking, section 7 conferencing, and CCAA policy (table 8.1). To help determine which method applies to a particular project, we have created a decision framework that identifies three categories of projects, each corresponding to a particular method (figure 8.1).

The first section of this chapter discusses how existing conservation banking and crediting policies can support Category 1 projects. This section further divides projects based on whether the banks are permanent or temporary. Next we discuss how section 7(a)(4) conferences can support Category 2 projects, which are targeted at conservation on federal lands. Finally, we discuss how CCAAs can support Category 3 projects, which are targeted at conservation on nonfederal lands. All projects will require a section 7(a)(4) conference because USFWS policy requires it to complete a conference on any natural resource decision it makes that affects a candidate species.

Category 1: Conservation banking projects

Conservation banking PLC projects are most appropriate in situations where the USFWS lacks a clear understanding at the time the PLC agreement is drafted of the future adverse impacts to be offset by the PLC actions. Without this information, the USFWS cannot evaluate the adverse impacts from those activities or issue a draft section 7 incidental

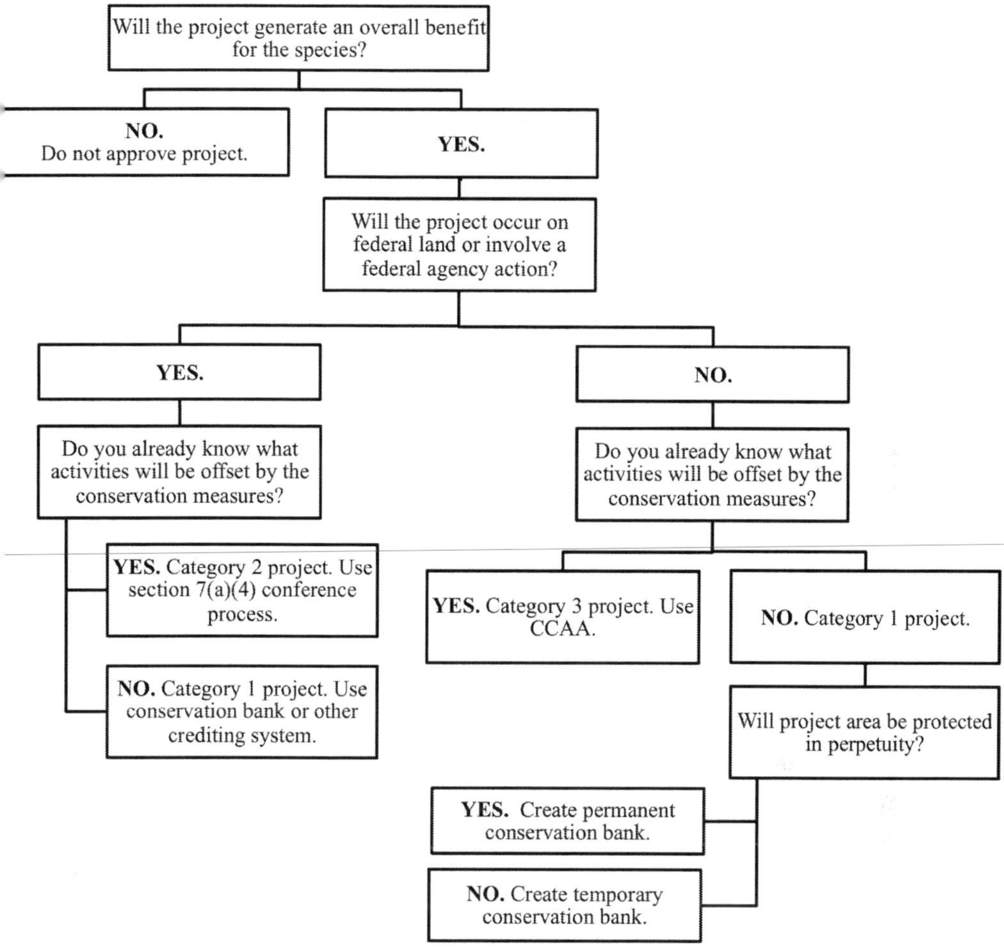

FIGURE 8.1. Decision framework for determining which existing ESA crediting-debiting method applies to a particular pilot project.

take statement or section 10(a)(1)(A) permit at the time the PLC agreement is finalized. As a result, Category 1 projects provide the least amount of regulatory predictability to participants. The USFWS can, however, offer participants two important guarantees: (1) that their PLC actions will be credited if those actions meet the conditions specified in the PLC agreement and (2) that valid credits can be used in the manner described in the agreement. By placing general sidebars on the use of those credits, the USFWS retains some control over deciding which specific future adverse impacts may be offset by the credits. For example, the USFWS could state that it will issue one credit for each individual of a species within a bank that survives to the age of two and that each credit may offset the incidental take of one individual that occurs within a 100-acre service area depicted in the PLC agreement. Participants can then begin accumulating a "bank" of credits, without having to know exactly how future incidental take might occur on those 100 acres.

Because Category 1 projects function as conservation banks for candidate species, the USFWS can create them based on existing banking policy and guidance designed for listed species. Two documents are the most applicable: the USFWS's 2003 Guidance for the Establishment, Use, and Operation of Conservation Banks (Banking Guidance) and the 2008 Recovery Crediting System (RCS) Guidance (USFWS 2003b; USFWS 2008). In our view, the most relevant distinction between the two crediting systems is the duration of the underlying conservation measures. Lands within conservation banks must generally be protected in perpetuity, whereas RCS conservation measures are not subject to this requirement.

The USFWS should consider supporting the creation of both permanent and temporary banks for candidate and other unlisted species, because each type of bank plays an important role in conservation (Carroll et al. 2008; Wolfe et al. 2012). Banks protected in perpetuity are important to the long-term recovery of species and can offset permanent impacts. Many landowners, however, are hesitant to enroll their property under a permanent easement (Sorice et al. 2013; Sorice and Abel this volume). For those participants, the ability to receive credits for conservation measures implemented for a limited time can lower the hurdles to participating in candidate conservation. Although these conservation measures are sometimes referred to as being "temporary," their effects on the species may well be permanent. For example, habitat protected for only one year can still result in permanent increases in population size. In our view, the relevant factor is not necessarily the duration of the effects but whether the underlying property is permanently protected through an appropriate legal instrument.

Crediting permanently protected conservation banks

As written, the Banking Guidance already provides the authority and overarching framework for creating permanently protected conservation banks for candidate species. The guidance states that it "can also be used to aid in the establishment of banks for candidate species." The guidance, however, lacks the specificity needed to create candidate species banks. For example, it does not describe how the USFWS will credit the benefits from candidate species banks or how those credits can offset any future incidental take. Further, it states that the "Service envisions that banks will mainly be used for candidates in conjunction with Candidate Conservation Agreements with Assurances or as a precursor to a multiple species Habitat Conservation Plan effort that covers listed and non-listed species." We envision a broader use of the Banking Guidance, one that allows the USFWS to credit PLC actions without having to determine precisely how those credits will be used in the future. Credits, for example, could potentially be used to satisfy mitigation requirements for single-species HCPs or to satisfy section 7 conservation measures if the species becomes listed.

We recommend that the USFWS revise the Banking Guidance to explicitly describe a process for creating and managing candidate species banks. In the meantime, the USFWS could issue an internal guidance document on creating PLC pilot projects, which would describe this process. In developing such guidance, the USFWS should consider the following three factors. The first is regulatory certainty. When the USFWS approves the creation of a bank for listed species, it must provide participants with certainty about when their efforts will result in credits and how those credits must be managed and used. Banks for candidate species must provide this same certainty and must do so with the added complication that credits issued before listing must be usable both before and after listing. The USFWS can provide this certainty by describing in each PLC agreement the process for issuing, managing, and debiting credits. Clear process and criteria for credit debiting are particularly important because Category 1 project participants are unlikely to know who will purchase their credits or when those purchases might occur. Each agreement can specify what types of debiting transactions the USFWS will accept and who qualifies as potential credit purchasers.

The second factor to consider is the section 7(a)(4) conference process for each PLC agreement. Because PLC banks would be designed to benefit a species and because future adverse impacts are unknown at the time the agreement is drafted, the USFWS would generally conclude with limited analysis that the decision to approve a bank will not likely jeopardize the species. As a result, no "formal conference" is required. Instead, only an "informal conference" is involved, resulting in a "conference report" that briefly describes why the approval of the agreement is "not likely to jeopardize" the candidate species. The third factor is the permanence of land protection. Similar to banks for listed species, candidate species banks should be permanently protected through fee title or a conservation easement by the time the first credit in the bank is sold. Further, credits would be sellable only after conditions for the long-term management and monitoring of the bank are met.

Crediting temporarily protected conservation banks

Many landowners may be willing to take PLC actions but are unwilling to permanently protect the underlying property through fee title or a conservation easement. The USFWS can encourage these landowners to participate in PLC by establishing a crediting system for projects that do not involve permanent land protection. We have found no existing USFWS guidance document or policy that has created such a system for unlisted species. We do believe, however, that the USFWS can create one based on the RCS Guidance (Robertson and Rinker 2010).

The RCS Guidance establishes a crediting-debiting system that allows a federal agency to help recover listed species by creating a "bank" of credits, which can be used at a later time to offset negative impacts from that agency's actions. Importantly, the system was designed to accommodate both temporary and permanent conservation actions. Unlike the USFWS's Banking Guidance, the RCS Guidance does not mention candidate species, nor does it imply any intent to cover candidates. Nonetheless, we believe that PLC projects can adopt the RCS framework of establishing a crediting-debiting process for conservation measures occurring on lands that are not permanently protected through the project. We recommend that the USFWS use the RCS Guidance as a template to draft a new guidance that describes a candidate banking system for PLC actions on temporarily protected lands. Below, we describe four key attributes of such a system and how it would differ from the RCS for listed species.

The first attribute is rollover assurance. Any system for crediting temporary conservation banks must provide participants with some assurance about when their efforts will result in credits. A PLC agreement can offer this guarantee by describing how credits will be established, managed, and used. Thus the agreement acts as a legal contract that requires the USFWS to follow through on its promise to issue credits if certain conditions are met. To "roll over" these credits after listing, the USFWS can rely on contract law, just as it does for permanent candidate species banks.

The second attribute is the section 7(a)(4) conference. When approving a PLC project, the USFWS should complete a section 7(a)(4) conference that covers the processes for both developing and debiting credits. This approach will provide participants with greater predictability about when and how they can use credits to offset future adverse impacts. The RCS Guidance adopts a similar approach, stating, "Ordinarily, a programmatic consultation will address both the crediting and debiting processes; in rare cases separate consultations may address the two processes."

The third attribute is application of PLC to nonfederal participants. Although the RCS Guidance is designed for federal agencies, we feel that the USFWS should consider creating a single PLC system that covers both federal and nonfederal participants. This is possible if the USFWS specifies in each PLC agreement the types of future adverse impacts that may be offset using PLC credits. For example, an agreement with nonfederal participants may specify that credits may be used to satisfy mitigation needs under both sections 7 and 10, provided the same method is used to calculate the net impacts to the species in both situations.

The fourth attribute is the potential lack of market demand for credits. Category 1 projects are the easiest to initiate because they do not require participants to know what adverse impacts they seek to offset under the project. But the post-listing impacts to a species may be so minimal that there are far more credits than will ever be needed. Thus participants assume a risk that their credits will have no tangible value after listing. This is perhaps less a concern if the participant is a federal agency, because those entities have an affirmative section 7(a)(1) obligation to help recover listed species. Nonfederal participants, however, have no such duty and, therefore, need to be informed of this risk. The USFWS could consider whether to create a program in which credits held by private entities are purchased by the USFWS or another federal agency, possibly in furtherance of the agency's section 7(a)(1) recovery obligations, assuming those credits are not used or purchased in the private market. A program of this type would incentivize candidate conservation by minimizing the risk borne by private entities. And it would result in far greater benefits to species because credits are retired without any adverse impacts to offset.

Category 2: Federal agency projects

We assume participants choose Category 1 projects because they lack a clear understanding, at the time they draft a PLC agreement, of the adverse activities to be offset by the projects. In some situations, however, participants will have this understanding. As a result, the USFWS can complete a section 7(a)(4) conference that covers both the beneficial PLC actions and the adverse activities. The USFWS can also issue a draft section 7 incidental take statement when it completes the conference, if the project involves a federal agency. We refer to these situations as Category 2 projects.

Most Category 2 projects will likely involve a federal agency authorizing an ongoing activity that harms a candidate species. If the species becomes listed, the activity will immediately be regulated under the ESA because it is "likely to adversely affect" the species. For the agency to continue the activity after listing, it must obtain an incidental take statement through a section 7(a)(2) consultation with the USFWS. As a condition of receiving the take statement, the agency may first need to modify the activity and avoid or minimize certain impacts to the species.

Instead of waiting until after listing to determine the ESA restrictions that apply to the activity, the agency could obtain regulatory predictability far earlier by creating a Category 2 project. As part of the project, the agency describes the specific activity that is expected to result in incidental take of the species after it becomes listed, while the USFWS determines what conservation measures, if any, would offset take to such an extent that the project produces an overall benefit for the species. Assuming this overall benefit standard is met, the USFWS and the federal agency would draft a PLC agreement. For the agency, greater regulatory predictability is the benefit for meeting this higher conservation standard.

Modified threshold for triggering section 7(a)(4) formal conference

After the terms of the PLC agreement are finalized, the USFWS, the agency, and any third-party participants sign the agreement. Because this approval by the USFWS is a discretionary natural resource decision that affects a candidate species, the USFWS's policies require it to complete a section 7(a)(4) conference on the approval. There are several ways to structure a conference. One way is by issuing a "conference opinion" on any PLC project intended to offset impacts from a federal action that is "likely to adversely affect" the species if it became listed. We recognize that under the USFWS's section 7 rules, a conference opinion is triggered not by a "likely to adversely affect" finding but by a "likely to jeopardize" finding (USFWS and NMFS 1998). For PLC pilot projects, we suggest that the USFWS consider using the lower "likely to adversely affect" standard for initiating formal conferences, because this standard triggers formal consultation for listed species. By adopting the same standard for initiating conferences and consultations, the USFWS can create a conference that mimics a consultation, thereby front loading much of the section 7 formal consultation that presumably must be completed if the species is listed.

The "likely to adversely affect" determination should be straightforward for a PLC project, as the Section 7 Consultation Handbook states that "if incidental take is anticipated to occur as a result of the proposed action, an 'is likely to adversely affect' determination should be made." An agency action that requires offsets will inherently cause some adverse impact on the species, thus triggering a "likely to adversely affect" finding. The only exceptions are if the effects are discountable, insignificant, or entirely beneficial (no negative effects whatsoever).

In a conference opinion, the USFWS could clearly explain how PLC actions would be treated under a section 7(a)(2) consultation if the species becomes listed. As a general matter, we believe these actions can be treated as section 7 "conservation measures." The USFWS defines conservation measures as "actions pledged in the project description that the action agency or the applicant would implement to further the recovery of the species under review" (USFWS and NMFS 1998). Thus the agency action subject to conference consists of the conservation measures that benefit the species and the proposed activities that will harm the species.

We believe that PLC actions can also be treated as "reasonable and prudent alternatives" under a section 7 consultation, but the need to do so is unlikely to arise. Reasonable and prudent alternatives are designed to avoid the likelihood of jeopardizing a species or destroying or adversely modifying critical habitat. If a proposed PLC project could result in either of these outcomes, its adverse impacts are likely too great to be compatible with our proposed "overall benefit" standard (see below).

Converting a conference opinion into a biological opinion

If the species becomes listed, the USFWS can use the final conference opinion to expedite a Section 7(a)(2) consultation. Specifically, the USFWS would convert the conference opinion into a final "biological opinion" with few or no changes, assuming certain conditions are met. To accomplish this conversion, the conference opinion could include a provision similar to the following, which comes from the Section 7 Consultation Handbook (USFWS and NMFS 1998).

> This concludes the conference for (action). You may ask the Service to confirm the conference opinion as a biological opinion issued through formal consultation if the (species is listed or critical habitat is designated). The request must be in writing. If the Service reviews the proposed action and

> finds that there have been no significant changes in the action as planned or in the information used during the conference, the Service will confirm the conference opinion as the biological opinion on the project and no further section 7 consultation will be necessary.

In addition to the requirement of "no significant changes," we believe another requirement should be that the PLC actions have resulted, or are likely to result, in an overall benefit to the affected species. If it appears at the time of listing that an overall benefit is unlikely to result because of unforeseen or changed circumstances, the participants should be required, as part of the PLC agreement, to take additional conservation measures or adopt additional restrictions on their project to meet the overall benefit standard. In other words, federal agencies and their permittees should not receive the same regulatory assurances through PLC projects as those provided for nonfederal activities. Offering such assurances would be inconsistent with the USFWS's interpretation of section 7(a)(1) as prohibiting federal agencies from receiving No Surprise and other regulatory assurances (USFWS and NMFS 1999). This lack of assurances should be clearly spelled out in the PLC agreement, so that participants are not given false expectations about their potential post-listing obligations. In evaluating whether an overall benefit standard is likely to be met, the USFWS could use the best scientific and commercial data available. Although this data standard applies throughout ESA decision making, it is particularly relevant to the conversion of a conference opinion into a biological opinion, because new scientific information on the affected species may have become available between the time of the conference and the time of the conversion.

Finally, as part of a conversion, the USFWS could evaluate whether the agency action triggers any of the four general conditions for reinitiating consultation (USFWS and NMFS 1998). If any condition is triggered, the USFWS could reevaluate the impacts to the affected species before issuing a formal biological opinion. If the USFWS does not consider all four conditions during the conversion, it may be required to consider them shortly after the biological opinion is issued, as the reinitiation triggers are certain to apply at that stage.

Category 3: Nonfederal projects

Category 3 projects are conceptually similar to Category 2 projects, except that they cover adverse impacts resulting from nonfederal activities. Under a Category 3 project, the USFWS would complete a confer-

Box 8.1. Examples of Candidate Conservation Agreements with Assurances (CCAA) that describe a "net benefit" as the desired outcome of the agreement

The Southern Idaho Ground Squirrel CCAA for the Soulen Company indicates that it may take ten years for the agreement to achieve a "net conservation benefit" for the species and that, "in order to qualify for approval, the Agreement and site-specific plan must result in a net improvement in ground squirrel habitat or populations."

The Programmatic Southern Idaho Ground Squirrel CCAA specifies that "in order to qualify for approval, the Participating Landowner's site-specific plan must result in a net improvement in ground squirrel habitat or populations on the enrolled lands."

The CCAA for the Lesser Prairie-Chicken and Sand Dune Lizard in New Mexico indicates that the certificates of inclusion used to enroll participants must "document that the Participating Landowner's proposed habitat enhancement or protection measures (conservation measures) will provide net conservation benefits" to the species.

ence on both the beneficial PLC actions and the proposed adverse impacts and issue a section 10(a)(1)(A) enhancement of survival permit that covers those adverse impacts. Because this is how the USFWS currently approves CCAAs, no new tools are needed to support Category 3 projects. Rather, Category 3 projects are CCAAs.

We believe current CCAA policy is adequate to create Category 3 pilot projects. The policy can be applied in a manner that allows the USFWS to explicitly recognize the benefits of PLC actions, including through the issuance of credits, and to describe how those benefits can offset adverse impacts to the species that occur both before and after listing. Further, the policy contains enough flexibility for the USFWS to require avoidance, minimization, and mitigation measures that could achieve an overall benefit for many species. We recognize, however, that the current approval standard for CCAAs is not explicitly based on an overall or net conservation benefit but rather on whether the agreement "would preclude or remove any need to list the covered species." We do believe this discrepancy is a minor obstacle that the USFWS can overcome through future policy or guidance revisions: we have identified at least three CCAAs that explicitly describe a "net benefit" as the desired outcome of the agreement (box 8.1). Several other CCAAs also refer implicitly to an overall or net benefit standard in their discussion of the anticipated effects of the agreement. Thus some USFWS offices have already been using the concept of net or overall benefit when approving CCAAs.

KEY LEGAL AND POLICY ISSUES

PLC requires the USFWS to make numerous legal and policy choices, each of which is within its discretion and authority. We identify three of these choices that we believe are critical to creating successful PLC pilot projects and offer recommendations on each. We emphasize that these are recommendations for pilot projects, not necessarily recommendations for a future comprehensive PLC program. The lessons learned from pilots will help determine whether these choices should be adopted or abandoned.

First policy choice: Overall benefit approval standard

The USFWS needs to determine the conservation standard for approving PLC pilot projects. Although several options are available, we believe that an "overall benefit" standard is appropriate. We define this standard as follows: the long-term benefits to the species resulting from a project exceed the adverse impacts to the species resulting from the activities offset under the project. Benefits to species can include certain adverse impacts avoided as a result of the project, such as commitments to forgo actions that would harm a species. In determining whether the overall benefit standard is met, the USFWS could evaluate benefits and harms using the same metric and ensure that it directly or indirectly informs the USFWS about the status of the species itself, as opposed to only the status of the species' habitat (see Gartner et al. this volume). For example, the USFWS could evaluate how a proposed housing development project would diminish a species' probability of survival and reproductive rate and compare that diminishment to the expected increase in both factors as a result of the avoidance, minimization, and compensatory mitigation performed under the PLC project.

Our definition, which focuses on effects to species, differs from a definition based exclusively on effects to habitat (e.g., comparing acres of habitat lost and preserved). The latter is inadequate to show whether the species experiences an overall benefit, because it alone does not relate habitat values to species values. When habitat is used as a proxy, the USFWS should describe how habitats lost and preserved affect the species' biological risk of endangerment by reducing the threats to the species. Without this clear translation between habitat impacts and species impacts, the USFWS risks erroneously equating improvements in habitat with improvements in a species' demographic status.

For any particular species, the USFWS may be able to achieve an overall benefit through different combinations of avoidance, minimization, and compensatory mitigation. For example, one project can rely heavily on avoidance and little on compensatory mitigation, while another project can rely heavily on compensatory mitigation and little on avoidance. Although both projects could in theory achieve an overall benefit, the latter may be less likely to do so because it relies more on compensatory mitigation, which often involves a greater degree of biological uncertainty than does avoidance. For example, habitat restoration requires creating a condition that does not yet exist rather than preserving a condition that already exists. In determining the appropriate balance of avoidance, minimization, and compensatory mitigation needed to achieve an overall benefit, avoidance should play the primary role in ensuring that a species is not inadvertently made worse off as a result of the project, and mitigation should play the primary role in ensuring that the species is made better off than the status quo. Put another way, avoidance serves as the backstop, while compensatory mitigation can advance the species' status and offset unavoidable impacts, such that an overall benefit is achieved. To meet this standard, the amount of compensatory mitigation required will commonly exceed a 1:1 benefit-to-loss ratio.

We recommend that the USFWS follow the hierarchy of avoidance, minimization, and mitigation in determining how PLC actions can satisfy any post-listing ESA requirements. Thus, an off-site conservation bank created for candidate species would be allowed to satisfy mitigation requirements only, because no on-site minimization or avoidance has been performed in advance. The USFWS should be clear with project participants about how the avoidance, minimization, and mitigation hierarchy affects their potential post-listing ESA obligations. The USFWS's RCS Guidance also reflects this hierarchical approach (USFWS 2008).

Second policy choice: Use of section 10(a)(1)(A) permits

When creating PLC projects for nonfederal participants (i.e., Category 3 projects), a key question is whether the USFWS may issue section 10(a)(1)(A) enhancement of survival permits to authorize future incidental take resulting from the projects or whether section 10(a)(1)(B) permits are required. Under current CCAA policy, section 10(a)(1)(A) permits are issued to cover adverse impacts resulting from not only the conservation activity but also certain nonconservation activities on the property. For example, the CCAA for the New England cottontail rabbit covers impacts from invasive species control (which benefits the rabbit), as well as farming, silviculture, and minor construction activities (which do not benefit the rabbit).

It is unclear, however, exactly what types of nonconservation activities could be authorized through CCAAs. The CCAA draft handbook could be read to imply that coverage is intended primarily for low-impact activities, especially "current" activities that have "traditionally" caused take (USFWS and NMFS 1999). All other activities, such as a housing development or a timber harvest, would require a section 10(a)(1)(B) permit and an accompanying HCP. Further support for this view comes from section 10(a)(1)(A) itself, which references enhancement of survival alongside other low-impact activities such as propagation enhancement, scientific research, and the establishment and maintenance of experimental populations. According to this interpretation of section 10(a)(1)(A), newly proposed, high-impact activities, such as a 1,000-acre wind energy installation, could be authorized through a section 10(a)(1)(B) incidental take permit.

Current CCAA practice, however, seems to deviate from this interpretation. One recent example is the Texas Conservation Plan for the Dunes Sagebrush Lizard (*Sceloporus arenicolus*), which consists of a CCAA and an HCP that authorize up to 21,257 acres of incidental take (USFWS 2011f). Both the CCAA and the HCP cover the same proposed activities, including oil and gas development, agricultural activities, and general activities such as hunting and off-highway vehicle use. Many of these activities are geographically broad and potentially high impact, particularly oil and gas extraction. Under the CCAA, however, the USFWS can authorize these activities using a section 10(a)(1)(A) permit, presumably on the theory that impacts to the species will be avoided, minimized, and mitigated to the point of satisfying the CCAA approval standard.

The USFWS's policy and practice on when it will issue a section 10(a)(1)(A) instead of a 10(a)(1)(B) permit are often unclear. However, a section 10(a)(1)(A) permit appears adequate to authorize incidental take under a PLC project, even for certain high-impact activities, but only if the USFWS adopts an overall benefit or other comparable standard.

This is because the overall effect of the PLC project, and the legal requirement for issuing section 10(a)(1)(A) permits, is the enhancement of survival, which connotes a net or overall improvement to the species' status. Thus our proposed "overall benefit" standard ensures not only that a species' status is improved as a result of a PLC project but also that the PLC agreement is legally consistent with the plain language of the ESA. We believe the USFWS should consider analyzing this issue in light of its past practices on issuing section 10 permits.

We caution, however, that there will likely be a point at which an activity becomes so adverse that no amount of avoidance, minimization, and mitigation could result in an enhancement of survival to the species and an overall benefit. We do not believe PLC projects are appropriate for those activities. To assess appropriateness, the USFWS should carefully evaluate every PLC project to determine whether adverse impacts to the species can be avoided and offset to a degree that generates an overall benefit. This analysis could then be reflected in the biological effects determination for the project and readily accessible to the public.

Third policy choice: Commitment to programmatic monitoring, evaluation, and transparency

While monitoring and periodic reevaluation are a stated component of CCAAs, HCPs, and other ESA tools, they have rarely been used to their full potential. A firm commitment should be made to not only collect but also evaluate all monitoring results from PLC projects and verify whether the projects are on track to meet their biological objectives. The USFWS could seek the help of academic and nongovernmental institutions, state wildlife agencies, and the proponents of the PLC project to undertake these analyses. Finally, transparency regarding the outcomes of pilot projects is important. We recommend creating a Web page that is periodically updated with monitoring results, annual reports, and the status of credits from all projects. This information will be used to guide the development of future policies or regulations on PLC and expand the tool beyond its pilot phase.

CHAPTER 9

A Primer on Biodiversity Measurement Systems

BOBBY COCHRAN AND NICOLE MANESS

ABSTRACT

Developing effective incentive programs and markets for species conservation requires tools to quantify biodiversity. Thus biodiversity measurement systems are critical for programmatic success. Measurement systems need to assess a target location rapidly, consistently, and accurately with objective indicators to assess the quantity and quality of habitats or populations relative to some reference condition. Many biodiversity measurement systems have common components: indicators, frameworks that filter those indicators, metrics that combine indicators into a single score, and processes to validate and improve the performance of the measurement system. While every market-based program will need to develop aspects tailored to its goals and local conditions, certain steps are universal to any biodiversity measurement system: define goals and conditions, assess the science, select indicators and metrics, test the system, and regularly reassess performance and make necessary modifications.

INTRODUCTION

Emerging conservation strategies such as payments for ecosystem services and market-based incentives have spurred the development of tools to better quantify conservation outcomes created by programmatic interventions. Measurement systems attempt to provide clear, reliable, and accurate information about the quality and quantity of a particular species' populations or ecosystem service on which payments and markets rely. Here we provide a brief primer on measurement systems for biodiversity, including but not limited to at-risk species and ecosystems. Biodiversity quality and quantity can be communicated as units of either (1) biodiversity benefits generated by additional actions taken on the land to protect and manage habitat and species populations or (2) impacts generated by activities on the land that reduce habitat or species populations. Those units are then translated into credits and debits, respectively, that can be traded in a marketplace to satisfy some regulatory requirement or used to determine payments to landowners for the restoration of habitat for at-risk species, including a main focus of this volume—candidate species under the US Endangered Species Act.

When based on principles of scientific credibility, transparency, and usability, biodiversity measurement systems can create a foundation wherein participants in incentive- or market-based programs can be confident that they are getting the conservation value for which they are paying. Developing an effective measurement system involves a set of explicit steps (Willamette Partnership 2011):

1. Selecting a set of quantifiable indicators that capture the biological, ecosystem, or biogeochemical changes that are of interest (i.e., the program's objective).
2. Translating those indicators into a metric that communicates the overall quantity and quality of a specific location with respect to the program's objectives through time (e.g., species or habitat).
3. Validating the outputs produced by the metric(s).
4. Evaluating and improving the metric(s) via adaptive management.

In 2011, Willamette Partnership conducted a review for the US Department of Agriculture Office of Environmental Markets of thirty-five existing biodiversity measurement systems used in incentive- and market-based programs (Willamette Partnership 2011). Drawing from that review, we provide some insights into how measurement systems can be applied to pre-listing conservation (PLC) programs that attempt to incentivize early conservation actions to protect and enhance habitat for candidate and other at-risk species. We first describe the main purposes of measurement systems for market-based programs. Second, we discuss the anatomy of measurement systems, including different approaches, common characteristics, and challenges. And third, we conclude with recommendations on designing biodiversity measurement systems for market-based programs that work both in the field and in the marketplace.

MEASURING BIODIVERSITY IN TERMS IN WHICH PEOPLE CAN INVEST

Measurements of biodiversity are undertaken for many different purposes (McDonald-Madden et al. 2010). Here we focus on measuring biodiversity in a way that informs credit calculation or monetary payment. Researchers and practitioners continue to struggle to develop approaches to quantify biodiversity and its complexity (Busch and Trexler 2003). To inform program design for biodiversity markets and other incentive programs, scientific knowledge needs to be organized into measurement systems in a way that is accessible and usable, such as the combination of multiple indicators into a single metric.

At a minimum, measurement systems need to assess a target location rapidly, consistently, and accurately with measurable indicators to assess the quantity and quality of habitats or populations relative to some reference condition. Program participants, meanwhile, need to be able to understand how a measurement system works and how it relates to land management decisions. Scale considerations in measuring benefits provided by conservation actions are both important and complex. Most landowner decisions are made at the land parcel scale, yet biodiversity characteristics (e.g., population or habitat dynamics) operate and need to be measured at a range of scales—from the parcel to the ecoregion. An effective measurement system attempts to address both landscape-level dynamics and the local scale where land management decisions are commonly made (Gartner et al. this volume).

THE ANATOMY OF MEASUREMENT SYSTEMS FOR BIODIVERSITY

Conservation practitioners have been developing and testing measurement systems for habitat and biodiversity for over four decades (USFWS 1980a; Harwell et al. 1999; Young and Sanzone 2002). Many biodiversity measurement systems have common components: indicators, frameworks that filter those indicators to meet program objectives, metrics that combine indicators into a single score, and processes

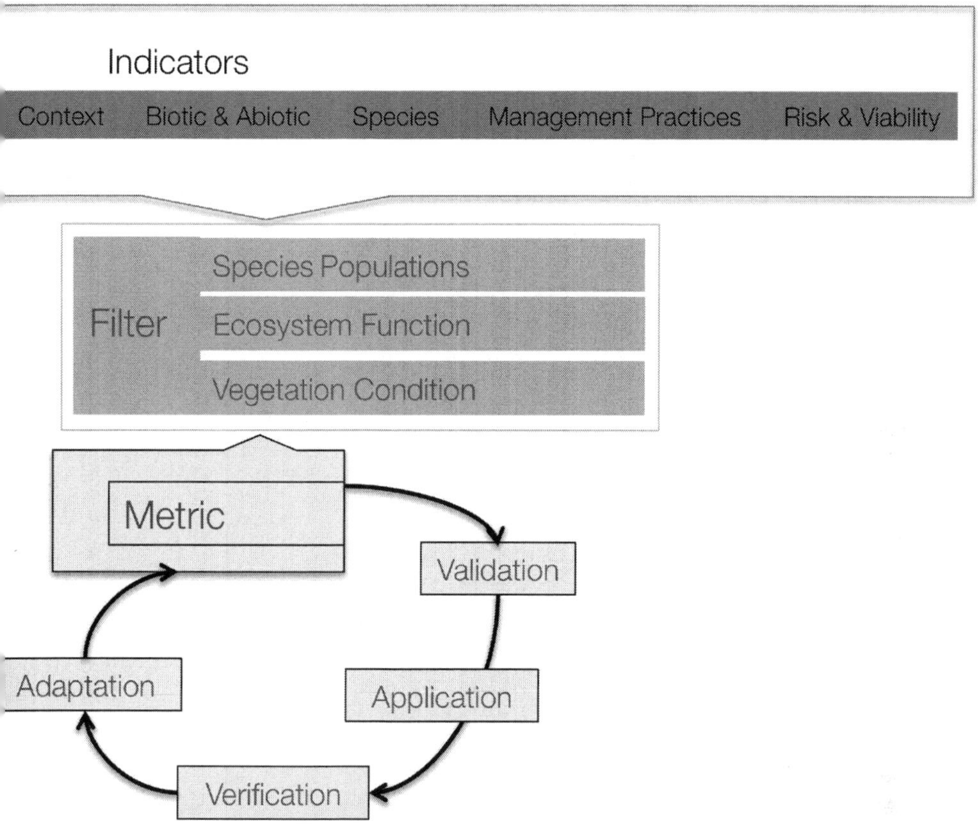

FIGURE 9.1. A framework for building and sustaining a biodiversity measurement system. Many biodiversity measurement systems have common components: specific programmatic indicators across different contexts (e.g., risk and viability), frameworks that filter those indicators to meet program objectives, a methodology that combines indicators into a single metric, and processes to validate and improve the performance of the measurement system.

to validate and improve the performance of the measurement system (figure 9.1). All of these components are necessary to ensure that an incentive- or market-based program is generating the promised biodiversity benefits. This is true whether the target of the program is at-risk species, habitat such as wetlands, or biodiversity-compatible agricultural practices. A major design challenge is to promote standardization in biodiversity measurement systems while also providing the flexibility that is often needed to address specific program objectives, needs, and conditions.

Indicators

Indicators capture site-specific information that measures the quality and quantity of habitat or species' populations. Program administrators are limited in terms of the number of indicators they can measure, and variability and subtle differences in how indicators are structured are common. Yet indicators seek to provide information in five broad categories (table 9.1):

1. Context: the contribution of a site and its biodiversity benefits within the broader landscape.
2. Biotic and abiotic: the condition of abiotic and biotic components of a site, such as soils, vegetation, water, and biogeochemistry.
3. Species attributes: the condition of populations and the suitability of habitat for particular species.
4. Management practices: how a specific location is managed (e.g., prescribed burning).
5. Risk and viability: the likelihood that a specific location will support the targeted biodiversity benefits over time given internal and external stressors.

These categories provide macro-level insights into the types of indicators that should be included in biodiversity measurement systems. Further, using these categories to characterize different types of indicators provides some consistency across programs.

Indicator Filters

Indicators are typically filtered through underlying approaches that shape how they are organized into a metric. Filtering a group of indicators through a particular programmatic framework influences how specific information from the indicators gets aggregated into an overall biodiversity or habitat metric. There are three dominant approaches: vegetation-based, species-based, and function-based.

Vegetation-based filters attempt to balance accuracy with practicality for evaluating biodiversity and habitat quality. The immobility of vegetation simplifies sampling, and on-the-ground assessments can be conducted rapidly and cost-effectively for many ecosystems (Gibbons and Freudenberger 2006). Many measurement systems use vegetation condition as a proxy for biodiversity or habitat quality by comparing the

TABLE 9.1 MAJOR INDICATOR CLASSES AND SAMPLE MEASURES

Indicator Class	Sample Measures
Context	
Connectivity	Proximity index, historic and current vegetation maps
Priority location	Located within or near a mapped conservation priority area (e.g., State Wildlife Action Plan, Eco-regional Plan)
Surrounding land use	Distance to each surrounding land use type
Biotic & Abiotic Conditions	
Native vegetation	Percent cover by strata or species, age classes, species richness, target plant species presence
Non-native vegetation	Percent cover, invasive species presence
Bare ground	Percent cover
Hydrology	Flow duration, depth and period of inundation, stream morphology, special features (e.g., springs and vernal pools)
Soil	Soil type, litter layer depth, texture, drainage, erosion
Geographic features	Elevation, aspect, slope
Disturbance	Fire return interval, wind regime, disease, flood regime
Climate	Precipitation
Species Attributes	
Target species	Richness, presence, species counts, species abundance, age structure
Site features	Breeding habitat, foraging habitat, species features (e.g., snags, large wood, boulders)
Management Practices	
Crops	Irrigation, crop type, crop rotation, soil conditioning
Inputs	Water, fertilizer, pesticide
Best management practices	Practices implemented
Human disturbance	Land use profile, fragmentation, pollution
Risk & Viability	
Threats	Roads, invasive species, high levels of predation
Stewardship	Legal protection, land tenure, existing use, ability to implement management practices

condition of a specific area with reference sites or states. For example, the Biobanking Assessment Methodology (Australia) uses Ecological Vegetation Classes as a reference site or target benchmark for restoring vegetation (Burgin 2008). Common vegetation indicators include native species richness, native plant cover, and abiotic attributes such as soil conditions. Relatedly, measurement systems are increasingly relying on remotely collected spatial data, which can be cost-effectively used to complement on-the-ground data collection. The differences between the project location and reference conditions can be used to calculate a similarity index. That index can then be used as a score or as a multiplier to arrive at a weighted score for habitat or biodiversity. One assumption in using reference sites or states as targets for restoration and management objectives is that the ecological characteristics of the reference sites are optimal for supporting a program's objective (e.g., habitat for an at-risk species). Two major challenges are to define the reference site or conditions and to determine whether historical conditions are the best predictor of desirable habitat (Gibbons and Freudenberger 2006; Hawkins et al. 2010; Ravenscroft et al. 2010). Pre-listing conservation (PLC) programs that adopt a vegetation-based filter for a measurement system should use the best available science to justify and document any reference sites or conditions used.

A species-based filter typically uses a suite of indicators that characterize species populations and desirable habitat for those target species (Gartner et al. this volume). The indicators can include habitat- and population-based data and characterize specific locations compared to baseline conditions or reference states. Research on habitat suitability for species has a long history, both in the literature and in practice (Schamberger and O'Neil 1986; Thuiller et al. 2010). For example, habitat suitability index models, in conjunction with the habitat evaluation procedures, have been used in the United States for over thirty years (USFWS 1980a). Species-based frameworks should be based on the best available science, and they should follow the guidance and recommendations of federal and state recovery plans (Willamette Partnership 2011). Species-based filters can be resource intensive, requiring expensive monitoring methodologies. Program administrators should work collaboratively with scientists and practitioners to develop species-based approaches that are accurate in documenting change while also pragmatic enough to be operational at scale. For PLC programs, species-based filters are likely to be the common approach since the underlying policy of the Endangered Species Act is species-focused (Li and Male this volume; Madsen this volume).

Function-based filters focus on ecological processes that characterize ecosystems. Measurement systems for wetlands provide the best examples. The Oregon Rapid Wetlands Assessment Protocol is a standardized methodology for assessing the function of wetlands based on a suite of site- and landscape-level indicators (Adamus et al. 2010). Desirable levels of ecosystem function serve as performance targets, which can be derived from the literature, on-the-ground assessments, ecosystem models, and expert opinion (Adamus et al. 2010). A major advantage of function-based filters is that they allow for the weighting of metrics based on function (e.g., wetland credits are expressed not only in size but also in the level of ecosystem function). Major challenges to this approach include defining and measuring ecosystem functions, as well as incorporating complex temporal dynamics of those functions (Auerbach and Bendor this volume).

Metrics

A metric is an index score used to communicate the benefit of actions, or potential actions, taken on a given site to produce conservation outcomes as defined by a program (e.g., high-quality habitat for an at-risk species). It is derived from a suite of indicators that are filtered through a framework unique to a particular program. For example, a PLC program focused on a candidate species is likely to have a species-based filter from which a group of indicators are based (Gartner et al. this volume; Ginger et al. this volume). Many measurement systems use a similar metric: an area of defined habitat type, weighted by a habitat or ecosystem quality index (Adamus et al. 2010). This type of metric has different names, such as habitat hectare, habitat credit, or functionally weighted acre (DSE 2004). Not all measurement systems, however, combine area with habitat quality and function. Many incentive programs report on acreage enrolled without documenting or quantifying habitat quality or the additional biodiversity benefits created from the conservation intervention. Other approaches include Resource Equivalency Analysis, which has been used and promoted for measurement systems focused on species, habitat, and landscapes (Dunford et al. 2004; Bruggeman et al. 2005; Wilcox and Donlan 2007; Cole 2011). Some species-based measurement systems combine demographic and habitat quality approaches (Gartner et al. this volume).

Validation and Adaptive Management

A measurement system is considered valid if it is both accurate and precise. Accuracy is the degree of closeness to the actual (true) value being measured, while precision is the degree to which repeated measurements under unchanged conditions show the same results (Legg and Nagy 2006). Precision can be broken down into two components: repeatability and reproducibility. Repeatability is the variation when efforts are made to keep sampling conditions constant (e.g., operators, instruments, and timing), while reproducibility is the variation when sampling conditions are different (e.g., different operators over long periods of time). Measurement systems should be evaluated for both accuracy and precision. While repeatability and reproducibility are relatively easy to evaluate, they are seldom reported. Relatedly, the sensitivity of individual indicators should be evaluated in terms of how they affect an overall metric score (Parkes et al. 2003). Mathematical techniques, such as sensitivity and power analyses, can provide insights into the ability of measurement systems to measure change and the influence of individual indicators (Morris and Doak 2002; Legg and Nagy 2006). In order to validate and evaluate a measurement system, it must be transparent (Ferraro and Pattanayak 2006). Measurement systems are increasingly adopting standardized protocols that define or guide methodologies. Doing so improves consistent application among users, as well as across sites in space and time.

Performance standards are an essential element of successful conservation programs (Kapos et al. 2008). They are used to define interim benchmarks as a site moves toward its full potential in relation to target conditions for species or a reference condition for vegetation. Assessments also include measures at multiple scales, for example, both site condition and landscape context, recognizing the importance of characterizing ecosystems beyond property lines or political boundaries.

In general, there is currently a lack of independent and structured validation of measurement systems with respect to their accuracy and precision. Each type of measurement approach (e.g., vegetation, species, and function filters) makes assumptions about the selected indicators and their relationships with a program's objective. In many instances, resources are spent in development of the initial version of a measurement system, with few resources reserved for validation and improvement. Program administrators should budget resources for validation and modifications of measurement systems.

A PROCESS FOR BUILDING BIODIVERSITY MEASUREMENT SYSTEMS FOR MARKET-BASED PROGRAMS

Every market-based program will need to develop aspects tailored to its goals and local conditions. However, certain steps are universal to building any biodiversity measurement system:

1. Define conservation goals, target users, and the objectives of the measurement system. What are the biodiversity or ecosystem outcomes that the program intends to produce? What are the interventions that are being conducted to produce those outcomes?
2. Assess the science and engage experts to identify important biological and ecosystem functions with respect to the program's objectives and select measurable indicators to track desirable outcomes. Existing measurement systems should be reviewed and adopted if appropriate. This step should involve representatives from regulatory agencies who may need to approve or certify a measurement system or the overall program.
3. Develop and field test indicators and metrics for accuracy, precision, and cost-effectiveness.
4. Finalize the measurement system, including detailed documentation and a peer-review process.
5. After a period of time, conduct a reassessment of the measurement system and make any necessary modifications based on performance to date.

For a PLC program, program administrators should carefully consider integrating the following factors into a biodiversity measurement system:

- Indicators and metrics should capture habitat quality and species demographic characteristics, both as baseline conditions and through time.
- A measurement system should incorporate the landscape context of the site (e.g., located in priority conservation area, fragmentation, and road density).
- A measurement system should be transparent: indicators should be clearly articulated and understandable, and the relationship between indicators and metrics should be clear.
- Indicators and metrics should be chosen and calculated, respectively, carefully and explicitly to closely track the program's objective (e.g., candidate species' demography).
- A measurement system should be designed a priori with sufficient statistical power to be able to detect expected changes with intended conservation actions.

- A measurement system should consider ease of implementation so that trained technicians can implement it in a reasonable amount of time.

The framework described above can act as a guide to designing a biodiversity measurement system that will interact with other aspects of market-based and incentive programs for biodiversity. Incentive-based programs for biodiversity conservation are growing in the United States and abroad. They range from US Farm Bill programs to payments for ecosystem services to new approaches such as pre-listing conservation. Each of these policy tools targets different stakeholders with different conservation objectives. The common need across all of these programs is to define conservation goals, develop standards for quantifying and tracking conservation outcomes, and scale proven mechanisms in order to increase public and private investment in the most effective actions landowners can take on their lands.

CHAPTER 10

A Landowner-Centered Approach to Incentivizing Participation in Pre-Listing Conservation Programs

MICHAEL G. SORICE AND TROY ABEL

ABSTRACT

Pre-listing conservation programs can motivate landowner investment in proactive recovery efforts for species at risk of being listed under the US Endangered Species Act. Despite the increasing popularity of including monetary and nonmonetary incentives in conservation programs, questions remain about achieving private landowner participation at levels sufficient to attain conservation goals across a landscape. Landowners face the risk that a collective failure of pre-listing efforts could lead to land use prohibitions. Studies investigating participation in conservation programs find many factors that influence participation, such as age, property size, trust, and risk perceptions. In designing pre-listing conservation programs, it is important to recognize that incentives inherent in the program structure and delivery also influence participation. Pre-listing conservation programs that take a landowner-centered approach in which program administrators directly involve private landowners in the design process will better recognize the social and ecological complexity of recovering at-risk species and result in greater participation.

INTRODUCTION

The first thirty years of US Endangered Species Act (ESA) implementation have revealed the constraints and unintended consequences of the law's approach to endangered species recovery. Funding problems, enforcement issues, an overreliance on biologists to solve social conflicts, a command-and-control approach to implementation, and a bureaucratic structure that precludes organizational learning and adaptability have all led to a policy that is ineffective at incentivizing conservation actions on private lands (Kellert 1994; Clark 1997; Bean 1998; Norris 2004; Murchison 2007). Further, past conflict related to endangered species and private lands in the United States has created a social memory whereby private landowners associate endangered species with land use prohibitions and loss of property rights. Such negative perceptions have contributed to a perverse incentive that discourages landowners from cooperating to manage land for the benefit of listed species. This inability to promote recovery on private lands is problematic given that land in the United States is primarily in private ownership and many endangered species rely on private lands for habitat (GAO 1995; Groves et al. 2000; Lubowski et al. 2006).

Although pre-listing conservation (PLC) efforts focus on increasing the abundance of imperiled species so as to eliminate the need for listing under the ESA, these efforts face challenges similar to those that focus on recovering listed species. It can be a risky proposition for private landowners to contribute to precompliance efforts if they perceive that a collective failure to provide sufficient habitat across a landscape mosaic potentially leaves them vulnerable to ESA regulation. Conservation programs seek to mitigate this risk by employing monetary and nonmonetary incentives so that at-risk species are more likely to be viewed by landowners as assets than as liabilities. These inducements can take the form of assurances against future regulation, cost sharing of land management practices, technical assistance, and direct financial payments to offset opportunity costs or increase income for landowners.

If designed appropriately, conservation incentive programs can be a useful tool to correct the high personal costs to landowners in supplying a good (i.e., biodiversity) from which society receives diffuse benefits. This inequity does not go unrecognized by landowners. For example, landowners in Colorado, Texas, Utah, and Indiana believe they should be compensated for protecting endangered species (Kreuter et al. 2006; Raymond and Olive 2008). Without changes to the current incentive structure, landowners may manage their property in ways that minimize the chance of an endangered species occupying it and restricting their future management options (Brook et al. 2003; Lueck and Michael 2003).

Conservation programs that seek to rearrange this perverse incentive structure promise to promote the recovery of at-risk species on private lands, but questions exist about how to achieve landowner participation at levels sufficient to prevent ESA listing. Using current research, we first discuss potential factors that influence landowner participation in conservation programs. We then suggest an approach to increase private landowner participation.

CHARACTERISTICS OF PARTICIPATING LANDOWNERS

Research examining who participates in species conservation programs generally evaluates an existing program and focuses on characteristics of private landowners, their land, and, to a lesser extent, social and psychological correlates of decision making. Generally, the term *private landowner* refers to private citizens (not corporations or companies) who own a sizable expanse of land in rural areas. Private landowners are a diverse population, comprising individuals who own farms, ranches, and forestland for traditional production-oriented reasons as well as for amenity-based reasons (Gosnell and Abrams 2009). Below, we briefly examine three case studies that analyzed the factors that influence landowner participation in conservation programs.

The US Fish and Wildlife Service has used the Safe Harbor conservation program to promote the recovery of the federally listed Red-Cockaded Woodpecker (*Picoides borealis*) on nonindustrial private forestlands in North and South Carolina (Bonnie 1997). This program provides landowners with assurances against future regulation provided that participants do not reduce the woodpecker's population below pre-agreement baseline conditions. This program, however, does not provide financial incentives. Factors positively related to private landowner participation in a Safe Harbor agreement include (1) ownership of more extensive acreage; (2) the possible presence of woodpeckers (estimated by the presence of active nests within one mile of a landowner's property and the amount of mature pine); (3) the use of methods to control forest understory; (4) landowner perceptions of the likelihood that woodpeckers will relocate on their land; (5) landowner attitudes toward the woodpeckers and endangered species protection; and (6) whether a consulting forester introduced the Safe Harbor program to the landowner (Zhang and Mehmood 2002; Mehmood and Zhang 2005). Only one variable was negatively related to participation: whether landowners believe the Safe Harbor program would weaken their property rights. In this case, risk mitigation seems to drive participation: landowners enrolling in Safe Harbor can protect their investments from future regulation and uncertainty.

In research in the Pacific Northwest, Langpap (2004) examined the demographic and land characteristics influencing participation in conservation programs designed to provide habitat for endangered species. Participation was positively related to (1) the importance a landowner places on the wildlife habitat provided by the forest, (2) the number of acres owned, and (3) membership in conservation organizations. Participation was negatively correlated with the landowner's age. Other findings included reduced participation related to years of ownership and the importance of aesthetic enjoyment of the forest. Participation was not related to the importance of investment or the commercial value of the forest, and landowners' perceived risk of regulation under the ESA did not influence participation. These results suggest that landowners who are more likely to participate in the program may be focused less on managing their land for profit.

In-depth qualitative interviews with landowners in central Texas explored the relationship between characteristics of landowners and their willingness to participate in cost-sharing conservation programs to enhance habitat for the federally endangered Golden-cheeked Warbler (*Dendroica chrysoparia*) and the Black-capped Vireo (*Vireo atricapilla*) (Cearley-Sanders 2005). Of the fifty-six respondents, 11 percent indicated no willingness to participate, 58 percent initially indicated no willingness but then said they would participate if certain conditions were met, 13 percent initially indicated a willingness conditional on having their concerns met, and 18 percent indicated a willingness to participate without stipulating conditions. Based on landowner characteristics (e.g., age, acres owned, membership in organizations), Cearly-Sanders and colleagues (2005) generated a landowner typology characterized by (1) a strong attachment to their land related to their livelihood and the previous generations who operated it, (2) a strong focus on production with less emphasis on attachment to the property itself, and (3) an emotional and psychological connection to their land even though they may not have been raised or lived in the rural community for many years. Landowners in this third group were the most likely to enroll in a conservation program; those in the second group were the least likely to enroll.

Current trends in rural land ownership indicate that people increasingly purchase land primarily for recreation, for its aesthetic qualities, and to experience the rural lifestyle rather than to engage in agricultural production (Theobald et al. 2005). Sorice et al. (2012) explored the relationship between the centrality of the ranching lifestyle and participation in hypothetical conservation programs intended to protect or maintain habitat for the Golden-Cheeked Warbler and Black-Capped Vireo in central Texas. Demographic characteristics (e.g., age, education, acres managed, income, absentee landowner, years property owned) failed to predict potential participation. Grouping landowners based on reported importance of the ranching lifestyle to their way of life predicted potential participation, with increasing importance negatively related to potential participation. This relationship, however, was fully mediated by landowners' attitudes toward participating. These results indicate that although landowner attitudes are better at predicting participation than a demographic analysis, this type of division may still miss key factors that influence attitudes toward participation in pre-listing conservation (PLC) programs.

In sum, research has not shown demographic factors to be consistently related to participation in conservation programs. Mixed outcomes do little to paint a clearer picture of whether landowners intend to enroll in conservation programs because they fail to account for the multiple reasons for owning, managing, and enjoying land (Bliss and Martin 1989; Koontz 2001; Knight and White 2009; Sorice and Conner 2010). Targeting programs to landowners based on demographic factors will not suffice to obtain participation at levels needed to achieve landscape-scale conservation outcomes because it does not account for unique, local conditions that shape landowner responses (Sorice et al. 2013).

LANDOWNERS OBJECTIVES AND PRIORITIES

If observing characteristics of landowners who do and do not enroll in conservation incentives programs is insufficient for obtaining needed participation levels, the next question must address what characteristics of conservation programs landowners desire. The literature is rife with factors that influence adoption of conservation behaviors. Studies focusing on at-risk species identify factors related to maintaining choice and control over how the land is managed even when regulatory assurances are provided (table 10.1). Additional research on endangered species has examined what landowners want by investigating how conservation program structure and administration are related to participation (Langpap 2006; Sorice et al. 2011; Sorice et al. 2013). This research demonstrates that the type and magnitude of both monetary and nonmonetary

TABLE 10.1 VALUES AND NEEDS OF LANDOWNERS IN AT-RISK SPECIES CONSERVATION PROGRAMS

- To operate land in ways that align with their own values and attitudes.
- To improve their land in ways that support their livelihood.
- To maintain their sense of place (e.g., family legacy, emotional attachment).
- To maintain their property rights.
- To avoid real and perceived risks associated with participation.
- To minimize economic costs and increase economic benefits of participation.
- To maintain a feeling of freedom and control over land use and management decisions.
- To trust that the program's decision processes are fair. To trust the institution administering the program and the individuals who represent the interests of the administering institution.
- To have adequate and timely information about the program, process, and species of interest.
- To avoid large amounts of paperwork and high transaction costs.
- To know if what they are doing actually helps at-risk species.

SOURCES: Zhang and Mehmood 2002; Mehmood and Zhang 2005; Womack 2008; Sorice 2012.

incentives matter but that landowners are willing to accept trade-offs between financial incentives, regulatory assurances, and other program components such as contract length. Financial payments to subsidize the cost of implementing land management practices (i.e., cost sharing) alone may provide a weak incentive relative to conservation programs with both cost sharing and assurances. Combining financial incentives with regulatory assurances may lead to greater participation and effort because it reduces risk while increasing benefits. Technical assistance may not be very important in the decision to participate, but its unavailability may be a significant disincentive (Sorice et al. 2011).

The influence of incentives on participation may vary considerably across landowners (Sorice et al. 2011). Landowners with positive attitudes toward participating may require very low financial incentives, be more willing to participate for a longer period, have little concern about regulatory risks, and be influenced by expected outcomes of helping the target species and improving the health of their land. Landowners with more neutral attitudes may be more strongly influenced by financial incentives and assurances and relatively less influenced by potential outcomes related to the target species or their land. They also may prefer participating for shorter periods. Finally, landowners with negative attitudes toward participating in programs are not likely to be influenced by incentives.

In sum, myriad factors are related to potential participation in conservation programs; there is no single driving factor that influences participation (e.g., Womack 2008; Sorice 2012). Amid this complexity, a pivotal question is how to devise a program that increases participation levels given that participation is absolutely critical to the success of a PLC program.

RETHINKING INCENTIVE PROGRAMS TO IMPROVE PARTICIPATION

The factors listed in the preceding section relate to the type of incentives meant to influence behavior (e.g., direct payments, assurances) as well as the way in which a program is structured and delivered (e.g., contractual obligations). Conservation programs that are designed in a top-down fashion by organizations based on the powerful assumption that simply getting the incentives right (i.e., financial payment or assurances) will be sufficient to obtain necessary participation levels are not guaranteed to achieve conservation outcomes. Enrolling in a program is itself an interaction with its own inherent set of incentives: landowners receive benefits and incur costs from the program's structure, the organization that provides the incentives, and the way in which it is administered. Thus both program structure and its implementation are key but overlooked elements that influence participation. Neglecting them will reduce participation.

Private landowners have many reasons for owning and operating their land and obtain many satisfactions from doing so. They view themselves as stewards with an ethic based on common sense (i.e., wisdom obtained from years of experience), independence (i.e., freedom to make ethical judgments about land use activities), and the human-land connection (i.e., the interconnectedness of human health and ecosystem health) (Peterson and Horton 1995; Bergmann and Bliss 2004; Knobloch and Cawley 2005; Schenk et al. 2007). Although procuring income to maintain one's livelihood is not a trivial component of landownership, landowners likely focus on noneconomic quality of life issues, such as well-being, sense of control of one's fate, safety and security, competence, and good social relations (Sheridan 2007; Kofinas and Chapin 2009). The programs through which incentives are delivered may act to discourage participation when, for example, they are administered in a strict and controlling fashion that undermines these values.

Given the many interacting factors that influence participation, a broad-brush approach to the design of PLC programs is likely to result

FIGURE 10.1. A landowner-centered approach to program design starts with learning directly from landowners by observing their daily lives and how they manage their land. A small group of program designers (foresters, ecologists, and social scientists) talk to a private landowner in the southeastern United States about his property and longleaf pine forest management.

in suboptimal levels of enrollment. The complex issues associated with conserving each at-risk species (e.g., habitat needs, life histories) occur in different social, political, cultural, and economic contexts. Some issues may lead to win-win outcomes that benefit landowners' livelihoods as well as the species, but other species management needs may threaten landowners' personal and cultural values and rights (Peterson et al. 2002; Sorice and Conner 2010). Thus PLC programs require a landowner-centered focus that incorporates the social complexity and ecological complexity inherent in at-risk species conservation by customizing programs to local landowner needs.

A landowner-centered approach to designing conservation programs is an exploratory process that involves on-the-ground research and action. Program designers enter a community to directly observe the daily lives of landowners as they manage their land, uncover latent needs, and establish prototypes of new ideas and refine them based on landowner feedback (Brown 2009; Brown and Wyatt 2010) (figure 10). The

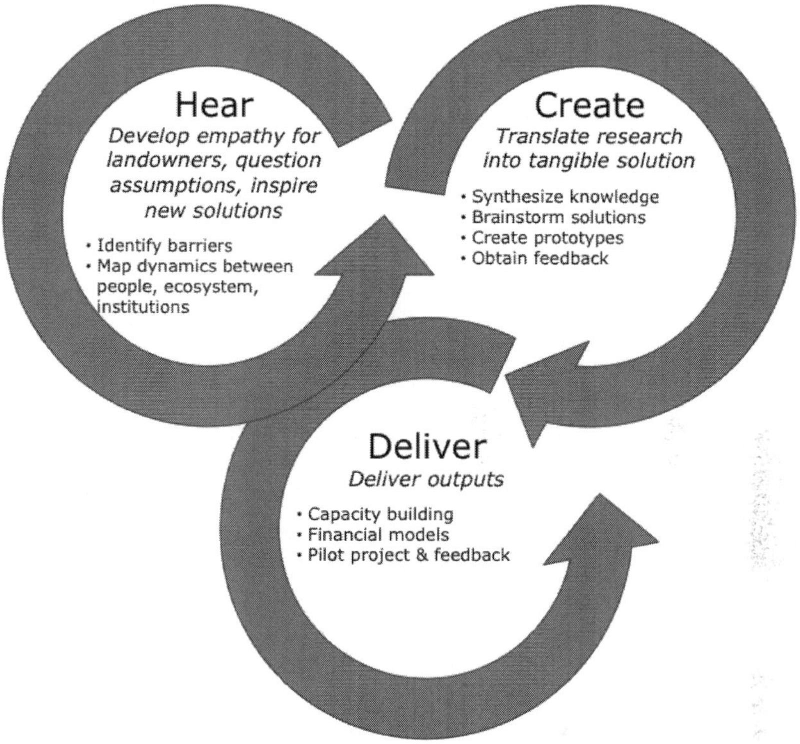

FIGURE 10.2. The three general phases of a human-centered design approach. Adapted from IDEO 2011.

goals of this approach are to construct a program collaboratively, from the bottom up, so that it fits the needs of landowners and to capitalize on innovations in ways that generate better conservation outcomes.

Three phases of participatory design methodology define this approach (IDEO 2011) (figure 10.2). Participatory design allows system designers to understand stakeholders' desires and needs during all phases of design (Bødker and Iversen 2002). This consultation improves landowner buy-in, leading to greater participation. Further, if landowners feel that programs are designed by them rather than for them, they may be more vested in the program's success. The process begins after clearly defining the problem to be solved, with the first phase emphasizing ethnographic research to understand the community's culture from the landowner perspective (e.g., unique land management challenges, how landowners interact with each other, trust or mistrust of organizations). In the second phase, this information is examined to identify themes and opportunities and to create prototypes of PLC programs through techniques such as storyboarding, creating video scenarios, and acting out the enrollment process. This phase is iterative as the community provides feedback. The third and final phase involves taking the top solutions to program structure and delivery, assessing both their technical feasibility and their financial viability, identifying the capabilities required to implement them, piloting the program, and measuring impact.

In sum, a landowner-centered approach should lead to greater participation because it puts landowner values at the forefront and leverages local expertise to develop innovative solutions. With this approach, a program is more likely to be structured and delivered in a way that supports landowners' basic needs for competence and autonomy. It will more likely achieve buy-in and engender trust in the organization delivering the program because, for example, concerns about trust may lead to completely new institutional arrangements or delivery systems. Further, the program itself will be better adapted to the local context.

CONCLUSION

Conservation programs use monetary and nonmonetary incentives to address the problem of asking private landowners to assume much of the burden of providing a public good. These programs can and do lead to improved conservation outcomes; however, participation can occur below the levels necessary to recover and sustain a target species across a landscape. Failure to achieve PLC program outcomes may result in a species being listed, which can further suppress participation due to landowner concerns about potential land use prohibitions.

Reduced participation can result from a failure to consider the culture and needs of all people living in a community. Given the importance of private landowner participation in achieving conservation goals, the design and implementation of conservation programs must avoid treating landowners as the object of analysis and instead involve them as active collaborators. The landowner-centered approach requires interaction with landowners, observing their lives and experiences, and using those insights to create innovative programs that are customized for landowners.

CHAPTER 11

Market Models and Finance for Upstream Species Conservation

C. JOSH DONLAN, ABHISHEK JAIN, AND BARBARA MÜLLER

ABSTRACT

A pre-listing conservation marketplace would offer federal and nonfederal project developers an efficient and cost-effective solution to managing their environmental risk regarding at-risk species (e.g., candidate species under the US Endangered Species Act) by allowing them to preemptively purchase conservation outcomes. Using the gopher tortoise (*Gopherus polyphemus*) as an example, we explore potential market structures of a pre-listing conservation program. To illustrate the factors that influence the cost of credits, we also present a financial analysis of gopher tortoise credits based on a suite of programmatic and financial assumptions. Those assumptions are based on work conducted in the southeastern United States focused on designing a pre-listing conservation pilot program for the gopher tortoise. Our main purpose is to illustrate a framework that can be used to explore the market and financial aspects of a pre-listing conservation marketplace. Our financial projections suggest that if certain programmatic targets can be met (e.g., ~15,000 acres enrolled in the program over five years), the minimum credit price and the overall cost of a pre-listing conservation program are not prohibitive. It is likely that a pre-listing conservation marketplace would be more cost-effective than current mitigation approaches in use downstream of the Endangered Species Act.

INTRODUCTION

A pre-listing conservation (PLC) program structured around market principles offers federal and nonfederal project developers an efficient and cost-effective solution to managing their environmental risk regarding at-risk species (e.g., candidate species under the US Endangered Species Act [ESA]) by allowing them to preemptively purchase conservation outcomes. Those outcomes would be based on some metric that allows for the demonstration of a net conservation benefit and would be represented in a distinct unit such as a species or habitat credit (Cochran and Maness this volume). In exchange for project developers mitigating their future environmental impacts in advance, the US Fish and Wildlife Service (USFWS) could provide those project developers with regulatory assurances that those purchased conservation outcomes (e.g., restored species habitat) will count toward any future regulatory requirements (Li and Male this volume).

Other potential buyers of PLC outcomes may be less concerned with assurances or regulatory predictability. For example, companies could purchase credits as part of their sustainability strategy or foundations and nongovernmental organizations (NGOs) could purchase credits as part of their investment and program strategies. Unlike many other biodiversity investments in the environmental sector (Ferraro and Pattanayak 2006), an upstream species conservation marketplace for PLC could be outcome-based: the conservation outcomes, verified by a third party, could be documented and delivered when the credits are bought and sold.

Regardless of the buyer(s) of PLC credits, a number of conditions must be met for any marketplace to function:

- A distinct product that can be bought and sold (i.e., credit).
- Sellers of that product.
- Buyers of that product.
- A robust, transparent transaction platform where the product can be registered and tracked.
- Oversight and regulation of the buying and selling.

Using the gopher tortoise (*Gopherus polyphemus*) as an example, we explore potential market structures of a PLC program. To illustrate the factors that influence the cost of credits, we also present a financial analysis of gopher tortoise credits based on a number of programmatic and financial assumptions. Those assumptions in turn are based on work conducted in the southeastern United States to design a PLC pilot program for the gopher tortoise (Gartner and Donlan 2011; Gartner et al. this volume). Our main purpose is to illustrate a framework that can be used to explore the market and financial aspects of a PLC marketplace.

MARKETPLACE STRUCTURE

Our marketplace structure for PLC gopher tortoise habitat credits is designed to be regulated, robust with respect to potential sellers and buyers, and liquid (i.e., credits can be sold easily, without significant movement in price). The market model includes a broker, in addition to buyers and sellers (figure 11.1). However, in some scenarios a broker may be unnecessary. Below, we briefly define the major components of the market model.

Pre-Listing Conservation Credit. A gopher tortoise credit is the currency that can be bought and sold in this example marketplace. An established protocol provides landowners and project developers with the details of the crediting and debiting system, including eligibility requirements and factors that are evaluated in determining habitat credits. For example, in our current PLC program structure, a land easement is required to be in place in order for a landowner to participate in selling credits. For the gopher tortoise, we developed a crediting-debiting methodology that integrates a species sampling approach with a habitat quality assessment (see Gartner et al. this volume for details). An initial landowner survey determines the number of credits available on a land parcel. Likewise, the project developer uses the same methodology to estimate the potential impact on his land; this could be conducted before or after the purchase of credits, depending on how much information is known about potential future impacts. For our current model, we used a contract length of forty years; this represents the longest contract length for which local landowners expressed a positive preference in a survey we conducted to quantify landowner attitudes toward the proposed program (Sorice et al. 2013; Gartner et al. this volume). However, the financial model could be adapted to a shorter or longer contract length. The credit price includes funds to manage, monitor, and audit the land parcel under contract producing the gopher tortoise credits, along with a profit margin for the seller. Required management activities included prescribed burning, invasive weed control,

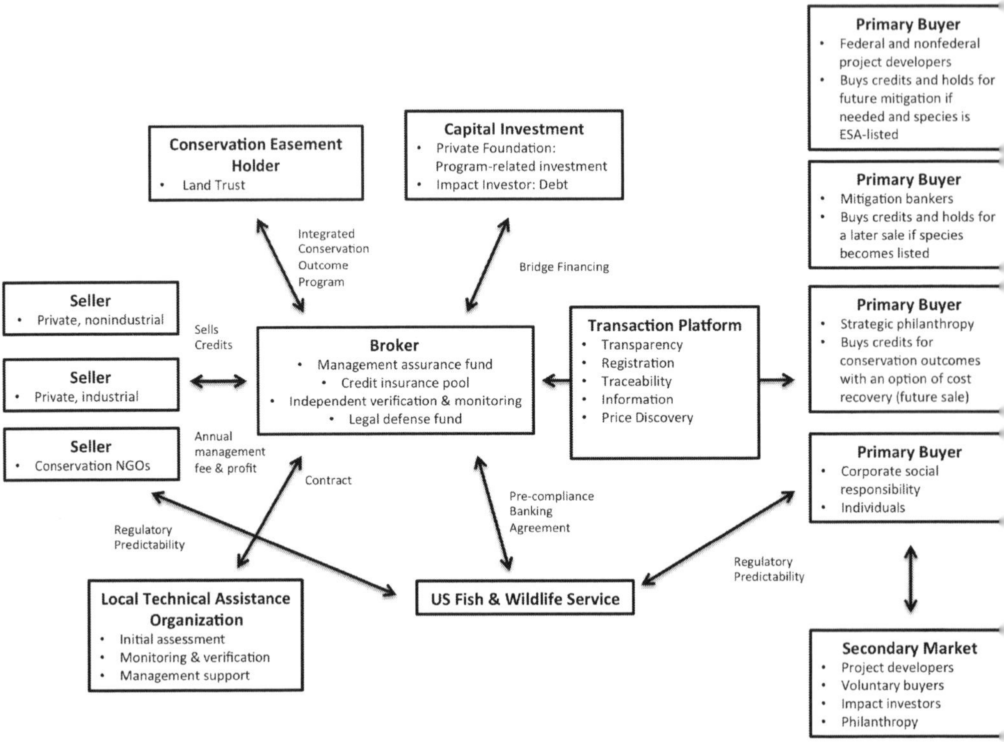

FIGURE 11.1. A potential marketplace structure for a pre-listing conservation program focused on the gopher tortoise, a candidate species under the US Endangered Species Act.

and a monitoring program, along with a comprehensive management plan (see Gartner et al. this volume for details).

Sellers. Potential credit sellers include private landowners of pine forests in the southeastern United States where gopher tortoises are present. This could include nonindustrial landowners, industrial landowners, and nonprofit or for-profit organizations. Potential sellers include private landowners operating sustainable timber operations, timber investment management organizations, NGOs, real estate investment trusts, and retiree landowners.

Buyers. Potential buyers include federal and state agencies or private parties interested in purchasing credits. The eligibility and restrictions of credit buyers must be balanced with the need to generate the necessary demand and liquidity to ensure a successful marketplace. Examples of potential buyers include the Department of Defense, the Department of Transportation, philanthropic foundations, corporations, mitigation bankers, and impact investors. Interest in buying credits could include

- The desire to voluntarily offset gopher tortoise impacts.
- The desire to manage the risk of needing to offset future environmental impacts under a regulatory scenario if the gopher tortoise becomes listed under the ESA.
- The desire to buy credits as a strategy to invest in conservation outcomes.
- The desire to buy credits as an investment, under the assumption that credit price will increase if and when the gopher tortoise becomes listed under the ESA and the USFWS is willing to provide regulatory predictability with the associated credits.

Broker. An independent nonprofit organization could serve as a market broker. Alternatively, a for-profit firm could also serve as a broker, assuming robust demand was present and risks were manageable. The broker facilitates the buying and selling of gopher tortoise credits. The broker manages the financial transactions, provides liquidity in the market, and manages the risk of potential default of credits. It does so both internally and externally, the latter with contractual relationships. The broker has fiduciary responsibility for a tortoise management assurance fund, which makes annual payments to landowners for the management costs of the habitat credits. It also makes profit payments to the landowner, either as annual or onetime payments. The broker is also responsible for the verification and monitoring of the credits; it may contract those duties to local technical assistance organizations (see below). The broker could manage default risk by holding a pool of unsold credits as insurance. This is similar to approaches used in the voluntary carbon market: project developers are often required to hold a percentage of projected carbon credits in escrow as a form of self-insurance to manage project risks. Last, the broker could maintain a legal defense fund in case of contract breach and the need for litigation. The broker maintains relationships with the landowners (i.e., sellers), the holders of the conservation easement (e.g., land trust), and investors; the latter may provide short-term debt for financing up-front costs and maintaining liquidity in the market (see below). The broker provides value with respect to scalability, accountability, and streamlining the implementation of the market.

Local Technical Assistance Organization. The broker may contract technical assistance organizations to conduct the initial credit assessment of potential sellers and the monitoring and verification of the habitat credits once they are sold. In addition, technical assistance organizations provide assistance with management support and the necessary due diligence and actions the seller may need to undertake prior to being eligible to sell credits.

Conservation Easement Holder. The broker maintains a mutually beneficial relationship with the credit seller's conservation easement holder (e.g., a land trust). Under our current model, a conservation easement is an eligibility requirement for market entry (i.e., credit sellers must have an easement in place on land where gopher tortoise credits are being generated and sold). The habitat credit program is complementary to conservation easement programs because it offers financial incentives to produce positive conservation outcomes on top of restrictive easements. The conservation easement provides the PLC program with a level of assurance that the credits will remain valid over the life of the contract.

Capital Investment. Access to affordable capital may be needed, in the form of debt or equity, to cover the up-front costs to initiate the market and maintain liquidity. In order to maximize the incentives for private landowners to enter the market as credit sellers, the broker covers the start-up costs of producing credits (and recovers those costs at the credit sale). Short-term debt could be provided in the form of a program-related investment by a foundation or investments by impact investing firms. Alternatively, initial investment could come in the form of grants from a foundation interesting in investing in outcome-based and market-based approaches to species conservation.

The US Fish and Wildlife Service. The USFWS regulates the market and maintains agreements with sellers, buyers, and the broker. A precompliance banking agreement is established with the broker and the USFWS (Li and Male this volume); the agreement could include an umbrella or programmatic approach, whereby brokers could issue subcontracts and individual permits, which would simplify and expedite the process. The USFWS also provides regulatory predictability both to the buyer and to the seller (Li and Male this volume). Regulatory predictability is likely critical to generate the necessary demand for the purchase of credits to create a functioning marketplace (Gartner et al. this volume). The USFWS also provides assurances to the seller against any future regulation for the net conservation actions undertaken that go beyond the credits sold. This type of assurance against future obligations is similar to Safe Harbor Agreements under the ESA and is an important program component to maximize landowner participation (Bean et al. 2001; Sorice et al. 2013)

Transaction Platform. Because credits may be bought, held for a period of time, and resold at a later date, a robust transaction platform is critical. A transaction platform provides scale by delivering transparency, registration, and traceability to the market (Silver this volume). It also provides a central location for information and price discovery. The platform is where credits are retired permanently when they are used to mitigate impacts, either in a voluntary or a regulatory scenario. Transaction platforms for environmental markets are available (Silver this volume; Van Patten this volume).

Secondary Market. A secondary market is where previously issued credits are bought and sold. At some point, it may be important to a functioning market because it provides liquidity. In this case, the secondary market would take place on the transaction platform. Potential buyers on the secondary market include impact investors, philanthropist, project developers, and private corporations.

FINANCIAL MODEL

Assumptions and Goals

The goal of our financial model was to estimate the minimum price of a credit over the life of a PLC program, operating in a marketplace similar to the one described above. Our hypothetical PLC program was based on a number of targets: the program would actively buy credits for five years and secure twenty-five 40-year contracts with a total area of 17,500 acres. Those acres and their landowners would be eligible to sell a total of 3,080 credits (table 11.1). The number of acres under the scope of our financial model would increase by 3,500 acres per year from year 1 to year 5, remain at 17,500 from year 4 through year 40, and then decrease by 3,500 acres per year from year 41 through

TABLE 11.1 TARGETS FOR A HYPOTHETICAL PRE-LISTING CONSERVATION PROGRAM FOCUSED ON THE GOPHER TORTOISE

Market structure	Broker Model
Program length	5 years
Total annual target	3,500 acres
Total target	17,500 acres
Estimated number of annual transactions	5
Estimated number of total transactions	25
Estimated average credits per transaction	123
Estimated total number of credits	3,080
Contract length with landowners	40 years

NOTE: The program assumes the credits are bought and sold for five years, while contracts with landowners last forty years.

year 44. Based on fieldwork in Georgia testing the crediting methodology (Gartner et al. this volume), we assumed the average land parcel under contract was eligible to sell 0.18 credits per acre. This is an conservative estimate based on the testing of our methodology on land parcels which resulted in a higher credit:acre ratio (e.g., 0.25). While our assumptions are based on empirical data, a real program will have more uncertainty, and thus our financial model is currently more descriptive than prescriptive.

In addition to the program targets above, our model adopted the following assumptions and approaches:

- We did not consider market forces such as inflation and taxes, which are difficult to predict. The minimum price of credit may increase after taking inflation into account. We assumed the broker operated as a nonprofit organization and had tax-exempt status.
- We assumed fixed costs estimates remained constant over the five years of buying activity (e.g., initial broker setup costs, ongoing broker costs, and transactions costs), and the stewardship costs that are paid to the landowner remained constant over the length of the 40-year contracts.
- We used a discount rate of 8 percent, discounting the future cash flows to current dollars.
- The number of credits sold (616 per year) and number of acres under the scope of the project (3,500 per year) remained constant over the five years of buying activity.

- There were no changes in the business model over the initial buying activity period (5 years) or over the length of the contracts (40 years).

We estimated the expenses to set up, initiate, and maintain the program. This included setup costs for the broker, ongoing broker costs, transaction costs, and payments to sellers (table 11.2). Broker setup costs included expenses to establish a nonprofit organization, the working fund to disperse payments to participating landowners, and a small legal defense fund in the event of contract breach. Ongoing costs for the broker included a director running the program (i.e., part-time), office and equipment costs, administrative costs, travel expenses, legal fees, and other miscellaneous costs.

We also estimated transaction-related expenses. This included the legal costs for drafting and executing contracts with landowners and fees associated with issuing, listing, and verifying the credits on a registry. Costs associated with the registry were based on an environmental crediting program run by the Willamette Partnership that uses the Markit Environmental Registry (J. Silver, personal communication). Other transaction-related costs included a baseline scientific survey to determine the number of credits that are initially eligible for sale (Gartner et al. this volume). Payments to participating landowners are broken into two separate expenses: stewardship costs and profit payment. Stewardship costs covered management activities required by the landowner to participate in the program; those costs were estimated at $20 an acre based on expert opinion (Gartner et al. this volume). Those costs include prescribed burning, invasive plant control, and monitoring; the costs are paid to participating landowners on an annual basis for the length of the contract. In addition to stewardship payments, a landowner receives a profit payment that is equivalent to 5 percent of the credit price for every credit sold. Landowners receive the profit payment in two installments: 50 percent in year 1 and 50 percent in year 5.

Estimating a Minimum Cost per Credit

One major argument in favor of PLC conservation approaches is that acting early should be more cost-effective than acting later (Donlan et al. 2013). Thus exploring the cost-effectiveness of PLC programs should be a priority. We used a net present value (NPV) approach to estimate the minimum cost per credit for our hypothetical PLC program. In our case,

TABLE 11.2 A FINANCIAL MODEL TO ESTIMATE THE MINIMUM CREDIT PRICE FOR A GOPHER TORTOISE PRE-LISTING CONSERVATION PROGRAM (CREDIT PRICE ESTIMATED USING NPV = 0)

Year	1	2	3	4	5
Revenues					
Estimated average no. annual transactions	5	5	5	5	5
Estimated average no. credits per transaction	123	123	123	123	123
Credits sold per year	616	616	616	616	616
Price per credit @ NPV=0	$1,911				
Total revenues	$1,176,982	$1,176,982	$1,176,982	$1,176,982	$1,176,982
		Expenses			
Initial setup costs at broker level					
Legal and administrative setup costs	$(7,000)				
Travel expenses in setup phase	$(2,000)				
Miscellaneous	$(5,000)				
Endowment fund setup costs	$(25,000)				
Legal defense fund setup costs	$(25,000)				
Total set-up costs at broker level	$(64,000)				
Ongoing costs at broker level					
Director salary (33% of time @ $80,000)	$(26,667)	$(26,667)	$(26,667)	$(26,667)	$(26,667)
Office and equipment costs	$(6,000)	$(6,000)	$(6,000)	$(6,000)	$(6,000)
Other administrative & general expenses	$(3,000)	$(3,000)	$(3,000)	$(3,000)	$(3,000)
Insurance costs	$(600)	$(600)	$(600)	$(600)	$(600)
Charges and taxes	$(600)	$(600)	$(600)	$(600)	$(600)
Travel expenses	$(5,000)	$(5,000)	$(5,000)	$(5,000)	$(5,000)

Accounting fees	$(1,200)	$(1,200)	$1,200)	$(1,200)	$(1,200)
External audit and tax advice	$(10,000)	$(10,000)	$(10,000)	$(10,000)	$(10,000)
Contract legal costs	$(25,000)	$(25,000)	$(25,000)	$(25,000)	$(25,000)
Other expenses	$(5,000)	$(5,000)	$(5,000)	$(5,000)	$(5,000)
Total ongoing costs at broker level	$(83,067)	$(83,067)	$(83,067)	$(83,067)	$(83,067)
Transaction-related costs at broker level					
Legal agreement costs (@ $1,000 per transaction)	$(5,000)	$(5,000)	$(5,000)	$(5,000)	$(5,000)
Baseline survey (@ $10,000 per transaction)	$(50,000)	$(50,000)	$(50,000)	$(50,000)	$(50,000)
Travel expenses (@ $1,000 per transaction)	$(5,000)	$(5,000)	$(5,000)	$(5,000)	$(5,000)
Other expenses (@ $1,000 per transaction)	$(5,000)	$(5,000)	$(5,000)	$(5,000)	$(5,000)
Markit registry account setup fee (onetime fee)	$(500)				
Annual access fee (fixed fee per year)	$(100)	$(100)	$(100)	$(100)	$(100)
Project listing fee (onetime fee)	$(24,000)				
Credit issuance fee (onetime fee)	$(70)				
Credit transaction fee (onetime fee)	$(420)				
Total transaction-related costs	$(90,090)	$(65,100)	$(65,100)	$(65,100)	$(65,100)
Ongoing payment to sellers					
Stewardship costs (@ $20 per acre)	$(70,000)	$(140,000)	$(210,000)	$(280,000)	$(4,796,135)
Annual profit payment for stewardship to sellers	$(29,425)	$(29,425)	$(29,425)	$(29,425)	$(156,306)
Total ongoing payment to sellers	$(99,425)	$(169,425)	$(239,425)	$(309,425)	$(4,952,441)
Total Expenses	$(336,581)	$(317,591)	$(387,591)	$(457,591)	$(5,100,608)
Net Income	$840,400	$859,390	$789,390	$719,390	$(3,923,626)
Present Value of Cash Flows Discounted @ 8%	$840,400	$795,732	$676,775	$571,075	$(2,883,983)
Net Present Value	$0				

estimating the NPV is challenging due to the uncertainty in key variables such as costs, revenues, and discount rates. Nonetheless, it is a useful first step in exploring the financial aspects of upstream conservation approaches. We focus on one key financial aspect,

$$\text{Net Income} = \text{Revenues}-\text{Costs}$$

By doing so, we can estimate a minimum cost of gopher tortoise credit while knowing little about potential demand.

Revenues were calculated simply by multiplying number of credits sold in a year (616 per year for five years) by the price of one credit ($1,911). As our goal was to estimate the minimum cost per credit (i.e., NPV = 0), we initially used an arbitrary number for the credit price and then adjusted it until NPV = 0. Total revenue is $1.17 million per year for the five years credits were sold (table 11.2). This is likely an underestimate since it does not include interest accumulated on the revenue generated, which a large portion of would be held in an endowment that makes annual stewardship payments to landowners over the 40-year contracts.

Initial setup expenses were estimated to be $64,000. Ongoing annual expenses at the broker level were estimated to be $83,067 per year for five years. This is an underestimate since there will be some annual cost necessary to manage the annual stewardship payments and monitor compliance during the length of the contract (i.e., 40 years) after the five-year credit selling period. Transaction-related expenses were estimated to be $90,090 the first year and $65,100 annually over the next four years. Annual payments to participating landowners are broken down into two components: stewardship costs ($350,000 annually after year 5) and a profit payment ($294,000 paid out over 9 years). Total expenses are between ~$300,000 and $450,000 annually over the five years of acting credit trading, followed by annual profit payments ($29,425 annually up to year 9, with a double payment of $58,849 in year 5) and stewardship payments (up to year 44, $350,000 annually between years 5 and 40). Since our program is only trading credits for five years, we have calculated the terminal value of all the dollars spent from year 5 through year 44 using an 8 percent discount rate and reported that value as expenses in year 5 ($4.9 million; see table 11.2).

The net income was calculated by the simple formula: Net Income = Total Revenues - Total Expenses (see table 11.2). Before the NPV of the marketplace was calculated, the net incomes for year 1 through year 5 were discounted to year 1 dollars by using a discount rate of 8 percent. The NPV is then calculated by adding the discounted Net Incomes from year 1 through year 5. After developing the overall model, we calculated the minimum price of a credit for which the marketplace breaks even (i.e., NPV = 0): $1,911.

CONCLUSION

One critical aspect of our financial model is the uncertainty surrounding our estimates of expenses. How sensitive is the credit price to changes in expenses? To help inform this question, we conducted a sensitivity analysis to explore changes in the minimum credit price due to increases in each type of expense while holding other expenses constant (table 11.3). The credit price was relatively robust to changes in all expense types (e.g., up to 80 percent increase). Even when we increased expenses by 80 percent, the credit price did not increase dramatically (see table 11.3). The credit price was most sensitive to increases in payments to sellers. Credit price was also relatively robust to the additional cost of longer contracts. For example, when we increased the contract length from 40 to 80 years, the credit price increased by only $77 to $1,988. The costs of increasing the contract length is related to the discount rate used in the model, which was 8 percent in our case. The minimum credit price was also relatively robust to changes in discount rate: a discount rate of 2 percent increased the credit price to $2,089, while a discount rate of 14 percent decreased the credit price to $1,753. In contrast to expenses, contract length, and discount rate, credit price was sensitive to the ratio of credits per acre. The minimum credit price decreases as the credit:acre ratio increases (figure 11.2). Since stewardship costs are a fixed cost on a per-acre basis and higher-quality gopher tortoise habitat results in more credits per acre, a high credit per acre ratio results in a more cost-effective overall program.

Though preliminary and case-specific, our financial model provides a foundation for exploring two financial challenges for piloting and scaling up PLC approaches. First, does the marketplace compensate a landowner sufficiently to cover her opportunity costs and incentivize her to participate in a program? Second, will PLC programs be cost-effective and financially feasible, and are they less expensive than current mitigation approaches that are being implemented downstream of the ESA? We use a case study based on a real property in Georgia to explore these two questions in relation to our financial model (Gartner et al. this volume).

TABLE 11.3 SENSITIVITY ANALYSIS TO EXPLORE CHANGES IN THE MINIMUM CREDIT PRICE ($1,911) DUE TO INCREASES IN EACH TYPE OF EXPENSE WHILE HOLDING OTHERS EXPENSES CONSTANT

Expense Type	+20%	+40%	+60%	+80%
Setup costs	$1,916	$1,921	$1,926	$1,931
Ongoing costs	1,939	1,967	1,995	2,023
Transaction costs	1,935	1,959	1,983	2,007
Payments to sellers	2,256	2,608	2,966	3,331

NOTE: Each expense type was increased up to 80% and the minimum credit price recalculated at NPV = 0. The financial model is relatively robust to changes in all expense types; minimum credit price did not diverge greatly from the original estimate of $1,911. The minimum credit price was most sensitive to an increase in the payments to sellers.

Our case study involves a landowner who owns a ~800-acre land parcel. The landowner chooses to enroll 200 acres in a gopher tortoise PLC program, and both the landowner and the land parcel meet the eligibility requirements of the program (Gartner et al. this volume). The initial scientific survey assesses both the tortoise population and the habitat quality on the property. The estimated tortoise population on the property is 105 individuals; the methodology employed also calculates the 95 percent confidence intervals around this mean estimate, which is between 75 and 147 tortoises. Using the conservative estimate of 75 tortoises, we then scale our tortoise estimate by the habitat credit score for the property (0.65). Thus the total number of credits the broker buys from the landowner is 49 (see Gartner et al. this volume for details). The broker would pay the landowner annual stewardship payments of $4,000 ($20 per acre over 200 acres) over the 40-year contact to conduct prescribed burning, invasive plant control, and monitoring. The broker would also pay the landowner a profit payment of $4,681 split between year 1 and year 5 of the contract. In total, the landowner would receive $164,681 in total payments over the life of the contract. The broker then must resell the credits for a minimum of $1,911 to cover their costs of operating the program. If the broker "shelves" a portion of the credits as a means of self-insurance, then the credit price would be slightly higher (e.g., 10 percent of credits shelved, the minimum credit price would be ~$2,100) Given that the landowner assumes little risk for entering into a contract as currently structured and the required management can be outsourced to a technical assistance organization, the proposed program may be an attractive opportunity for landowners to improve the ecosystem health of their property while

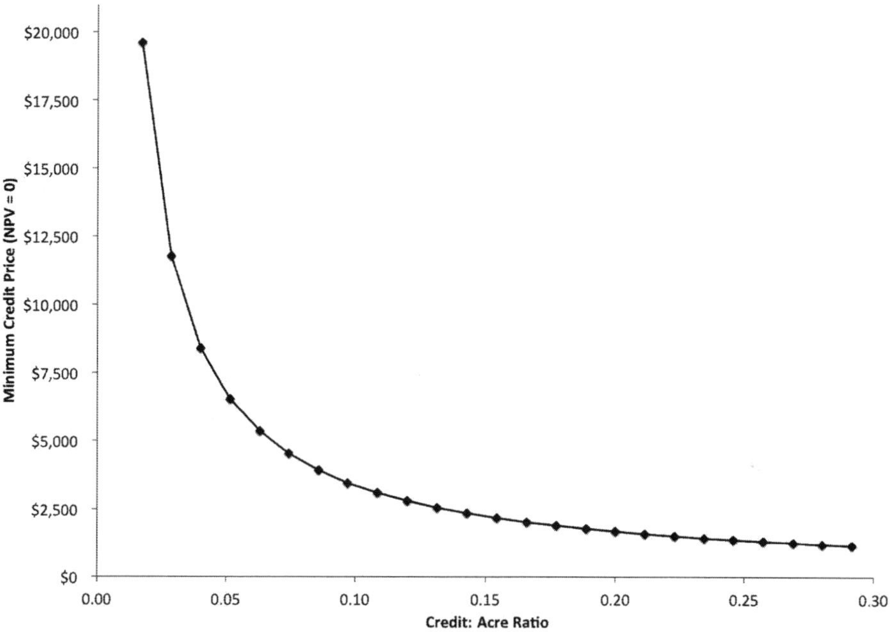

FIGURE 11.2. The effect of the credit:acre ratio on the minimum credit price. As gopher tortoise habitat quality decreases, the minimum credit price increases because there are fewer credits per acre being generated.

also receiving an alternative revenue stream that is compatible with other land use activities, such as timber harvesting (Gartner et al. this volume). While financial payments are only one of many factors that influence a landowner's decision to opt in to a voluntary conservation agreement (Sorice et al. 2013; Sorice and Abel this volume), our preliminary financial analysis suggests that our program may be attractive to some landowners in the southeastern United States (Johnson and Snieckus this volume). Further, increasing the profit payment could be a potential option if it resulted in increased program participation, assuming that the resulting increase in minimum credit price does not substantially affect demand (see table 11.3).

Due to the proprietary nature and scarcity of financial data on mitigation programs under the ESA, it is difficult to assess the cost-effectiveness of a PLC approach compared to traditional methods that are in place, such as conservation banking (Fox and Nino-Murcia 2005). Nationally, acreage-based credits for ESA-listed species range between $2,500 and $300,000 (mean $33,168), and available information on gopher tortoise conservation banks suggests that credits range from $12,000 to $20,000 (Madsen et al. 2011). Our model and analyses suggest a PLC approach could be comparable, if not more cost-effective. Our crediting methodology is based on both the species and habitat quality, as opposed to acres. However, based on our place-based case study (Gartner et al. this volume), our credit price ($1,911) transforms into an acreage-based credit is $10,616. From a per tortoise perspective, our credit price transforms to $2,925 per tortoise. However, our case study was conducted at a location that was of medium-quality gopher tortoise habitat (habitat score of 0.58). The cost-effectiveness per tortoise (i.e., conservation benefit) will increase with the habitat quality of the land that is enrolled in the program (figure 11.2).

Initial results of our market framework and financial model suggest that a PLC program for a candidate species, the gopher tortoise, is not cost-prohibitive and may be more cost-effective than mitigation programs downstream of the ESA. This may be particularly the case when the possibility of upstream conservation programs to reduce endangered species litigation is considered: over $15 million in taxpayers' dollars have been spent on attorney fees over the past four years (Hastings 2012). While PLC programs for other species will have important differences, we hope that our example can inform the design of upstream conservation programs that leverage markets and financial incentives.

CHAPTER 12

Tools to Promote Transparent and Efficient Markets for Species Conservation

JOANNA SILVER

ABSTRACT

For market-based environmental programs such as pre-listing conservation to be successful, the markets that underpin them must operate transparently and efficiently. One tool to increase these essential qualities is market registries: publicly available digital infrastructure that tracks each credit within a market throughout its life cycle. By providing a record of each credit's transaction history, registries reduce the potential for double selling credits and assist regulators. Accessible, up-to-date information on a given market's characteristics such as size, volume, and price over time also increases buyers' and sellers' confidence and improves market efficiency by reducing information imbalances. Although fully integrated market registries may not be possible to incorporate initially into emerging markets, tracking credits accurately on a registry platform from the outset is critical to build credibility and confidence in new marketplaces. Registries will also enable alternatives such as auctions and introductory platforms to increase transparency while accounting for the challenges of newly developing markets.

INTRODUCTION

Markets rely on transparency to sustain participant confidence. This relationship plays a major role in financial markets, where the availability of information is critical for buyers and sellers and drives risk tolerance, investment decisions, demand, and, ultimately, asset values. Market transparency means ensuring that accurate, up-to-date information about a market is readily available. When the voluntary carbon markets emerged in the mid-2000s, they lacked transparency and confidence due partly to the absence of carbon offset standards and registries. When registries began providing transparency to the marketplace and participants adopted various industry standards, the market grew dramatically due to increased confidence (Peters-Stanley et al. 2011).

Providing maximum transparency and credibility must be a priority for market-based environmental program design. One way to ensure this is the use of registries. A registry is a platform of technology and rules designed specifically to ensure accurate, efficient, and transparent recording of environmental credits throughout their life cycle (see http://tinyurl.com/proactive-strategies-12–1). The life cycle begins with issuance of the credits by a regulator or third party with the authority of an environmental standards body. Credits are then transferred from seller to buyer and eventually surrendered or retired to compensate for some environmental impact of the buyer.

Unfortunately, many environmental payment-based programs to date do not use registry infrastructure. As a result, they have suffered from a lack of transparency, which directly hampers growth and confidence. For instance, US species conservation and wetlands mitigation banking programs lack a centralized registry, resulting in difficulties in accessing and tracking information (Madsen et al. 2010). The difficulty of tracking wetland banks has been mitigated in part by the increased use of the US Army Corps of Engineers Regulatory In-Lieu Fee and Bank Information Tracking System, which now covers all but two districts (Madsen et al. 2011). In contrast, US species conservation banking lacks any system that attempts to function like a registry; ownership of species conservation banking credits is not centrally tracked.

In interviews with species conservation banking actors, many expressed frustration with existing regulatory tracking databases and noted the challenges created by existing systems, including out-of-date information, inability to track third-party transactions, and no real-time data tracking. Credit holdings are recorded in various ways across state, regional, and federal offices, ranging from paper ledgers and Microsoft Excel spreadsheets managed by private conservation bankers to fully fledged databases operated by regional government offices. Few of these systems are publicly available. Consequently, accessing a real-time view of credit availability and a consolidated overview of the marketplace is a challenge. While up-to-date market information may appear less important for an emerging environmental program, it becomes critical when transactions involve different types of buyers. For example, accounting problems and risks of double selling credits can arise when third parties (e.g., noncompliance buyers) buy credits and those transactions are not reflected on ledgers maintained by regulatory agencies. To ensure accountability and to avoid potential fraud in a market, a regularly updated and centrally controlled ownership registry is critical.

A lack of transparency in many environmental markets has also left potential participants unable to understand the market profiles, including considerations like size, volumes, levels of participation, price information, growth trends, and other core factors necessary to create strategies for investors and stakeholders. For companies wishing to take a leadership role and participate in early market opportunities, the lack of transparency makes it difficult to understand risk profiles, create a strategy for involvement, or to demonstrate actions publicly with confidence. Thus many market-based environmental programs, such as those focused on species conservation, have been placed in a high risk–low return category. These barriers must be overcome to advance market-based species protection such as pre-listing conservation (PLC) approaches on a larger scale.

REGISTRIES AND TRANSPARENCY IN ENVIRONMENTAL MARKETS

Irrespective of the volume of credits being issued and sold in an emerging environmental market, all credits should be tracked from the initial issuance stage through the end of the credit's life cycle. This aspect of transparency will be particularly important with PLC credits, since credits created and sold in a precompliance setting need to be traceable later in a compliance context in order prevent double selling and to ensure validity (Donlan et al. this volume).

Credit visibility will also be of great importance for potential buyers in PLC programs. A number of factors will directly impact how companies or other credit buyers will be able to brand their participation PLC markets: how the credit is created; the role that local stakeholders, regulators, and government agencies play in the verification or review processes; and how efficiently and transparently credits can be bought and retired. Traceability of assets in markets is becoming increasingly important for consumers, investors, and companies. This is particularly the case in food and clothing markets, where consumers increasingly wish to connect with the food they eat and know the origins of the clothes they wear (Verbeke 2001; Elkington 2010). While environmental markets are much smaller than food or textile markets, traceability and transparency are still important since those factors do and will continue to drive market confidence.

Market participants commonly seek transparency across the full spectrum of the credit life cycle.

- Premarket activity: the nature and design of the project generating the environmental benefit, the standard(s) followed, the validation and verification processes, and the creation of the credit.
- Market activity: linkage to a transaction platform, pricing of the transaction, and a record of who is involved in transactions.
- Postmarket activity: the end use of the credit (i.e., credit retirement and removal from circulation in order to compensate for some impact).

A registry designed specifically for a market-based environmental program achieves transparency by tracking all stages of a project and credit and storing the necessary information throughout the life cycle (see http://tinyurl.com/proactive-strategies-12–2). A registry in this context is electronic infrastructure designed specifically for an environmental market to ensure accurate and transparent recording of credits that have been issued or allocated, their respective environmental benefits, and the status of those credits. Verified environmental credits are issued with unique serial numbers that enable the credit to be traced through the registry infrastructure throughout its life cycle and track the quantified environmental benefits back to the original project activities undertaken. A registry provides visibility to the environmental standards and verifications that were used to create credits by providing project and verification documentation. When used exclusively, registries verify and record the transfer of ownership. The registry provider issues the verified quantity of credits into the accounts of project owners (e.g., species conservation bankers) and enables those account holders to transfer credits to accounts of buyers in the registry. Ultimately, the registry facilitates the retirement of the credits in order to compensate some environmental impact of the credit buyer. Registries are therefore the structural link between the development and creation of environmental assets and the marketplaces in which those assets transact.

REGISTRIES AND MARKET ACTIVITY

A registry is not an exchange or transaction platform itself, but it plays an important role as a tool the seller can use to transfer the assets to the buyer, enabling market transactions to take place. Mature financial markets are often not linked directly with a registry. This is because risks in asset delivery are managed in other ways: at the market entry point (e.g., only regulated brokers can enter trades) and at the settlement stage (e.g., participants have collateral requirements, centralized clearinghouses are utilized, and penalties exist for nondelivery). In contrast, participants in emerging environmental markets are often not traditional financial market participants, and trading infrastructures are still in their infancy with fewer regulatory or central counterparty structures to manage delivery risk. Addressing delivery risk up front with operating infrastructure that connects to a registry enables credits to be secure when offered on a transaction platform and ensures that credits are available for settlement and delivery once a transaction takes place. Environmental credits listed on a transaction platform should be linked to a registry, and that linkage should be exclusive, preventing credits from being bought or sold elsewhere at the same time a transaction is taking place on the linked platform.

Price transparency is also a critical element in any emerging market to build confidence and to facilitate equal access to information for all participants. All market participants benefit from clean, aggregated, and anonymous price data. A registry can capture key trade information, including price, volume, and date. Publishing such information even in early stages of transactions creates a pathway to price transparency in the marketplace and gives early indications of market behavior and price expectations. In addition, transparency of price information further educates sellers and buyers before they participate on transaction platforms such as auctions. Program administrators may wish to consider requiring price reporting to a registry. Initially, many participants may be reluctant to provide price and volume information for fear of losing commercial advantage to competitors. However, with systems and processes in place that ensure the dissemination of price information only in the aggregate and anonymously, such sensitivities can be preserved while better informing the market.

IMPORTANT DESIGN CONSIDERATIONS FOR A REGISTRY

A registry for a PLC program should be centralized so that all information is captured and transparent in a single system and with the appropriate level of coverage (e.g., national, regional, or state). A nationwide registry can enable easy data capture, wider participation, and increased transparency of various subprograms for participating companies, regulators, investors, consumers, and the larger public. However, registry infrastructure must also have the flexibility to provide for the particular needs of specific locations and species, along with the different stakeholders that will use the registry. To increase the transparency of the PLC programs, project documentation should be in the public domain, including documents related to management plans, crediting-debiting methodology, credit ratios, verification, and monitoring. This information will be important in order to provide visibility, confidence, and accessibility. Models for registries are already online for other environmental markets, where each project links to project documents, issuance requirements, quantity held by each account holder, and other relevant information.

Security and flexibility are core design considerations for any registry. Since a registry stores sensitive information, security is necessary to ensure confidence and trust of the users. The registry must be flexible enough to facilitate the registration of various types of projects under a range of standards while also capturing project- and credit-specific information, such as location coordinates, project documentation, environmental benefits, and units of measurement.

A core component of an environmental market is that credit sellers are ultimately paired with buyers who wish to compensate their negative environmental impacts by purchasing credits. For this to happen, a purchased credit must be transferred to a regulator or retired on the registry. "Retirement" in this context means that the credit is taken out of circulation so that it no longer exists in the registry as an active unit and cannot be resold to other buyers. For PLC programs, regulators such as the US Fish and Wildlife Service will play an active role (Li and Male this volume). A PLC registry should facilitate a regulatory review and approval process in cases where regulators are willing to provide certainty on how credits will satisfy requirements under the US Endangered Species Act if and when a species becomes listed. Such a function would enable the regulators to view and approve all PLC projects within their regional jurisdiction and potentially approve the issuance of PLC credits that would have future compliance validity.

In general, program administrators should rely on existing registry systems, as opposed to building one themselves. Existing registries can be custom-tailored to meet the needs of any market-based program, including PLC programs. Customizing a registry involves set-up and ongoing costs, as well as a shift in practices and procedures for all users. However, a well-designed registry is intuitive, and experienced environmental markets registry providers can provide cost-effective and high-quality products and services such as user guides, training webinars, and a help desk.

ALTERNATIVE TRANSACTION PLATFORMS FOR ENVIRONMENTAL MARKETS

High transaction costs can be a barrier to a successful market (Ribaudo et al. 2008). Therefore, new environmental marketplaces should strive to keep transaction costs low for buyers and sellers while still ensuring credibility and confidence in transactions. Achieving this balance will facilitate scalable marketplaces that will encourage broad uptake and participation. Uptake and participation—a pool of willing sellers and buyers who can transact assets easily and efficiently—are needed for liquidity.

Maximum liquidity and participation is achieved when assets are standardized and fungible (i.e., interchangeable or capable of mutual substitution). The European Union Emissions Trading Scheme (EU ETS) is an example of a fungible and liquid environmental market, where emission allowances are assets allocated and tradable across the European Union. Emission allowances trade on exchanges, which publish daily prices (Heimdal et al. 2012). Exchange platforms serving the EU ETS enable high levels of trade orders to be automatically matched and settled between buyers and sellers.

Most environmental markets, however, trade differently, largely due to the nature of their environmental assets and demand drivers. Whereas the emissions reductions credits transacted on the EU ETS are fully fungible across participating countries, market-based programs that are focused on biodiversity are regional in nature and have a variety of credit and project types (Jenkins et al. 2004). Consequently, buyers tend to be local or regional in nature as well. Sometimes buyers and sellers in a biodiversity market-based program already know each other. As biodiversity markets increase and scale up, however, this scenario will likely become less common. Because of differences in scale, traditional transaction platforms may be of minimal utility for some new programs focused on biodiversity conservation. Emerging alternative transaction methods, such as introductory platforms and auctions, may be more strategic in many cases for generating participation and volume. Linked to an independent third-party registry, these alternative transaction methods can ensure credibility and confidence in the transactions while also being low in cost for both buyers and sellers.

Program administrators, such as government agencies, are increasingly enlisting third-party providers such as Markit to set up environmental auctions for specific credit types. Auction platforms are an alternative transaction platform where assets are relatively fungible yet still regional in nature and defined by time, geographic area, and asset type. An example of an auction platform is a water nutrient trading program in the United States operated by the Pennsylvania Infrastructure Investment Authority (Pennsylvania Infrastructure Investment Authority 2013). In two Pennsylvania watersheds, phosphorous and nitrogen credits are bought and sold via spot and forward auctions, held by Markit, which acts as the independent third-party provider. The auction provider administers the auction on behalf of a state agency using proprietary technology. Auction platforms allow buyers and sellers to connect in a more concentrated and custom-tailored fashion. Preapproved participants are able to enter bids and offers confidentially during a specified window of time. When an auction closes, the auction provider determines the results based on prespecified auction rules and notifies program operators, participants, and the broader public of the auction winners, the quantity traded, and the final prices at which the trades will proceed. Auction training sessions, participation rules, schedules of future auctions, and past auction results are publicly available.

Auctions can be based on spot or forward contracts. Spot contracts are when transactions are settled within a few days of the auction closing and credits were in existence at the time of the auction (i.e., credits are delivered to the buyer in exchange for money). Environmental markets, however, are often forward-looking: investments in environmental improvements are generally multiyear and a buyer's compliance requirements are often annual and ongoing. Therefore, these markets naturally lend themselves to forward contracts, that is, contracts requiring the seller to deliver credits on some future date for an agreed upon price. Auctions offer a controlled and transparent setting where prices can be set fairly, liquidity is concentrated, and participants are subject to the same auction rules and have access to all outcomes and information.

TABLE 12.1 DIFFERENT CHARACTERISTICS OF THREE DIFFERENT CREDIT TRANSACTION PLATFORMS: EXCHANGES, AUCTIONS, AND INTRODUCTORY PLATFORMS

	Exchanges	Auctions	Introductory Platforms
Fungibility	Very fungible	Somewhat fungible	Not fungible
Compliance area	International, national, large-scale regional	International, national, regional, local	International, national, regional, local
Participant type	Sophisticated, regulated	Registry member with coordinator approval	Registry member

Online introductory platforms can also offer a place for buyers and sellers to connect. Operating like an electronic noticeboard, these platforms enable a seller to display credits for sale, along with associated information such as quantity, quality, and price. Buyers can review and respond privately. The two parties can then negotiate pricing and execute a bilateral transaction. These types of transaction are often referred to as "over-the-counter" transactions because there is no intermediary system directly connecting the buyer and seller; rather, they transact directly. Such platforms can result in less visibility of the transaction and limited transparency of volume and pricing. However, introductory platforms bring sellers and buyers together in a low-cost and efficient way. When only introductory platforms are linked to a registry, buyers can have more confidence in the credits they are buying due to the reduced risk of double selling. In addition, price information can be captured and displayed in an aggregated and anonymous way, increasing market transparency.

Traditional exchanges may have an important role to play in environmental markets when programs become large and fungible. In the meantime, alternative tools like auctions and introductory platforms that are linked directly to registries can assist in generating transactions for biodiversity-based market programs while concurrently promoting transparency and confidence (table 12.1).

CONCLUSION

Market-based mechanisms are a powerful tool to incentivize investment in species conservation upstream of regulation. When applying market principles to biodiversity conservation, there is real value in leveraging tools designed specifically for transacting. These tools can assist in creating scalable programs that are transparent and efficient. Only once a trading program is transparent can confidence, participation, and investment increase (Peters-Stanley et al. 2011). Transparency facilitates trust and encourages broader understanding and support. Efficiency is equally important: lengthy, paper-based processes frustrate market participants and hamper investment. Transparency and efficiency in environmental markets can be achieved by utilizing registry infrastructure designed specifically to track market activity. The project boundaries and details are defined on the registry, project documentation is reviewed and made public, and an environmental credit is created and made available for sale. A registry can interface with transaction tools such as auction platforms, introductory platforms, and exchanges. Once sold, the credit can then be transferred from the seller to the buyer on the registry and ultimately retired on the registry to compensate for some impact by the end buyer.

For markets to function, it is important that sellers can efficiently find buyers and engage in transactions cost-effectively. In emerging PLC markets, credit volume and the number of buyers and sellers will be low. Credits will be, and will likely remain, local and regional. Consequently, emerging PLC markets will not likely be best served by traditional exchanges. However, auctions and introductory platforms could be valuable tools for PLC market administrators and participants to leverage in order to concentrate activity and facilitate transactions in a low-cost and time-efficient manner.

ACKNOWLEDGMENTS

Opinions, estimates, and projections expressed in this chapter are solely that of the author and constitute the current judgment of the author as of the date of this chapter. They do not necessarily reflect the opinions of Markit Group or its affiliates. Markit Group and its affiliates do not warrant the accuracy or completeness of information contained herein.

CHAPTER 13

The Role of Electronic Marketplaces in Scaling Environmental Markets

MICHAEL VAN PATTEN AND AARON MARTIN

ABSTRACT

Markets focused explicitly on biodiversity have lagged behind other environmental markets but continue to grow and expand under both regulatory and voluntary frameworks. Yet businesses are increasingly internalizing environmental externalities in their goods and services. For a variety of reasons, businesses struggle to identify and locate investment opportunities that will allow them to reduce their environmental impacts. The use of transaction platforms and exchange technology can help increase the visibility and access for businesses wishing to engage in actions to reduce their net environmental impact. The Mission Markets Earth Marketplace is an example of a centralized marketplace that aggregates all credit types related to environmental markets. The exchange connects potential buyers directly with local project developers who seek to promote their projects and sell credits and/or provide ecosystem services to potential buyers. Since most environmental markets are regional, the Mission Marketplace also provides a foundation for customized exchange portals that aggregate and standardize data and fees while providing large institutions on the buy side with a suite of products related to minimizing their negative environmental impacts. Without marketplace mechanisms like exchanges and centralized marketplaces, most environmental markets will remain opaque and underutilized by major stakeholders, such as corporations and governments, for which these markets could otherwise serve effectively.

INTRODUCTION

Over the past decade environmental markets have grown exponentially (Madsen et al. 2010; World Bank 2011). Markets focused on carbon and water have been leading the way; the carbon market, for example, was valued at $142 billion in 2010 (World Bank 2011). Markets focused explicitly on biodiversity have lagged behind other environmental markets but continue to grow and expand under both regulatory and voluntary frameworks (Madsen et al. 2010; Bull et al. 2013). In 2010, a minimum of $3 billion to $4 billion in transactions took place in programs related to biodiversity offsets (Madsen et al. 2011).

Businesses are increasingly internalizing social and environmental externalities in their goods and services. Furthermore, more businesses are beginning to do so not only because it is a potential liability but also because it is a potential asset that can result in increased sales and customers. Sustainable practices are becoming necessary in many sectors for businesses to remain competitive and innovative (Nidumolu et al. 2009).

As businesses seek to avoid, minimize, and mitigate their environmental impacts with respect to their operations and products, they will face a number of challenges. First, they must identify and quantify their impacts. Second, because specific species and ecosystems are often limited spatially, options to offset environmental impacts can be limited. Third, the expertise required to create and quantify a biodiversity offset often falls outside the expertise and networks of many businesses. Businesses are often unaware of the options available that would allow them to reduce their net environmental impact.

The use of transaction platforms and exchange technology can increase visibility and access for businesses wishing to engage in actions to reduce their net environmental impact. Environmental exchanges can serve regulatory or voluntary markets and provide a central location for the buying and selling of credits, tied to programs such as wetland and species banking, land easements, fishing quotas, sustainable agro-commodity certification, water quality, and other ecosystem-based programs.

Here I briefly discuss how environmental exchanges and technology can be leveraged to create regional exchange portals that are connected to each other and to a central aggregation platform. Such a framework will facilitate transparency and the effective monetization of environmentally based credits. Over 80 percent of current biodiversity markets are not transparent enough to estimate their market value (Madsen et al.

2010). Exchanges are a primary tool that will allow for increased transparency, and consequently a better understanding of environmental markets by the variety of stakeholders.

Exchanges are a critical component if any market-based environmental approach based on the buying and selling of credits is going to reach the scale necessary to achieve positive landscape-level impacts. Because demand is often the limiting factor in emerging environmental markets (Gartner et al. this volume), exchanges are particularly important because they focus on delivering product efficiently and effectively to potential buyers.

MISSION MARKETS EARTH: AN EXAMPLE OF AN ENVIRONMENTAL EXCHANGE

The Mission Markets Earth Marketplace (MME; www.mmearth.com) was created in 2010 with the goal of providing a centralized marketplace to aggregate all credit types related to environmental markets. It was created under the assumption that businesses and other stakeholders will want to access a single, centralized platform in order to locate and purchase multiple environmental projects or credits (e.g., carbon, water, and biodiversity). The MME assumes that the bundling and stacking of ecosystem services credits will become a standard practice and that market and regulatory signals will eventually incentivize companies to voluntarily offset their environmental actions. The MME facilitates multiple transactions at a single location, as opposed to having to search out transactions at different venues in order to comply with various regulatory mandates or voluntary in-house corporate responsibility policies. The exchange connects potential buyers directly with local project developers who seek to promote their projects and sell credits and/or provide ecosystem services to potential buyers. It provides standardized documentation on environmental credits and the projects behind the credits.

The MME supports multiple environmental markets. Currently, most exchanges support just one or two environmental markets, such as carbon, renewable energy credits, or water quality nutrient credits. Such fragmentation can result in less transparency and increases the difficulty for businesses to efficiently identify projects or credits that meet their environmental compliance requirements. In contrast, the MME strives to provide the key functions needed for a marketplace to a variety of users (table 13.1).

TABLE 13.1 KEY FUNCTIONS AND SOME USERS OF AN ENVIRONMENTAL MARKETPLACE EXCHANGE

Key Functions of an Environmental Exchange

1) Gives stakeholders a central location to search for projects (credits), which are searchable by multiple attributes (e.g., project type, country, city, etc.).
2) Provides a platform where buyers and sellers can negotiate discreetly online.
3) Increases liquidity for environmental credits.
4) Provides price history and other data for past transactions.

Examples of Environmental Exchange Users

Agricultural producers
Environment project developers
Fisheries quota brokers
Impact investment funds
Real estate brokers
Regional environmental credit exchanges
Water rights brokers

THE ROLE OF CUSTOMIZED PORTALS

Most environmental markets are regional (Jenkins et al. 2004). This is particularly true for water and biodiversity. Thus exchanges often function best when customized for specific regional markets. A hub-and-spoke model provides a framework to provide turnkey solutions for regional, credit-specific markets while also leveraging economies of scale. Future exchange models will improve on the hub-and-spoke model and resemble more a series of networked hubs. The MME provides a foundation for customized exchange portals that aggregate and standardize data and fees while providing large institutions on the buy side with a suite of products related to minimizing their negative environmental impacts.

Customized exchange portals should be promoted in order to service emerging environmental markets such as pre-listing conservation (PLC) programs. Such portals provide customized exchange platforms that allow for specific, private transactions while concurrently being connected to a centralized platform. The centralized platform provides standardized registry and ownership transfer protocols (Silver this volume), as well as benefits from technical and marketing support.

The Environment Bank in the United Kingdom is a recent example of a customized exchange portal. In February 2012, the Environment

Bank launched an online marketplace for exchanging environmental credits under a biodiversity offset scheme. The Environmental Markets Exchange allows conservation groups, farmers, and landowners to register their wildlife sites and provide conservation credits, which then are available to developers for purchase to offset their biodiversity impacts (Environment Bank 2012). Biodiversity offsetting is new to the United Kingdom and is currently operating under a voluntary framework for project developers. The government supports biodiversity offsets, however, and has recently launched six pilot projects (Government of the United Kingdom 2011).

Any potential offset site can be registered on the Environmental Markets Exchange if the project developers have a management plan in place that aims to create or restore habitat. Following an expression of interest, an Environment Bank staff member visits the property to get further details to assess eligibility and assess potential credits. There is currently no cost to register a project on the platform, and no initial obligations or commitments. The Environment Bank is currently leading a biodiversity offset pilot project in Essex, and the Environmental Markets Exchange will serve as the transaction platform.

CONCLUSION

Without centralized marketplaces that provide information and connect buyers and sellers, both large and small environmental markets will remain fragmented and difficult to scale. Environmental markets must demonstrate that they can provide information and perform in order to attract mainstream players. Electronic marketplaces help provide the price discovery, project information, and other data that large organizations need for decision making. Without marketplace mechanisms like exchanges and centralized marketplaces, most environmental markets will remain opaque and underutilized by major stakeholders, such as corporations and governments, for which these markets could otherwise serve effectively.

PART THREE

Case Studies

CHAPTER 14

Prospects for Pre-Listing Conservation Approaches in Freshwater Ecosystems

DANIEL A. AUERBACH AND TODD K. BENDOR

ABSTRACT

Freshwater species across the United States are highly threatened. The US Endangered Species Act assures a final measure of protection for species and their habitat, but the listing process can entail conflicts and costs that further expose vulnerable species to extinction. Formal contractual commitments to conserve species prior to threatened or endangered status may favor the long-term viability of freshwater populations by hastening management changes and fostering collaborative relationships. Pre-listing conservation mechanisms offer regulatory certainty via advance permits applicable under endangered status as an incentive for regulated entities to modify harmful practices or engage in conservation actions. We discuss pre-listing conservation in the broader context of freshwater biodiversity threats, describe two examples of aquatic Candidate Conservation Agreements, and review existing stream and wetland mitigation markets. These precedents illustrate some of the challenges and potential benefits associated with a pre-listing conservation approach to freshwater species conservation. We highlight factors likely to advance the success of future pre-listing conservation initiatives in freshwater ecosystems. In certain instances, freshwater species and regulated entities can mutually benefit from pre-listing conservation agreements that facilitate spatial and institutional coordination to promote the protection and restoration of aquatic ecological processes.

INTRODUCTION

Impaired water quality and altered flow patterns threaten freshwater biodiversity by degrading habitat and reducing native populations (Baron et al. 2002; Richter and Thomas 2007; Strayer and Dudgeon 2010; Carpenter et al. 2011). While the long history of human modification of inland waters shapes our perception of the severity and scale of ongoing damage (Wohl 2005; Doyle and Shields 2012), many aquatic species depend on habitat and flow conditions that conflict with societal expectations for irrigation, transportation, and flood control (e.g., easily navigable channels and predictable water supply). Consequently, species that rely on freshwater ecosystems face a host of impacts from water infrastructure and land use changes such as riparian development, dams, groundwater pumping operations, trans-basin diversions, dredging, channelization, levees, and road crossings. In addition, river, lake, and stream habitats accumulate toxins, sediment, and excess nutrients from terrestrial sources, while the linear, branching form of river and stream habitat makes it especially vulnerable to fragmentation (Lowe et al. 2006).

Freshwater conservation is complicated by a variety of factors, including (1) the mosaic of public and private landownership in most US watersheds, (2) the divided regulatory authority over water quality and quantity, and (3) the spatial separation between actions and their effects that can disconnect culpable parties from penalties and beneficial actors from adequate credit (Dyckman and Paulsen 2012). Terrestrial protected areas often inadequately sustain freshwater species (Herbert et al. 2010), many of which may have limited appeal as conservation targets given that they are often small, hard to observe, and invertebrates. The combined effect is a crisis in freshwater biodiversity (Richter et al. 1997; Ricciardi and Rasmussen 1999; Strayer and Dudgeon 2010). The conservation status of many freshwater taxonomic groups, including amphibians, fish, mussels, and crayfish, is well documented and declining (Williams et al. 1993; Taylor et al. 1996; Burkhead 2012). Many aquatic invertebrates have also likely experienced comparable declines due to shared threats (Richter et al. 1997; Ricciardi and Rasmussen 1999).

Over the past decades, the importance of healthy aquatic ecosystems has sparked both widespread voluntary conservation actions and statutes that regulate land and water uses that affect freshwater species and ecosystems. This includes statutes such as the US Clean Water Act, US

Wild and Scenic Rivers Act, and US Endangered Species Act (ESA). The ESA offers a final measure of protection for freshwater species and their habitat, but the listing and recovery process is often costly and controversial (Scott et al. 2005; Schwartz 2008). Pre-listing conservation (PLC) approaches offer regulatory predictability and avoided costs as incentives to take conservation actions for species prior to regulatory triggers. Aquatic PLC actions could take the form of habitat banks that provide advance mitigation when specific future impacts are uncertain or Section 7 consultation and Candidate Conservation Agreements with Assurances (CCAA) for federal and private stakeholders, respectively, when ongoing or planned activities result in known impacts (Li and Male this volume). We discuss existing freshwater mitigation markets and CCAAs to highlight several factors likely to influence the success of aquatic PLC initiatives, then provide some perspectives for potential future programs. If PLC programs can serve as the nexus for coordinated functional restoration at a watershed scale and can foster durable collaboration among stakeholders, then they have the potential to increase the effectiveness and efficiency of aquatic conservation under the ESA.

PRECEDENTS

Freshwater Candidate Conservation Agreements and mitigation banks illustrate important issues for the design and implementation of aquatic PLC programs. These precedents serve as case studies, demonstrating strengths and shortcomings, as well as providing templates for future applications.

Private landowners entering into a CCAA commit to actions that are intended to prevent the listing of an at-risk species (e.g., candidate species) as federally threatened or endangered under the ESA (USFWS 2003a). Participants who meet contractual obligations receive the assurance of an enhancement of survival permit defining the extent of regulation in the event of listing and may be eligible for technical and financial assistance (Li and Male this volume). In addition to agreements with individual parties, the US Fish and Wildlife Service (USFWS) works with delegated entities such as state wildlife agencies to develop programmatic CCAAs (USFWS 2003a). Programmatic CCAAs simplify the negotiation and review process by specifying a shared set of threats and potential beneficial actions, thereby enabling numerous landowners to enroll as conservation partners under a shared assurance (Womack

2008). Both the individual and the programmatic approach provide for changing legal and biological conditions such as ownership transfers or natural catastrophes and are binding for a fixed duration, usually a minimum of five years.

Robust Redhorse CCAA

A consortium of agencies, environmental advocates, and industry groups formed the Robust Redhorse Conservation Committee following the scientific rediscovery of the robust redhorse (*Moxostoma robustum*) in the coastal plain rivers of Georgia and the Carolinas (figure 14.1). The committee sought to determine the basic life history and habitat requirements of this large catostomid ("sucker") fish while providing guidance during the Federal Energy Regulatory Commission relicensing of the Sinclair hydropower dam on the Oconee River in Georgia. The committee drafted a detailed conservation plan that documented several conservation concerns, including (1) small populations and limited recruitment due to migration barriers; (2) harmful effects of excess sedimentation due to watershed development, particularly the loss of clean gravel bars for spawning; and (3) the spread of predatory flathead catfish (*Pylodictis olivaris*) (Nichols 2003; Grabowski and Isely 2006).

In 2002, the USFWS signed a CCAA with Georgia Power and the Georgia Department of Natural Resources to protect and expand the range of the robust redhorse (USFWS 2002). Capitalizing on the work of the Robust Redhorse Conservation Committee, the agreement had the stated purpose of monitoring and reestablishing the robust redhorse along 19 miles of the Ocmulgee River. The agreement specified stocking of hatchery-reared and transplanted fish to supplement the resident population (whose condition was unknown) and committed the signatories to fund and conduct studies measuring population trends, individual movement patterns, and microhabitat use (USFWS 2002). These latter provisions increased the value of the CCAA for robust redhorse conservation at a regional level.

The CCAA provided a time line and the resources to study the effects of a dam on a population of concern, both detrimental (e.g., disrupting spawning cues and migrations) and beneficial (e.g., trapping excess upstream sediment input and obstructing flathead catfish spread). Reporting on a portion of this research, Grabowski and Jennings (2009, 175) observed that "the use of hatchery-reared robust redhorse to establish a refugial population in the Ocmulgee River seems to be a viable strategy

FIGURE 14.1. The robust redhorse (*Moxostoma robustum*). © B. Gratwicke.

to aid in the recovery of this species." But they went on to strongly caution that the study results did not yet indicate the persistence of a self-sustaining population in the target area. Recent surveys in the neighboring Oconee River have yielded no observations of robust redhorse, and the status of the fish remains precarious (RRCC 2011).

The robust redhorse CCAA helped to secure the economic value of dam operations over time, while providing critical data for the design and implementation of conservation practices Similar arrangements may appeal to other private hydroelectric dam operators as a means to clearly define planning horizons and ensure the availability of information to support later regulatory or operational decisions (e.g., public pressure to remove, reengineer, or switch from peak to run-of-river releases) (Richter and Thomas 2007). A comparably structured Section 7 consultation process could likely appeal to divisions of the US Bureau of Reclamation or the US Army Corps of Engineers that are responsible for federal irrigation or flood control infrastructure. The robust redhorse CCAA and the ongoing work of the Robust Redhorse Conservation Committee demonstrate how PLC arrangements can foster collaborative relationships between the private sector, academia, and government agencies. More broadly, this example indicates that PLC approaches have the potential to deliver useful information, initiate beneficial management changes, and avoid antagonism that undermines the effectiveness of species recovery plans. However, PLC initiatives must address several challenges if this potential is to be realized (see below).

Arctic Grayling CCAA

Public-private partnerships have also been formed to improve conditions for Arctic grayling (*Thymallus arcticus*) that occupy the Big Hole River in Montana (figure 14.2). This partnership was formed despite a protracted dispute over the ESA listing status of Big Hole River population, the last in the lower forty-eight states of a once-abundant fish (USFWS 2010b). An advisory committee convened by Montana Fish, Wildlife, and Parks (MFWP) identified management changes needed to address the threats posed by low flows, warming water temperatures, increased sedimentation, and negative interactions with non-native salmonids (MFWP and USFWS 2005). Subsequently, a programmatic CCAA was approved, authorizing MFWP to extend the provisions of an enhanced survival permit covering agricultural and ranching activities to landowners willing to participate (MFWP and USFWS 2005).

The CCAA capitalized on the local expertise and working relationships built by MFWP staff, with support from the US Natural Resources Conservation Service and the Montana Department of Natural Resources and Conservation (MFWP and USFWS 2005). After an initial property assessment, parcel management plans are developed and submitted for approval. The plans detail committed actions such as restricted near-bank grazing, native tree planting, and the repair or installation of head gates to control flow into irrigation ditches. In addition to habitat structure enhancements, supplemental flow agreements provide the option to define thresholds in discharge magnitude and timing that trigger reduced water diversions. For example, in order to gain approval of a property-specific plan, the landowner might agree to limit withdrawal for irrigation during certain summer weeks, contingent on readings from a designated streamflow gauge.

Implementation of the Arctic grayling CCAA included prioritizing parcels at a watershed scale. Taking advantage of existing survey data, numerous river segments and associated landholdings were ranked according to their capacity for (in order of importance) (1) the protection of existing populations, (2) the improvement of known spawning areas, and (3) the reestablishment of populations within historical habitat (MFWP and USFWS 2005). These rankings and the division of the project area into five subsections have allowed the Montana Department of Natural Resources and Conservation to allocate resources strategically and transparently (MFWP 2010). As of 2010, more than thirty landowners were participating in the CCAA, which represents over

FIGURE 14.2. The Arctic grayling (*Thymallus arcticus*). © A.K. Smith.

160,000 acres along the Big Hole River. The Arctic grayling CCAA has persisted through a variety of property transfers and de-enrollments, as well as ongoing changes in listing status (MFWP2010; USFWS 2010), further demonstrating the institutional viability of a freshwater PLC approach. Notwithstanding these organizational successes, the influence of the program on the Arctic grayling population remains unclear.

Conservation Banking Approaches

In addition to direct agreements between agencies and regulated entities, PLC programs could involve intermediaries that broker compensation for nonspecific and anticipated impacts on candidate species (Li and Male this volume). "Conservation banking" refers to restoration and protection performed by an intermediary seeking to mitigate or offset another responsible party's harmful impacts via a regulated transaction. Banking, as originally conceptualized, requires compensatory actions to occur *prior* to degradation (Page and Wilcher 1990; DOD et al. 1995). Research into the timing of compensatory mitigation relative to impacts suggests that biodiversity conservation activities performed *after* permitted impacts can result in large, permanent declines in ecosystem services and biodiversity (Bendor 2009; Moilanen et al. 2009). Biodiversity offset programs in which impacts precede compensatory mitigation are therefore likely to conflict with the goal of preventing near-term population declines and are likely to be inappropriate for candidate species in most cases (Urban et al. 1999; Wilkinson 2009).

Conservation banking can expedite the regulatory process and fund property acquisition (e.g., riparian parcels and water rights) and restoration (Marsh et al. 1996). The USFWS recognizes habitat banking as a useful strategy for protecting some species, and the construction of freshwater fisheries banks is already ongoing, primarily in California (USFWS 2003b; Fox and Nino-Murcia 2005; Cannon and Brown 2008). However, current aquatic species banks have experienced less activity relative to markets for wetland and stream credits, and much less information is available. We therefore focus on stream and wetland mitigation banks to illustrate issues for freshwater PLC taking a banking approach.

Permiting overseen by the US Army Corps of Engineers under Section 404 of the Clean Water Act has served as an important mechanism for aquatic ecosystem protection in the United States (NRC 2001; Hough and Robertson 2009). Development that involves the discharge of fill material into wetlands or streams requires permits that often stipulate compensatory mitigation to offset aquatic habitat damage or wetland loss. Permittees have the option to purchase mitigation credits from wetland and stream banks rather than perform the necessary actions and monitoring themselves (DOD et al. 1995; DOD and EPA 2008). The desire to meet Section 404 requirements without incurring substantial project delays has spurred the creation of a substantial stream banking market (Lave et al. 2008; Doyle and BenDor 2011). A "stream bank" typically consists of restored channel and riparian zone habitats, often accompanied by some upland area. An interagency team evaluates the credits generated by these banks, which may then be sold to land developers, state transportation agencies, or other permittees required to mitigate damage (DOD and EPA 2008; Lave et al. 2008; BenDor et al. 2011).

While mitigation is intended as the final option after avoiding and minimizing impacts (Page and Wilcher 1990; DOD et al. 1995), controversy has arisen over the frequency of compensatory mitigation via restoration versus the preferred avoidance and minimization measures

(Mann and Goldman-Carter 2008; Murphy et al. 2009). Despite a broadly adopted "no net loss" standard for wetland acreage and function, mitigation requirements and the growth of wetland banking have raised debate over the actual quantity and quality of protected wetland habitat (NRC 2001). Empirical evidence of shortcomings has prompted the revision of federal guidelines for stream and wetland mitigation (NRC 2001; DOD and EPA 2008). The possibility of irreversible and irreplaceable loss is a primary concern for aquatic species banks, indicating a need for additional research into how banks might be designed to rehabilitate the habitat function and structure needed for self-sustaining populations.

Getting the Currency Right

Successful mitigation requires a currency of credits to quantify the environmental cost of permitted impacts and the environmental benefits produced by banks or individual CCAA participants (Gartner et al. this volume). Yet significant conceptual and practical difficulties surround the definition of precise and accurate measures of species demography and ecosystem function (Turner et al. 2001). These difficulties have prompted the use of acreage and stream reach length as easily quantified surrogates for wetland and stream function, despite uncertainty as to how size and structural features serve as proxies for processes such as flood attenuation, nutrient retention, and wildlife habitat quality (Hill et al. 2010; Doyle and BenDor 2011).

When the specific impacts of an action on an aquatic candidate species are unknown, the use of habitat banks will require clear definitions of the ecological benefits provided by the actions credited for trade (Salzman and Ruhl 2000; Ruhl et al. 2005; Scheerer and O'Neill 2010). If the goal of candidate conservation is species persistence, then credited habitat improvements (e.g., the addition of large woody debris to channels) warrant direct links to population increases measured by surveys of abundance. However, quantifying such benefits can require intensive, prolonged monitoring and analyses that influence the price of credits and potentially the demand for habitat banking (Ruhl et al. 2005; Scheerer and O'Neill 2010). Moreover, the unresolved challenges of defining credits for even a single management target suggest that, at least for the time being, PLC banking initiatives should avoid credit stacking, whereby different benefits of the same conservation action are sold in multiple markets (e.g., exchanging credits from a restored riparian parcel in contexts driven by the ESA, the Clean Water Act, and carbon emissions) (Robertson and Mikota 2007; Doyle and BenDor 2011).

Conservation banking also involves the definition of a "service area" within which the mitigation credits generated by a bank may be traded. Federal guidance on wetland and stream banking constrains impacts and compensation to the same watershed, but differing interpretations have allowed the thirty-six District Engineers to delineate a service area considered most locally appropriate (DOD and EPA 2008). Consequently, the size of service areas varies widely in conjunction with underlying environmental and economic differences (BenDor et al. 2011). Service area size is a key determinant of economic and ecological success (Bonnie and Wilcox 2008; Womble and Doyle 2012). Large service areas risk concentrating impacts in "hot spots" of pollution or habitat destruction while locating mitigation activities at distances that limit their value. On the other hand, the possibility of more buyers within a larger service area creates greater incentives for private bankers to proactively restore habitat, and a small service area may limit demand (Salzman and Ruhl 2000). Trading ratios set the credits required for a given impact (e.g., three mitigation credits per one impact debit), and ratios that address the distances among impacts and between impacts and mitigation may offer a means to define larger service areas while controlling the undesirable aggregation of negative impacts (BenDor and Brozović 2007).

The rationale for defining service area size may differ between species banking programs and stream or wetland banks due to the different effects of trading ecosystem function versus habitat loss and gain within a watershed. Exchanging habitat loss at one site for protection or restoration elsewhere may be defensible or even preferable for some species. Banks that are large, contiguous, and strategically located to protected habitat may also offer advantages relative to mitigation actions taken at the impact site (Mead 2008). In contrast to impacts, the spatial concentration of conservation efforts may allow more efficient monitoring and enforcement and yield conservation benefits not possible in small, fragmented areas (Schwartz 1999; BenDor and Brozović 2007; Templeton et al. 2008). Unfortunately, the widespread threats to freshwater ecosystems may limit opportunities for the beneficial concentration of habitat improvements to at-risk species with patchy distribution, limited movement requirements, and proximity to unimpaired catchments. The effects of spatial attributes on the biological and economic success of habitat banks will demand additional research as the practice becomes more common.

REALIZING THE POTENTIAL OF PLC IN FRESHWATER ECOSYSTEMS

Given the expectation that a species may be listed as threatened or endangered under the ESA, a contractual agreement or purchased credits that provide clarity regarding future ESA regulation may appeal to private hydroelectric operators, individual landowners, and federal water and land management agencies. Yet what benefits does PLC offer aquatic species relative to the current listing process? Addressing this question requires understanding that a PLC approach augments and supplements existing policy, with the intent of promoting cooperation over contention, and expediting conservation actions. Nonetheless, gauging the general desirability of aquatic PLC is not straightforward. Stream and wetland banking approaches have shown limited success as a means to control the degradation of aquatic habitat, but they are generally designed to meet ecosystem criteria rather than the needs of individual species. Further, their implementation has been a moving target, with changing policy guidelines. Current CCAA guidelines emphasize the legal standard of preventing endangered status rather than a net conservation benefit (Li and Male this volume), and freshwater species banks and CCAAs are simply too new and few to support a comprehensive, formal assessment of successes and failures.

In many instances, merely determining what to measure impedes evaluation of freshwater conservation mechanisms. Aquatic population surveys may involve challenging logistics, but structural proxies (e.g., stream length) risk inaccurately portraying program effectiveness. High levels of natural variability, species migrations, and spatially linked stream chemistry complicate assigning short-term responsibility for conservation actions to certain individuals inhabiting a certain property, much less the long-term effect of a particular agreement on the status of at-risk population or species. Information to date suggests that neither the robust redhorse nor the Arctic grayling CCAA has yet to result in net conservation benefits. Any freshwater conservation approach (including traditional species recovery planning under ESA) is likely to be hindered by (1) the low reproductive potential of slowly maturing species, (2) the continued spread of invasive species, and (3) the intensifying effects of climate change (e.g., warming temperatures and reduced precipitation). Nonetheless, aquatic species banking and CCAA policy could build on recent policy changes for wetland and stream banking to define rigorous crediting and monitoring standards based on ecological function rather than surrogate variables (Bernhardt et al. 2005; Ruhl et al. 2005; DOD and EPA 2008; NRC 2001). For example, Scheerer and O'Neil (2010) describe a promising example of such a crediting method for a threatened minnow. More research is needed to develop cost-effective and biologically sensitive indicators that will enable aquatic PLC programs to defensibly assert that net conservation benefits have occurred. In the meantime, aquatic PLC programs must address three primary challenges to be effective: functional restoration, watershed planning, and organizational coordination.

Functional Restoration

While new protections for any remaining intact habitat will constitute a top priority, aquatic PLC projects are almost certain to involve restoration at some scale, from planting native riparian trees to releasing captive-bred individuals to removing or modifying dams. Critiques of stream restoration efficacy and monitoring have shown the consistent difficulty of regenerating lost biological processes through structural manipulations (e.g., reconfiguring channel and floodplain topography), and few studies to date have documented that restored habitat serves the needs of populations as effectively as pre-impact habitat (Bedford 1996; Salzman and Ruhl 2000; Doyle and Shields 2012). As stream restoration practitioners work to develop regionally appropriate techniques and evaluation standards, the integration of habitat reconstruction with a return to some degree of natural flow and sediment regime has emerged as a key practical guideline (Palmer et al. 2005; Bernhardt et al. 2007; Beechie et al. 2010; Doyle and Douglas Shields 2012). Neglecting flow variability may undermine other elements of an aquatic PLC initiative (Beechie et al. 2010). For instance, eradicating a non-native predatory fish may not benefit an at-risk species that is also impacted by lowered base flows or the absence of flood spawning cues.

An appealing consequence of expanding aquatic PLC programs could involve more widespread establishment of environmental flow standards or tighter adherence to existing commitments throughout US watersheds. An environmental flow regime defines a varied discharge schedule designed to balance human and ecological needs (Poff et al. 2010; Richter et al. 2012). The Arctic grayling CCAA demonstrates that participants may agree to modify their water use patterns, and efforts such as the Sustainable Rivers Project, a partnership between the US Army Corp of Engineers and the Nature Conservancy, demonstrate the feasibility of large-scale adaptive flow management (Susskind et al. 2010; Konrad et al. 2011). Nonetheless, established water rights, interstate compacts, and competing demand from other water users are likely to influence environmental flow negotiations for many PLC agreements (Susskind et al. 2010). Achieving net conservation benefits for an at-risk species may warrant changing dam operations or reengineering levee systems, but the potential for such functional restoration will likely decrease with the economic importance of the infrastructure responsible for impacts.

Watershed planning

Restoration is widely necessary in part because river and stream networks progressively accumulate terrestrial and upstream impacts and because freshwater species movements are subject to hierarchical network structure. For instance, dams or dewatering may impact populations over areas that are disproportionately large relative to the size of the obstruction. The resulting habitat fragmentation can interfere with reproduction or prevent a subpopulation from rescuing a threatened neighboring subpopulation (Lowe et al. 2006; Brown et al. 2011). In addition, high levels of natural environmental variability and low reproductive rates of some species will likely require project durations of many years. Yet, longer project durations increase the likelihood that aquatic PLC will be subject to climate change and changing human water demand. Thus, management changes that exceed the authority or spatial domain of a single owner or agency are often needed, making watershed-wide planning integral to freshwater conservation (Bernhardt and Palmer 2011).

Long-term, whole-watershed aquatic PLC programs will be better positioned to accommodate the uncertainties associated with the above spatiotemporal factors. Fortunately, both programmatic CCAAs and carefully planned species banking arrangements are suited to coordinate management improvements across multiple sites and over prolonged time frames. Spatially extensive aquatic PLC efforts could leverage the branching configuration of freshwater habitat, so that limited conservation resources have positive effects over a large area when obstructions are removed or threats are reduced. As demonstrated by the numerous studies examining dam removal on the Elwha River (Washington, USA), removing obsolete downstream dams may rapidly restore access to substantial amounts of habitat, possibly without the costs commensurate with reach-by-reach improvements (Kuby et al. 2005; Brenkman et al. 2012). Aquatic PLC may accommodate long-term planning if participating stakeholders are open to long-term contracts, comparable to the time frames for relicensing infrastructure such as dams. In such settings, agreements could provide for persistent monitoring and facilitate restoration when hydrological patterns are most appropriate (e.g., species reintroductions concentrated in years of favorable precipitation levels). Finally, establishing public or private protected areas along river corridors, particularly adjacent to established protected areas, could compound the value of habitat improvements under a PLC program, which could increasing the cost-effectiveness of species conservation (Lawrence et al. 2011).

Organizational Coordination

Administrative complexity dominates water resource issues (Gardner 2011). Statutes ranging from local ordinances to international treaties obligate numerous agencies, regional planning councils, municipalities, and private interests to engage in decisions concerning aquatic species. These mandates frequently differ from USFWS policy. Many landowners and businesses are already familiar with navigating particular regulatory or legal frameworks (e.g., prior appropriation and riparian water rights). Thus PLC programs will have to integrate with these existing standards.

The multistakeholder coalitions central to the robust redhorse and Arctic grayling CCAAs illustrate the opportunity for aquatic PLC programs to provide a common platform with which to strengthen existing relationships, capitalize on disparate sources of technical expertise, and coordinate basinwide management. If local watershed protection groups favor PLC objectives, these organizations might act as intermediaries among stakeholders, or contribute to promoting and monitoring a PLC agreement (Donlan et al. this volume). Moreover, a freshwater PLC initiative might also seek to integrate financial or administrative elements of existing programs, such as flood or crop insurance. For example, landowners familiar with programs that improve irrigation (e.g., drip or center pivot systems) might be predisposed to participate in a PLC arrangement that modifies in-stream flows. Likewise, commercial developers might be attracted to PLC agreements that incorporate a memorandum of understanding between the USFWS and the US Army Corp of Engineers that specifies priority permit reviews for participants.

OPPORTUNITIES AND CONCLUSIONS

The many candidate species that depend wholly or partially on freshwater habitat reflect the crisis in aquatic biodiversity in the United States. PLC programs may be a desirable conservation approach for a number of these species, whereas prompt listing under the ESA and subsequent protection may be more appropriate for other species. Successful aquatic PLC initiatives will depend on whether net conservation benefits can be achieved without a complete cessation of economically important activities that are responsible for impacts. If the main threats are mutually exclusive with net conservation benefits for the target species, then a PLC agreement may be merely deferring regulation until after development has occurred and the species is further at risk.

Aquatic species that are threatened by extractive industrial activities and with few prospects for rapid functional restoration will be unlikely to benefit from PLC approaches. For example, many mining and fossil fuel production methods permanently destroy habitat or introduce persistent toxins into surface and groundwater. Similarly, some water control infrastructure (e.g., dams) may irreversibly impair populations and preclude PLC arrangements. PLC approaches hold more promise for at-risk species that are primarily threatened by the activities of stakeholders with long-term interest in overall watershed health, particularly if specific interventions are known to improve target populations. For instance, many agricultural and recreational activities may be compatible with the needs of some at-risk aquatic species. A detailed assessment is needed, but several examples serve to illustrate the interplay of factors that influence the potential applicability of PLC to aquatic species (table 14.1).

Once widespread, the Rio Grande cutthroat trout (*Oncorhynchus clarkii virginalis*) is now restricted to a few headwater reaches of the Rio Grande, Canadian, and Pecos drainages in Colorado and New Mexico. Like other native western trout, the Rio Grande cutthroat is threatened by loss and fragmentation of habitat due to overgrazing, flow withdrawal, road crossings, and ecological interactions with non-native trout species (RRCC 2011). A PLC agreement targeting the Rio Grande cutthroat would include a suite of potential stakeholders: federal (US Forest Service, US National Park Service) and state agencies, tribal authorities, private landowners, and nearby municipalities with a desire or obligation to steward the watersheds inhabited by the species. Agencies or municipalities seeking regulatory certainty might serve as anchor partners to fund land or water rights purchases and habitat improvements. Individual landowners

TABLE 14.1 EXAMPLES OF CANDIDATE SPECIES FROM MAJOR FRESHWATER TAXONOMIC GROUPS THAT COULD POTENTIALLY BENEFIT FROM PLC APPROACHES

Species	Relevant Threats	Potential Conservation Actions	Possible Stakeholders	Key Considerations for PLC
Rio Grande cutthroat trout *(Oncorhynchus clarkii virginalis)*	Flow diversion and withdrawal, non-native interactions and disease	Securing in-stream flows; Non-native removal; Barrier monitoring; Captive breeding	Multiple tribes, state and federal agencies, private landowners	Public perception of complex genetic divisions
Great Basin pyrgs (*Pyrgulopsis sp.)*	Groudwater pumping, grazing, recreational abuse	Limiting water demand; Fencing & education; Possible captive breeding	Municipal water authorities, BLM, private landowners	Regional scale groundwater hydrology; Extreme vulnerability of single populations
Obey crayfish *(Cambarus obeyensis)*	Surface mining; pollutant discharge; watershed development within small range	Land use prohibitions; Runoff & discharge control	Private developers	Intensity of planned development; Very narrow range
Chamberlain's dwarf salamander *(Eurycea chamberlaini)*	Poorly described; direct damage to seepage spring habitat; general amphibian threats	Protection of current known populations; education	Private developers, Department of Energy (Savannah River Site)	Little data on threat severity or locations of greatest concern

NOTE: We are not recommending a particular conservation strategy for the species listed; rather, we use them to illustrate some major factors in a potential PLC program.

not already engaged in conservation actions may be receptive to outright compensation or in-kind support (e.g., irrigation system improvements) to implement the necessary management actions (MFWP and USFWS 2005; Womack 2008). Information is known regarding the protection of remaining habitat and potential restoration, and a multistakeholder management team already exists (CBD 2009; RRCC 2011). Functional conservation measures such as limiting flow diversions, improving riparian grazing regimens, and prohibiting recreational abuses could be implemented relatively rapidly. Furthermore, support for captive breeding programs might immediately supplement populations as more gradual habitat improvements take effect. A programmatic CCAA could be used to coordinate local efforts over larger spatial and temporal scales, with the Arctic grayling CCAA potentially providing a template that could be modified into a PLC agreement with stronger incentives (see Li and Male this volume). Species banking is also conceivable for the Rio Grande cutthroat, especially if planned in conjunction with existing protections (e.g., wilderness areas and regional land trusts) and climate change projections (e.g., deemphasizing reaches expected to exceed thermal tolerances).

A number of freshwater invertebrate species could potentially benefit from a PLC approach. Many Great Basin springsnails (small grazing gastropods) are threatened by altered hydrology, grazing, and recreational damage to freshwater habitats in Nevada, Utah, and California (Hershler 1998). Stakeholders include a range of public and private entities, and demand for regulatory predictability could be high among development interests in the greater Las Vegas region. Planned development includes major groundwater extraction with the potential to destroy many small desert springs (CBD 2009). However, the hydrologic complexity of regional groundwater dynamics and the high endemism of springsnails mean that a PLC approaches must exclude agreements with a risk og irreversible losses (i.e., extinction that follows habitat loss for species with a single extant population, such as the Lake Valley pyrg, *Pyrgulopsis sublata*). Watershed development in the southeastern United States threatens numerous aquatic species, such as the Obey crayfish (*Cambarus obeyensis*) and Chamberlain's dwarf salamander (*Eurycea chamberlaini*) (Harrison and Guttman 2003; Williams et al. 2006). While species-specific information is not comprehensive, planned development activities are expected to impact these species via water quality degradation and changes in fluvial geomorphic conditions (USFWS 2012b). This species-rich area warrants further study to determine if a CCAA or species bank—drafted under a PLC agreement—could offer a degree of immediate protection while supplying resources for additional ecological data collection for these at-risk species.

Continued success under the ESA warrants an expanded set of options that foster a shift from triage to proactive management. PLC approaches have the potential to promote collaborative, efficient, and effective conservation for aquatic species. Yet the design and implementation of PLC programs will require addressing the complex hydrological, biological, and economic conditions that surround many at-risk freshwater species. Aquatic PLC programs face an uphill battle given the profound conflicts between many current societal expectations and the ecological conditions needed to sustain freshwater species. With increased agency resources and leadership, however, PLC has the potential to nurture comprehensive freshwater stewardship, transforming adversarial relationships and delivering durable net conservation benefits.

ACKNOWLEDGMENTS

We wish to thank N. T. Hitt and R. Lave for helpful comments and the editors for the invitation to participate. D. Auerbach also thanks Y. Li for additional perspective on pre-listing conservation.

CHAPTER 15

The Greater Sage-Grouse, Energy Development, and Pre-Listing Conservation

SHAUNA GINGER, SARA VICKERMAN, AND BRUCE TAYLOR

ABSTRACT

Although widely distributed across the western United States, the Greater Sage-Grouse has been declining due to habitat loss and fragmentation. In 2010, the US Fish and Wildlife Service determined that protection of the Sage-Grouse under the US Endangered Species Act was warranted but precluded. While states hold the primary responsibility over Sage-Grouse management, federal agencies manage almost two-thirds of sagebrush habitat. In response to increasing pressure for energy development and the need to demonstrate adequate regulatory mechanisms to avoid an Endangered Species Act listing of the Sage-Grouse, states and federal agencies are implementing policy strategies that fit within their current legal parameters. Each of the eleven range states has a Sage-Grouse conservation strategy; however, only a subset has plans that describe avoidance or minimization measures for impacts that permanently destroy or fragment sagebrush habitat. When mitigation activities have occurred to minimize impacts to the Sage-Grouse, they have been implemented on a project-by-project basis and inconsistently within and across states. A Sage-Grouse pre-listing conservation

This chapter is based on information available to the authors up to early 2013. Sage-Grouse science and mitigation policy have evolved considerably in recent years and this evolution is likely to continue. The details may change, but the authors believe that key messages in this chapter will be valid well into the future.

program should (1) be structured as a private-public partnership, (2) be proactive in terms of designing solutions for accommodating energy development, and (3) help mobilize new conservation funding. Conservation success for the Sage-Grouse will require the integration of mitigation frameworks in a landscape-scale conservation strategy.

INTRODUCTION

Populations of the Greater Sage-Grouse (*Centrocercus urophasianus;* hereafter Sage-Grouse) once occurred across thirteen US states and three Canadian provinces in western North America (figure 15.1). They have declined to nearly half their historical range due to land use changes that have reduced and degraded sagebrush (*Artemisia* spp.) ecosystems (Schroeder et al. 2004) (figure 15.2). Often considered an icon of the American West, the Sage-Grouse is viewed as a surrogate for the over 350 other species that depend on sagebrush for their existence, including many endemic and at-risk species (Suring et al. 2005; Knick and Connelly 2011). In 2010, the US Fish and Wildlife Service (USFWS) determined that protection of the Greater Sage-Grouse under the US Endangered Species Act (ESA) was warranted but precluded by other, higher-priority listing actions (USFWS 2010a). A litigation settlement requires that a listing decision be made by September 2015 (Environment News Service 2011).

There are a variety of efforts under way to conserve the Sage-Grouse, driven in part by the goal to preclude the need to list the species under the ESA. These efforts are hindered by several factors, including those related to climate change (e.g., increased drought, fire, and invasive species) and the intersection of sagebrush habitat with lands used for rangeland agriculture, natural resource development, and, most recently and increasingly, energy development. The combination of mixed and multiuse land tenure patterns and the vast areas Sage-Grouse need to survive and flourish requires that all stakeholders must cooperate on a conservation strategy if it is to be successful (box 15.1). Integrating landscape-level conservation planning with the mitigation hierarchy for development (i.e., avoid, minimize, mitigate; see Madsen this volume) will be important for Sage-Grouse conservation in the context of future impacts. Given that development will almost always have residual environmental impacts, compensatory mitigation programs, including prelisting conservation (PLC) approaches, provide the opportunity to achieve a goal of net zero impact or even a net conservation benefit (see

FIGURE 15.1. The Greater Sage-Grouse (*Centrocercus urophasianus*). © J. Stafford-USFWS.

Li and Male this volume). Mitigation programs set in the context of an overarching conservation strategy and implemented prior to ESA listing could result in cost-effective benefits and incentivize voluntary actions necessary to ensure the long-term conservation of the Sage-Grouse. Here we discuss aspects that will play critical roles in designing and implementing successful PLC and mitigation programs for the Sage-Grouse. In particular, we examine the roles of landscape planning, stakeholder coordination, land tenure, and regulatory certainty in existing and future conservation programs.

CURRENT STATUS OF THE SAGE-GROUSE AND CONSERVATION PROGRAMS

The distribution of the Sage-Grouse is currently estimated at over 258,000 square miles (~670,000 km^2), which represents 56 percent of their potential distribution prior to European settlement (Schroeder et al. 2004) (figure 15.2). This distribution is not uniform. Much of the population resides in a fraction of its current distribution; these core population areas make up only 25 percent of the species range but contain over 75 percent of the breeding population (see figure 15.2). Sage-Grouse require large, interconnected expanses of intact sagebrush habitat with minimal human disturbance or development (Connelly et al. 2011a; Wisdom et al. 2011; Knick et al. 2013). The annual home range

Box 15. 1. Balancing economic development and Sage-Grouse conservation

The stakeholder challenge of balancing economic development and Sage-Grouse conservation is one that has been prominent in the media throughout the western United States.

The future of the economy of the West is probably tied to the future of the sage grouse.

Salt Lake Tribune (Loomis 2012)

Farmers and ranchers can do more to save the sage grouse through voluntary, incentive-based conservation measures than an ESA listing would.

(Farm Bureau News 2013)

This effort, as far as federal, state, tribal and private people working together, is just unheard of, but it needs to be. If we continue doing business the same way we have been, that bird is going to get [ESA] listed.

Las Vegas Sun (Demirjian 2013)

We don't want to lose any more habitat, but I drive a car. I fly in airplanes. We have to be realistic.

Salt Lake Tribune (Loomis 2012)

We're trying to find a happy medium where we can still produce and capture the energy that we need, and still keep the birds protected. Everyone needs to give a little.

Bismarck Tribune (Nicholson 2013)

of the Sage-Grouse can cover more than 1,000 square miles (2,700 km^2), with seasonal ranges that can be separated by more than 49 miles (80 km; Dalke et al. 1963; Connelly et al. 1988; Schroeder et al. 1999; Leonard et al. 2000). Males gather in the spring to perform courtship displays in relatively open areas called leks. Availability of dense shrub-steppe cover for nesting, shelter, and food is a key factor influencing lek locations, and Sage-Grouse exhibit strong site fidelity to breeding locations, as well as other seasonal habitats (Connelly et al. 2011b). Because the state and extent of sagebrush habitat across the landscape influences

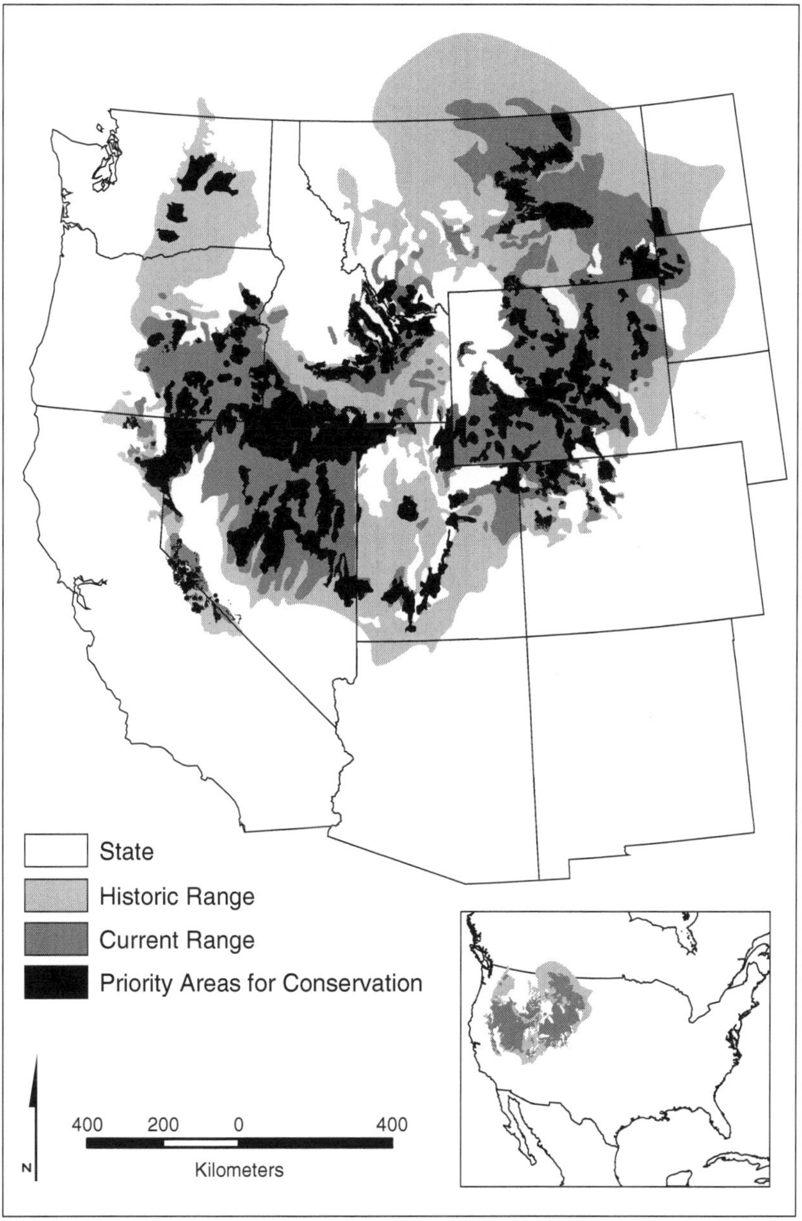

FIGURE 15.2. Historic (maximum range from 1800s to early 1990s) and current (occupied since the late 1990s) distribution of Greater Sage-Grouse in North America (Schroeder et al. 2004) overlaid by Priority Areas for Conservation (PACs) derived from habitat maps from states (USFWS 2013b). PACs represent key areas across the landscapes necessary to maintain redundant, representative, and resilient Greater Sage-Grouse populations (USFWS 2013b).

Sage-Grouse population dynamics, understanding and addressing both species ecology and ecosystem dynamics are vital to Sage-Grouse conservation programs, including those with mitigation components (Knick and Connelly 2011).

The sagebrush ecosystem extends across much of the western United States (Miller et al. 2011). Sagebrush communities are sensitive and can take decades to recover from disturbance events. The processes and practices to restore healthy sagebrush communities are not well known, and restoration is often limited by financial and logistic resources (Knick et al. 2003; Miller et al. 2011). Loss of suitable sagebrush habitat is the underlying cause for declines in Sage-Grouse populations. Habitat loss and fragmentation negatively affect the Sage-Grouse via a number of mechanisms including reduced courtship activities and degradation of leks, degraded winter habitat, reduced recruitment and annual survival, and reduced quality of nesting and brooding sites (Aldridge and Boyce 2007; Walker et al. 2007; Doherty et al. 2008; Holloran et al. 2009). Primary factors that threaten Sage-Grouse by contributing to habitat loss and fragmentation include wildfire, invasive species, energy and natural resource development, urbanization, agricultural conversion, infrastructure development, and the inadequacy of regulatory mechanisms to conserve sagebrush habitats (USFWS 2010a).

States hold the primary responsibilities for the protection and management of species not listed under the ESA. State laws and regulations have an impact on Sage-Grouse in three main ways: (1) they provide specific authority for conservation activities on lands that are state-owned, (2) they provide broad authority to regulate and protect wildlife on all lands within state borders, and (3) they provide an indirect mechanism for conservation through the regulation of threats to the Sage-Grouse (e.g., invasive plants). All state wildlife agencies across the Sage-Grouse's range manage the species as a resident native game bird, with the exception of Washington, where it is listed by the state as threatened. As of 2013 all eleven states within the species' range have a statewide Sage-Grouse conservation plan. Although the conservation plans share certain commonalities, they vary widely in how mitigation is addressed.

While it is the states that hold primary responsibility for Sage-Grouse management and conservation, federal agencies manage almost two-thirds of sagebrush habitat in the western United States. The US Bureau of Land Management (BLM) manages just over half of Sage-Grouse habitat rangewide, and the US Forest Service is responsible for managing approximately 8 percent of the species' habitat (Knick 2011). Other federal agencies in the Departments of Defense, Energy, and Interior, including the Bureau of Indian Affairs, the USFWS, and the US National Park Service, are responsible for managing less than 5 percent of sagebrush habitat (USFWS 2010a). The Sage-Grouse is designated as a sensitive species on all BLM lands. Management guidance for species of concern under BLM states that "sensitive species will be managed consistent with species and habitat management objectives in land use and implementation plans to promote their conservation and to minimize the likelihood and need for listing under the ESA" (BLM 2011b).

Variation in land use and tenure across the range of the Sage-Grouse presents conservation challenges (Knick 2011). Federal and state agencies, nongovernmental organizations, and private landowners have been working collaboratively to address the conservation challenges facing Sage-Grouse and their habitat. These collaborations come in a variety of forms and scales, from multiple efforts led by the Western Association of Fish and Wildlife Agencies to statewide task forces to local working groups that prioritize conservation efforts within states (WGA 2011; USFWS 2012d). Regional-scale efforts are being led by federal agencies such as the BLM, the US Department of Agriculture Natural Resource Conservation Service (NRCS), and the USFWS (box 15.2).

Scientists and practitioners are taking steps to improve scientific information and provide guidance on Sage-Grouse management. For example, multiscale habitat assessment tools such as the *Sage-Grouse Habitat Assessment Framework* and ecologically based models have been developed to provide analytical tools to inform conservation and planning efforts (Stiver et al. 2010). Other tools are focused on the development of metrics to support landowner incentive and habitat credit-trading programs (Defenders of Wildlife 2012). Application of consistent methods, based on the best available science, to measure ecological condition at local and landscape scales, and across jurisdictions and land tenures, will cost-effectively expedite planning and program implementation.

For wide-ranging species like Sage-Grouse, there are many challenges to developing landscape-level conservation plans that include meaningful mitigation strategies. Despite the increasing amount of scientific information documenting the threats to the Sage-Grouse, an overarching conservation strategy that comprehensively addresses mitigation has yet to be implemented. Several general frameworks, however, provide starting points:

Box 15.2. Some examples of federal programs focused on Sage-Grouse conservation

Under its 2011 National Greater Sage-Grouse Planning Strategy and in close coordination with US Forest Service, the BLM is reviewing its land use planning process in over 80 Resource Management Plans. The BLM aims to incorporate objectives and conservation measures into Resource Management Plans by September 2014 with the goal of providing adequate regulatory mechanisms to conserve Greater Sage-Grouse and its habitat on lands managed by the agency (BLM 2011a).

Launched in 2010 by the NRCS, the Sage-Grouse Initiative harnesses Farm Bill programs to address Sage-Grouse conservation on private lands. In the first two and a half years, more than 700 landowners participated the Sage-Grouse Initiative, and NRCS invested $145 million and generated $70 million in partner matches. As of 2013, this multistate effort included securing over 240,000 acres in conservation easements, conducting 200,000 acres of habitat improvement through removal of encroaching trees, and implementing new grazing systems on 2 million acres (SGI 2013).

The USFWS is working with the BLM, local governments, and private landowners in many states to develop Candidate Conservation Agreements and Candidate Conservation Agreements with Assurances. These voluntary agreements are focused on managing habitat to remove or reduce threats to species at risk of being listed under the ESA. In 2013, USFWS entered into a CCA with the BLM and Oregon Cattlemen's Association that covers over 10 million acres of Sage Grouse habitat on BLM managed lands. The goal of the agreement is to reduce or remove threats to Sage-Grouse on enrolled BLM grazing allotments in Oregon, while supporting livestock grazing practices that are beneficial or neutral to Sage-Grouse.

- In 2006, the Western Association of Fish and Wildlife Agencies published the *Greater Sage-Grouse Comprehensive Conservation Strategy*, which recommends that a rangewide off-site mitigation policy be developed and gives broad guidance on how to do so (Stiver et al. 2010).
- The BLM created the National Technical Team composed of state and federal resource professionals that produced a report with habitat management recommendations as the agency amends its Resource Management Plans to incorporate new Sage-Grouse protection measures (BLM 2011b). The report

provides avoidance and minimization measures for many potential impacts on priority Sage-Grouse areas and recommends effective mitigation to offset impacts as appropriate (i.e., as determined by local options and needs). The mitigation actions, however, are not described in detail.

- In 2013, the Conservation Objectives Team comprising state and USFWS representatives produced a report to help inform Sage-Grouse conservation efforts by identifying objectives and measures for each habitat threat identified in a 2010 assessment (USFWS 2013b). The report stresses avoidance of impacts as the priority strategy, followed by meaningful minimization and compensatory mitigation of impacts. It also, however, does not provide prescriptive details.

ENERGY DEVELOPMENT AND THE SAGE-GROUSE

If the grouse is listed it is going to have a pretty big impact on energy companies and private landowners.

—David Wolfe, Environmental Defense Fund

The Sage-Grouse faces a number of complex conservation challenges: development pressures that interact with historical land use, high-intensity grazing, invasive species, and altered fire regimes (Oregon Biodiversity Project 1998). Energy development and a lack of regulatory mechanisms to ensure impact avoidance and appropriate mitigation, however, have emerged as the priority conservation issue. Energy independence is a matter of US national security, and energy consumption is expected to grow 10 percent by 2035 (EIA 2012). Consequently, there is increasing pressure to develop both nonrenewable and renewable domestic energy sources; the latter is projected to be the fastest growing sector over the next twenty-five years. The federal government has declared a goal of wind power comprising 20 percent of the country's energy supply by 2030 (DOE 2008). Research suggests that an additional 19,300 square miles (50,000 km^2) of land, with an actual infrastructure footprint of ~965 square miles (2,500 km^2), would be needed for wind development to meet the 2030 goal (DOE 2008). The majority of the potential wind capacity occurs west of the Mississippi River (NAS 2008). Yet, even with renewable energy goals, fossil fuels will continue to be the dominant energy source, and many of the nation's oil and gas resources are located on sagebrush habitat (EIA 2011; Knick et al. 2011). The impacts of wind, oil, and gas energy development, particularly its infrastructure and associated fragmentation, are a growing concern throughout the western United States.

In the eastern range of the Sage-Grouse (i.e., portions of Colorado, Montana, North Dakota, South Dakota, Utah, and Wyoming), 44 percent of federal mineral estate lands have been authorized for oil and gas exploration (Naugle et al. 2011). Over 38 percent of core habitat areas for Sage-Grouse in the eastern range are at risk from wind, oil, and gas development (Doherty et al. 2011). Declines in Sage-Grouse populations due to oil and gas development are well documented (Aldridge and Boyce 2007; Walker et al. 2007; Holloran et al. 2009). Overall, the Sage-Grouse is predicted to decline 7 to 19 percent from 2007 levels due to the negative effects of oil and gas development (Copeland et al. 2009). Since comparable types of infrastructure are required, the effects of renewable energy development are likely to be similar to those of oil and gas development. Over 30 percent of Sage-Grouse habitat has high potential for wind power (USFWS 2010a).

On public land, development pressure coupled with multiple-use management policies (e.g., Federal Land Policy and Management Act) leads to wildlife conservation objectives competing with energy production and other natural resource development. Sage-Grouse require habitat with low levels of human land use, possibly as low as 3 percent near leks (Knick et al. 2013). Population declines are attributed to the effects of human disturbance, linear features that fragment habitat (e.g., roads and power lines), habitat disturbance by infrastructure, increases in avian and mammalian predators, plant invasions, and noise pollution near leks (Naugle et al. 2011). These impacts negatively affect lek attendance, nest success, chick and yearling survival, and winter habitat use (Aldridge and Boyce 2007; Walker et al. 2007; Doherty et al. 2008; Holloran et al. 2009; Johnson et al. 2011; Knick et al. 2013).

The USFWS has concluded that current regulations and guidance for energy development do not adequately ameliorate impacts to Sage-Grouse (USFWS 2010a). Further, because energy development is expected to continue to expand, the USFWS suggests that "unless protective measures consistent with new research findings are widely implemented via a regulatory process, those measures cannot be considered an adequate regulatory mechanism" (USFWS 2010a). Discretionary measures by the USFWS, federal land managers, and state conservation agencies are likely to have a significant impact on energy development in Sage-Grouse habitat and thus will heavily influence the future of the species.

In response to increasing pressure for energy development and the need to demonstrate adequate regulatory mechanisms to avoid an ESA listing of the Sage-Grouse, states and federal agencies are implementing policy strategies that fit within their current legal parameters. These strategies are one way to both define and incentivize frameworks for PLC programs. These approaches are primarily based on mapping key or core habitats, based on leks and population centers, and setting rules to avoid or limit development in those areas. Identifying key habitats essential for Sage-Grouse conservation is a crucial component of producing analytical frameworks to prioritize conservation efforts, including the assessment of trade-offs between conservation and energy development (USFWS 2013b). The mechanisms employed by states vary in scope and regulatory strength, from utilizing existing laws to issuing executive orders. Colorado and Nevada provide two examples.

- The Colorado Oil and Gas Conservation Commission (COGCC) requires that permittees and operators determine whether their proposed development location overlaps with *sensitive wildlife habitat* or is within a *restricted surface occupancy* area (COGCC 2009). For Sage-Grouse, sensitive wildlife habitat and restricted surface occupancy area are defined as areas within 4 miles (6.4 km) and 0.6 miles (1 km) of an active lek, respectively. Any potential overlap with these areas triggers a consultation with the development proponent and Colorado Parks and Wildlife to identify measures to avoid impacts, minimize the extent and severity of impacts, and offset impacts that cannot be avoided or minimized.
- Nevada issued an executive order in 2008 calling for the preservation and protection of Sage-Grouse habitat. In 2010, the governor's Sage-Grouse Conservation Team produced the *Nevada Energy and Infrastructure Development Standards to Conserve Greater Sage-Grouse Populations and Their Habitats* (State of Nevada 2010). The document outlines site selection criteria and best management practices for energy development and associated infrastructure as well as a mitigation framework based on five habitat categories (NDOW 2013).

Agencies with primary jurisdiction over sage-grouse and siting of energy and other development play an important role in efforts to reduce impacts of development on the species. The states of Wyoming and Oregon are two examples where jurisdiction over Sage-Grouse and energy development differs. In both states, impact avoidance in key Sage-Grouse areas and minimization in other habitat areas are the foundation for management, but regulatory authority and implementation vary greatly.

Wyoming: Leading by Executive Order

Approximately 35 to 40 percent of the entire population of Sage-Grouse resides in Wyoming (BLM 2012). Of states in the eastern half of the species range, Wyoming contains the largest breeding population. It also has the highest energy development risk (Doherty et al. 2011). Because over half of its core habitat areas has the potential for wind, oil, and gas development, Sage-Grouse conservation success in Wyoming will depend heavily on leasing and permitting policy decisions (Doherty et al. 2011).

Established by gubernatorial executive order in 2008 and renewed in 2011, Wyoming's Sage-Grouse core area conservation strategy defines and limits development in important habitat areas (State of Wyoming 2011). Composed of industry representatives, private landowners, conservation practitioners, and government officials, the governor's Sage-Grouse Implementation Team identified core population areas as important Sage-Grouse breeding areas. Although they represent less than a quarter of Sage-Grouse habitat in Wyoming, these core areas include approximately 80 percent of the total breeding population in the state and cover approximately 15 million acres (WGFD 2009; USFWS 2010a).

Commercially viable development projects in Wyoming, regardless of land tenure, go through the Industrial Siting Commission, which in turn must comply with the executive order. Under Wyoming policy, any new state or federally permitted energy development project that contains core area habitat cannot disturb more than 5 percent of the total surface area (i.e., an average of 640 acres). Surface facilities are prohibited within 0.6 miles of occupied leks, and an average of one new (or existing) oil and gas well pad per 640 acres is permitted (State of Wyoming 2011). To the extent that the state has regulatory authority, restrictions apply to multiple activities, including drilling, agriculture, and mining. Wind development is not permitted in core areas. In non–core habitat areas, minimization measures are required to maintain habitat conditions such that there is a 50 percent likelihood that leks will persist over time (WGFD 2009).

A potential weakness of the Wyoming plan is that it relies heavily on avoidance in core areas as the primary conservation strategy. Impacts to non–core habitat are considered offset by impact avoidance in core habitats. Thus success of the plan in reducing the decline of the Sage-Grouse rests on the definition and importance of core areas and in assuring those areas are not degraded. This entails the assumption that protection of core areas will sustain population dynamics over the long term. A 2013 study looking at predictive models of oil, gas, wind, and residential development in Wyoming suggests that Sage-Grouse populations could decline 14 to 29 percent under the core area policy plan alone (Copeland et al. 2013). In addition, the plan only pertains to new energy developments that require state or federal permits. Much of the Sage-Grouse habitat in eastern Wyoming is primarily on private lands or a mixture of public and private lands that may not fall under the current policy. Ongoing or new impacts from existing permitted activities are not covered, and thus those projects may continue to threaten the Sage-Grouse and its habitat.

Among the plan's strengths are the state's ability to use existing authority under an executive order to unify the missions of state agencies around Sage-Grouse conservation. This has facilitated the implementation of a conservation plan faster than doing so through legislative channels. Also, because the Industrial Siting Commission must comply with the executive order, the state is given new authority for prioritizing conservation over more development projects. This allows for a central clearinghouse, streamlining both the permitting process for developers and the reviewing process for the state. From a local regulatory perspective, it allows Wyoming to maintain jurisdiction and thus control of potential restrictions on energy development. The current policy has the potential to significantly reduce new activities within core Sage-Grouse habitat and is the justification for leniency in permitting activities outside core areas, which greatly aids in development planning. An improved, revised policy that includes the core area policy and targeted conservation easements has been recommended to further reverse future Sage-Grouse decline (Copeland et al. 2013).

Oregon: All-Lands, All-Threats Approach

Natural resource–based industry is a major driver of the Oregon economy, making up 37 percent of the state's annual domestic product and employing over one-third of its residents (State of Oregon 2012b). Oregon's land use planning laws provide relatively strong protection for lands zoned for farm and forest uses. As a result, development on lands outside of urban growth boundaries is more constrained compared to other states. Southeastern Oregon, however, is a focus area for potential commercial wind development and for new transmission lines carrying power from both renewable and nonrenewable sources to and from other states (USFWS 2013b). Other types of natural resource exploration occurring in the state include geothermal, solar, and mining (EIA 2013; State of Oregon 2013). Eastern Oregon contains large areas of relatively unfragmented sagebrush-dominated landscapes, important for sustaining connectivity between sage-grouse populations in Oregon and the greater Great Basin area (Knick and Hasner 2011). In Oregon, the majority of occupied Sage-Grouse habitat is located on BLM land (i.e., ~70 percent), compared to 21 percent on private land, and the remainder occurs on lands managed by the state, the US Forest Service, and the USFWS (Hagen 2011a).

Oregon's regulatory environment for siting energy projects is governed by multiple agencies at the local, state, and federal levels. Wind projects greater than 105 megawatts and utility-scale transmission and energy projects are reviewed and approved through a formal state process that leads to a site certificate issued by the Oregon Energy Facility Siting Council. The Council's siting standards require that the proposed facility comply with habitat mitigation goals and standards defined by the Oregon Department of Fish and Wildlife. Under a core habitat area approach described in the state's 2011 Sage-Grouse Strategy, a mitigation framework identifies guidelines for mitigating impacts to Sage-Grouse resulting from energy projects located in core habitat and non–core habitat areas (Hagen 2011a; Hagen 2011b). Generally, Oregon Department of Fish and Wildlife staff recommends avoidance of impacts to Sage-Grouse habitat that occur in core areas and mitigation with a *no net loss with net benefit* standard for impacts to Sage-Grouse non–core habitat areas.

Projects of less than 105 megawatts are approved through a local land use procedure requiring a conditional use permit. For projects not falling under the Energy Facility Siting Council jurisdiction but with a federal nexus, the federal entity will seek input from the Oregon Department of Fish and Wildlife and the USFWS on species and habitat impacts through the National Environmental Protection Act process. For projects not falling under Energy Facility Siting Council jurisdiction but on private land, the county decides whether or not to consult with wildlife agencies and therefore whether to require compliance with the Sage-Grouse conservation and mitigation standards. Therefore, small-scale utility projects and wind projects under 105 megawatts on private land with impacts to Sage-Grouse may not be assessed or reviewed by wildlife agencies. To date, all proposed wind power projects in Oregon counties that overlap with Sage-Grouse habitat have been less than 105 megawatts in capacity.

The 2011 Oregon Sage-Grouse Strategy for mitigation has several key strengths and weaknesses. While there is support for alternative approaches that leverage market-based principles, the state has not defined priorities and a policy framework that are needed to target mitigation actions to achieve the greatest conservation benefit. Also, without the impact assessment requirements for projects of less than 105 megawatts, there will continue to be knowledge gaps about Sage-Grouse impacts, and wildlife agencies will have limited ability to recommend avoidance, minimization, and mitigation measures.

Given the need for more renewable energy producing facilities, Oregon is considering changes to its energy siting statutes and rules. In 2012, the governor released a ten-year plan that included proposals for updated standards, new landscape-level planning and mitigation policies, and recommendations for state actions to facilitate better agency coordination and public participation (State of Oregon 2012a). Landscape-level planning is a key element in Oregon's efforts to develop a comprehensive *all-lands, all-threats* approach to Sage-Grouse conservation. Co-convened by the governor's Natural Resource Office, the BLM, and the NRCS, the *SageCon* partnership brings together a wide range of state, federal, non-profit, and private partners in monthly coordination and work group meetings. The partnership is intended to help preclude ESA listing of the Sage-Grouse, or at least minimize the impacts of a listing if it occurs. Development of a consensus on a shared set of geographic conservation priorities and appropriate development requires the engagement of a broad range of stakeholders, often with conflicting views and opinions. Mustering the political will to implement a shared vision for these landscapes will require collaboration on a scale with few precedents.

The Potential Role of PLC Programs for the Sage-Grouse

Ultimately, multiple threats and not just energy development must be successfully managed to ensure the persistence of Sage-Grouse populations and sagebrush ecosystems. Integrating mitigation measures and programs into state and federal plans can serve as principal regulatory mechanisms to assure adequate conservation measures for the Sage-Grouse and its habitat. As demonstrated in Wyoming and Oregon, the conservation and management setting for Sage-Grouse varies greatly across jurisdictions. A Sage-Grouse PLC mitigation program should (1) be structured as a partnership between the private and public sectors, (2) be proactive in terms of designing solutions for accommodating energy and other development, and (3) help mobilize new funding for Sage-Grouse conservation (Doherty et al. 2010). Taking into account the range of threats to Sage-Grouse and the cross-jurisdictional complexity of management, there are a variety of ways PLC programs can be developed.

Whether developed locally or regionally, a successful PLC program will transparently address the mitigation hierarchy (i.e., avoid, minimize, mitigate), have clearly identifiable sources of both demand and supply for mitigation activities and outcomes, operate under a robust science-based transactional infrastructure that provides full accounting for habitat impacts (debits) and offsets (credits), and fit within a larger conservation landscape. The ultimate outcome must be net conservation benefits, ensuring measurable outputs in the form of stability and enhancement of Sage-Grouse habitat and populations. For species with large geographic ranges like the Sage-Grouse, this objective comes with many opportunities and challenges (table 15.1). Our previous examples of conservation plans in Wyoming and Oregon offer a framework for analyzing the potential for fostering a PLC mitigation program from a demand, supply, and transactional infrastructure perspective.

Overall, the 2011 Wyoming state plan lacks a clear driver for a compensatory mitigation-based program because it relies on avoidance in core areas as its primary strategy. However, as some activities may still be permitted in core habitat, compensatory mitigation may be needed. The plan does not outline in detail how mitigation activities (i.e., offsets) should be structured or where supply would come from for credits generated by mitigation activities. Without programmatic guidance, project-by-project mitigation is favored. This piecemeal approach, reminiscent of early wetland mitigation programs, is unlikely to meet landscape-level goals (Auerbach and Bendor this volume). The plan does provide the basis for transactional infrastructure within its impact assessment methodology, which defines and limits disturbance. If this methodology were adopted and clarified for use in compensatory mitigation activities, the Wyoming plan could be used not only as a protection plan, but as a means of achieving net conservation benefits via mitigation activities under the auspices of a PLC program.

In Oregon, the consultation, permitting, and implementation processes of the 2011 state mitigation strategy drives some demand for offsets framed within the mitigation hierarchy. The process does not

TABLE 15.1 SOME OPPORTUNITIES AND CHALLENGES IN DEVELOPING A SAGE-GROUSE PLC MITIGATION PROGRAM, DIVIDED INTO THREE MAIN PROGRAMMATIC FACTORS: DEMAND, SUPPLY, AND TRANSACTIONAL INFRASTRUCTURE

	Opportunities	Challenges
Demand for mitigation comes from impacts to species and habitat, incentivized primarily by regulation or the potential of future regulation, but sometimes by public pressure or environmental ethics.	• In many states, regulations and policy already exist for the siting and permitting of development. • Federal processes (e.g. NEPA) require consideration of impacts on federally managed land, which represents nearly two-thirds of the Sage-Grouse range. • Potential for ESA listing in 2015 is generating interest and demand. • Interest in sustainability programs within the private sector, especially renewable energy, is increasing.	• Some states or local areas have no regulations for development. • The rules for assessing and mitigating impacts are often vague or applied inconsistently within and across jurisdictions, especially between states. • Especially where local regulations or policies are unclear, state and federal agreement on when and where to require mitigation can be a cumbersome process. • The level and timing of mitigation may be difficult to predict.
Supply arises from available habitat managed as offsets for a length of time commensurate to the impact, often in perpetuity.	• Readily available state-mapped priority areas for Sage-Grouse could be used to prioritize mitigation sites. • Large privately held rangelands exist throughout the range of the Sage-Grouse, and landowners have expressed interest in participating in PLC programs. • Public rangelands may also offer some mitigation opportunities.	• There may be resistance in areas where grazing practices need to be modified for Sage-Grouse conservation. • There is limited experience in restoration or enhancement of sagebrush habitats to benefit Sage-Grouse. • Multiuse management mandates on federal land may conflict with Sage-Grouse conservation needs. • Split mineral estate issues need to be resolved on conservation areas.

		• Landowners may be unwilling or unable to perform long-term management. • A clear mechanism to deliver regulatory certainty from the USFWS needs to be developed.
Transactional Infrastructure provides the metric or common currency behind mitigation activities and a platform on which to trade impacts for offsets (e.g., credits).	• Several metrics have been developed or are currently being developed. • Programs and groups are available to provide a trading platform to implement a program.	• Additional science and resources may be needed to fully develop infrastructure. • A robust program requires multiagency and stakeholder collaboration. • Scaling up rangewide so that conservation is meaningful will be challenging.

explicitly cover all types of energy development, and it is voluntary for projects on private lands that only require county approval. While the strategy includes an impact assessment methodology, it lacks detail or a defined metric. On the supply side, the strategy offers sideboards for siting offsets but lacks detail on stewardship assurances (e.g., financial and real estate) and does not offer a metric to assess habitat quality at the site level. The strategy, however, does offer a base framework to develop a PLC program, which could take many forms, from traditional conservation banking to broader habitat credit-trading schemes. To engage with development projects that do not require a formal review, the USFWS and the state should collaborate on a program that delivers the necessary regulatory certainty to strongly incentivize the demand for advance mitigation when and where it is appropriate.

In the face of development pressures, integrating landscape conservation planning with the mitigation hierarchy is critical to successful Sage-Grouse conservation (Kiesecker et al. 2011). The mitigation hierarchy, however, should have some flexibility. For example, while avoidance is a key priority, it is not always feasible or even ultimately desirable compared to other potential actions. Minimization works only when the science is well known, and in some cases greater conservation benefits may be realized from conservation actions off-site as opposed to minimizing impacts on-site. Demand for mitigation activities comes from clearly defined rules that are integrated with avoidance and minimization guidelines, and such activities will succeed only if there is supply and a common currency. By viewing the mitigation hierarchy through a landscape lens, we can better ensure that overarching conservation goals are met.

For cross-jurisdictional and wide-ranging species like Sage-Grouse, the challenge is to design and to implement solutions at sufficient scale to meet the specific species requirements in the broader ecological context, and to do so while embracing regional social and political realities. For Sage-Grouse, implementing lasting conservation programs will also require working with local stakeholders to maintain rural ways of life while also incentivizing long-term stewardship of sagebrush habitats. Finally, conservation planning must also include planning for development, both in terms of project siting and in terms of mitigating unavoidable impacts. A primary objective of PLC is to promote early conservation actions of a declining species that does not yet have statutory protection. For the Sage-Grouse, this will require developing a landscape-scale strategy and action guidelines that promote overall ecosystem function and habitat protection.

To implement a successful PLC mitigation program for Sage-Grouse, the following key factors must be addressed:

- *Planning.* With clearly identified conservation priorities, decision makers could direct development to less contentious areas and more strategically target mitigation investments to sites that provide greater long-term conservation value. Robust state mitigation plans that align with the BLM and complement conservation strategies are fundamental in this endeavor.
- *Permitting.* With more efficient permitting processes for energy and other natural resource developments, combined with a landscape approach to mitigation, offsets for unavoidable impacts can be achieved at lower costs while still generating net conservation benefits.
- *Quantification.* Assessment methodologies will need to be improved to quantify habitat impacts and benefits in ways that are both credible and cost-effective (Cochran and Maness this volume). Application of consistent methods to measure ecological and demographic conditions at the landscape and local scale, and across jurisdictions and land tenures, will cost-effectively expedite planning and project implementation. The various tools and methodologies in development provide a means to leverage environmental markets to meet overall goals for sagebrush and Sage-Grouse conservation.
- *Private sector.* Adoption of market-based approaches that incorporate strict crediting protocols could incentivize private sector investments. Capital-intensive developments like those associated with large-scale development of renewable energy facilities and transmission lines in sagebrush habitats may prove to be principal drivers for these kinds of investments.
- *Adaptive management.* Current knowledge of the long-term effectiveness of restoration techniques and other management actions is limited. PLC programs should incorporate adaptive management strategies to address emerging issues.
- *Collaboration.* The USFWS, BLM, state agencies, and other stakeholders should collaborate on programs that deliver the necessary regulatory certainty to fully incentivize appropriate mitigation and drive demand for offsets for those impacts deemed unavoidable.

Successful landscape-level Sage-Grouse conservation plans that address development issues will likely need to include both regulatory and voluntary measures. PLC programs could play an important role and facilitate the opportunity for development projects to result in net conservation benefits for the Sage-Grouse (see Li and Male this volume for a discussion on net conservation benefit in a PLC context).

In our view, there are two important next steps for developing a PLC approach with mitigation for the Sage-Grouse. First, pilot projects in which demand is strongly incentivized are needed. This will be easiest where stakeholders, including the USFWS, have collaborated on a conservation plan and there are regulatory incentives already in place at the state level (e.g., Wyoming's executive order) and with the USFWS (i.e., through use of agreements). Second, policies need to be developed, utilizing existing tools, that demonstrate net conservation benefits. In the context of ongoing habitat losses driven by climatic factors and other ecosystem changes, a no-net-loss policy will not be sufficient. Policies at the highest levels of government, in collaboration with major land users, state governments, and the public, should be developed that can act as an umbrella and connect local efforts. To conserve the sage-grouse to the extent necessary, we will need to demonstrate the ability and political will to manage habitats across scales that match the biological needs of the species and its supporting ecosystem. We must be open-minded when thinking about solutions. Implementing local and scalable PLC programs for Sage-Grouse will help demonstrate our ability to conserve species, habitat, and biodiversity at large scales.

ACKNOWLEDGMENTS

This chapter benefited greatly from input by state and federal biologists across the range of the Sage-Grouse. Earlier drafts were significantly improved by reviews by P. Deibert, J. Everett, D. Mead, C. Rowland, A. Sitz, R. Szlemp, and anonymous individuals. We would also like to thank D. Weisbaum for expertly crafting the range map and J. Stafford for providing the handsome Sage-Grouse portrait. The USFWS and Defenders of Wildlife supported the writing of the manuscript. The findings and conclusions in this chapter are those of the authors and do not necessarily represent the views of the USFWS.

CHAPTER 16

The Gopher Tortoise, Military Readiness, and Pre-Listing Conservation

TODD GARTNER, C. JOSH DONLAN, MICHAEL G. SORICE, JAMES MULLIGAN, MARY SNIECKUS, AND RHETT JOHNSON

ABSTRACT

In 2009, the World Resources Institute, Advanced Conservation Strategies, the American Forest Foundation, and the Longleaf Alliance set out to design and implement the first market-based pre-listing conservation program: a candidate conservation banking pilot program focused on the gopher tortoise (*Gopherus polyphemus*) in the southeastern United States. Our work included engagement with stakeholders on both the demand side and the supply side of the market, development of a crediting methodology and transactional infrastructure, and engagement with state and federal wildlife agencies. Our approach focused on the ecology of the gopher tortoise and the design and generation of demand, supply, and transactional infrastructure that could result in net conservation benefits. We discuss the implications of our program design for conservation outcomes and offer key insights we have learned from our efforts. Although the program is still in the development stage, lessons learned from this pilot initiative have important implications for the design and implementation of other programs emerging throughout the United States that aim to conserve candidate species prior to their listing under the US Endangered Species Act.

FIGURE 16.1. The gopher tortoise (*Gopherus polyphemus*). © R. Browning-USFWS.

INTRODUCTION

Before European settlement, longleaf pine (*Pinus palustris*) forests spanned 90 million acres in the United States, stretching from Virginia south to Florida and west to eastern Texas. Frequent low-intensity fires that occurred throughout the Southeast defined the historical distribution of these forests (Finch et al. 2012). In the late nineteenth century, these expansive stands were among the most sought after timber and resin trees in the country. But due to land conversion, agriculture, invasive species, and fire suppression, only 3 million to 4 million acres of longleaf pine forest remain today. Many species that depend on these forests, including the gopher tortoise (*Gopherus polyphemus*), have consequently experienced population declines (McCoy et al. 2006) (figure 16.1).

The ecology and management of the gopher tortoise is well studied (Diemer 1986; Mushinsky et al. 2006; Ashton and Ashton 2007). The species plays important ecological roles in the longleaf pine forest ecosystem, including increasing local biodiversity by promoting landscape heterogeneity via burrow construction (Kaczor and Hartnett 1990). In

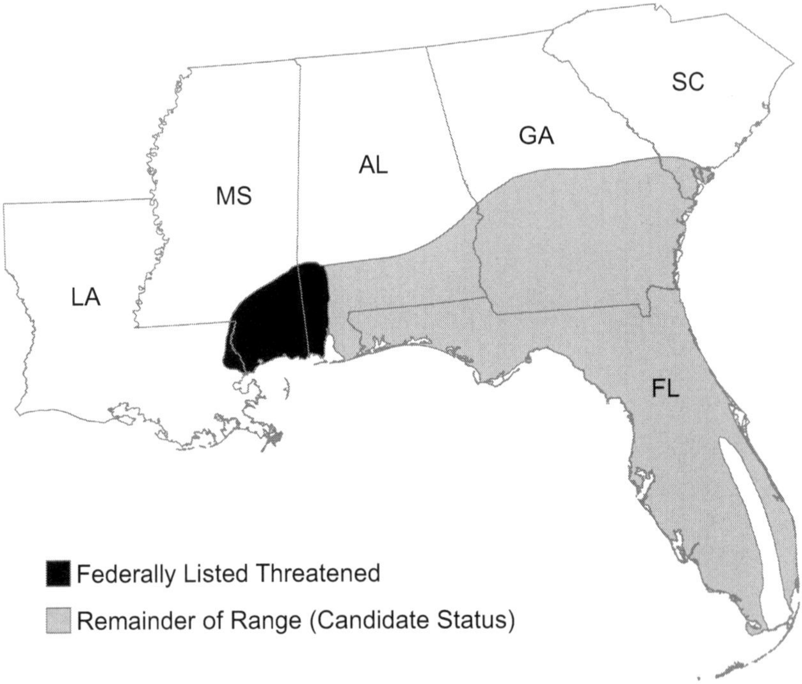

FIGURE 16.2. The distribution of the gopher tortoise and its status under the US Endangered Species Act.

addition, gopher tortoises provide habitat for a suite of vertebrates and invertebrates: over 360 species have been recorded using their burrows (Jackson and Milstrey 1989).

The gopher tortoise is federally listed as threatened under the US Endangered Species Act (ESA) in Mississippi, Louisiana, and the Alabama counties west of the Mobile and Tombigbee Rivers (figure 16.2). The US Fish and Wildlife Service (USFWS) has designated the eastern population of the gopher tortoise as a candidate for possible future listing under the ESA (USFWS 2011c). The eastern portion of the gopher tortoise's range includes Alabama (east of the Mobile and Tombigbee Rivers), Florida, Georgia, and southern South Carolina. Increased efforts to protect and restore longleaf pine forests will be needed to prevent the eastern population of the gopher tortoise from further decline and listing under the ESA. Since 87 percent of southern forests are privately owned, this task lies primarily in the hands of private woodland owners (Hoctor and Beyeler 2010).

Species and ecosystem conservation on private lands faces a number of challenges (Norton 2000; Best 2002). Some private landowners may be interested in managing their forests for wildlife benefits but lack the necessary financial and technical resources (Johnson and Snieckus this volume). Further, the perceived legal threat of land use restrictions from the ESA can create a disincentive for landowners to cooperate in managing their land for the benefit of at-risk species (Brook et al. 2003; Lueck and Michael 2003). Efforts and incentives are needed that turn management for declining species on private lands from a perceived liability into an asset.

In 2009, the World Resources Institute, Advanced Conservation Strategies, the American Forest Foundation, and the Longleaf Alliance set out to design the first market-based pre-listing conservation (PLC) program: a candidate conservation banking pilot program focused on the gopher tortoise. Our objective was to create a scalable, voluntary, and science-based framework that would generate net conservation benefits for the gopher tortoise through the sale of conservation credits prior to regulatory triggers (i.e., the ESA). We designed the PLC program as a marketplace and developed different program components within this market-based approach. This included a policy strategy, a market structure, a financial model, and a science-based methodology that could support the program design and transactional infrastructure needed for success. In this chapter, we focus on demand, supply, program design, and transactional infrastructure and report on the progress and challenges we experienced in our efforts. Other aspects of the program are discussed elsewhere in this volume (Donlan et al.; Li and Male; see also Donlan et al. 2013).

CREATING AN UPSTREAM CONSERVATION PILOT PROGRAM

The pilot program was designed around supply, demand, and infrastructure (Gartner and Donlan 2011). An interested and eligible private landowner can receive a financial payment to conserve and restore longleaf pine forests on her property if it is capable of supporting a healthy population of gopher tortoises. In doing so, the landowner generates gopher tortoise credits that can be sold to a buyer or a broker (Donlan et al. this volume). Potential sellers include nonindustrial family landowners, industrial forest owners, nonprofit organizations, and state- and county-owned lands. Buyers can use credits to mitigate impacts on gopher tortoises elsewhere at a predetermined mitigation ratio (e.g., two credits needed to offset one debit on an impact site). Buyers can thereby meet a voluntary no net loss biodiversity commitment (Ten Kate et al. 2004), or they can bank credits for later use to potentially meet mitigation requirements for an incidental take permit if the species becomes listed under the ESA (Li and Male this volume). Other buyers might purchase credits as part of a philanthropic strategy or as an investment, under the assumption that credit prices will increase if the gopher tortoise becomes listed under the ESA. For the gopher tortoise, prospective credit buyers include the Department of Defense, federal and state departments of transportation, businesses, mitigation bankers, impact investors, and philanthropic foundations.

A gopher tortoise credit is the actual currency that can be bought and sold, and it is designed to quantitatively represent the effect of successful mitigation efforts for the species. The number of credits a landowner is eligible to sell is determined via a science-based and peer-reviewed method. Because of its legislated responsibility to carry out the ESA, the USFWS serves as the regulator in the marketplace and will ultimately decide on certain factors like mitigation ratios. The agency approves the crediting methodology and maintains agreements with buyers and sellers. The USFWS may also provide regulatory predictability to buyers by allowing gopher tortoise credits to be used toward mitigating future impacts under a regulatory scenario if the gopher tortoise is listed under the ESA in the eastern portion of its range (Li and Male this volume). Further, the USFWS could provide assurances to the seller against any future regulation for conservation actions undertaken that go beyond the credits sold.

Here we discuss key components of creating a PLC program focused on enabling the buying and selling of credits. First, we discuss demand and supply for the program. Next, we present the crediting-debiting methodology (hereafter, crediting methodology) that we designed for the pilot program. We then discuss the implications of program design for stakeholder engagement, regulatory predictability, and achieving a net conservation benefit. Finally, we offer key insights from the lessons learned during the three-year process.

DEMAND: GENERATING COMMITMENTS FROM BUYERS

Without robust demand, any conservation program designed around market principles will struggle to produce landscape-level conservation benefits. In our attempts to generate demand, we opted to focus on major buyers. A PLC program will be most appealing to entities that anticipate reasonably large impacts to at-risk species over the foreseeable future. Identifying these buyers early on in the process and helping them understand the risks they may face if a candidate species becomes listed is an important first step in lining up potential investors and identifying feasible market opportunities. Early efforts to understand the needs and concerns of potential major buyers will also be useful during the early phases of program design.

While demand for gopher tortoise credits generated from our proposed candidate banking program could potentially come from numerous public and private entities, we targeted the US Army as a potential early buyer because of the potential impacts their on-base training activities may have on existing gopher tortoise populations and their habitat. The US Army could buy and use PLC credits to mitigate potential future negative impacts on gopher tortoise populations. Doing so would help the Department of Defense maintain military training and readiness (Orndorff this volume). The Army Species At Risk policy memorandum specifically identifies the gopher tortoise as a priority species (US Army 2009). The policy encourages proactive management efforts for gopher tortoises and their habitats before federal protection under the ESA is necessitated and further encourages installations to capitalize on partnerships and agreements when managing for such species. Military bases in Florida, Georgia, and Alabama are concerned that listing could result in delays or other complications in military training. These bases are seeking innovative solutions and partnerships in order to maintain training flexibility for military readiness on these installations, particularly given that development pressures are increasing around the bases (US Army Environmental Command 2010). Installations have the authority to work with partners to protect and restore habitat outside the installation if those activities are deemed beneficial to sustaining the military mission.

As we discuss later, our effort to secure commitments from US Army bases to purchase credits revealed that regulatory predictability would be key to generating demand from the Department of Defense (Li and Male this volume; Orndorff this volume). While the US Army continues to express interest, the USFWS had not yet offered clear regulatory predictability for the program by the end of initial design activities and thus no transactions have yet occurred.

SUPPLY: MAXIMIZING LANDOWNER PARTICIPATION

An often overlooked but key factor to the success of any voluntary conservation agreement is the level of landowner participation. A critical mass of landowners and acreage is needed in order to produce the landscape-level benefits needed for the recovery of at-risk species. Given the voluntary nature of conservation agreements, landowners must actively opt in to any program. Thus it is critical to understand landowner perspectives in order to design a program that maximizes their participation. Landowner focus groups and survey research are useful tools to capture perceptions and incentive structures that can be incorporated into program design and tested before full introduction of the program (Sorice et al. 2013; Sorice and Abel this volume).

Over three years, we held a series of one-day workshops with landowners. Participation was geared to landowners with an interest in conservation forestry and already enrolled in a forest stewardship program or a cost-share program under the US Department of Agriculture (USDA) Natural Resources Conservation Service. Workshops were focused on providing tools, resources, and technical advice to enhance the restoration and management of longleaf pine forests, including gopher tortoise conservation. Topics covered included controlled burning, invasive species control techniques, and the commercial viability of longleaf pine timber operations. We also leveraged the landowner workshops to introduce the candidate banking pilot program concept and discuss ways it could complement and provide additional value to traditional forest management and timber production. In addition to the workshops, we met individually with landowners who were particularly interested in gopher tortoise conservation in order to get input and feedback on program design (Johnson and Snieckus this volume).

Specific to the design of the pilot program, we used focus groups and a mail survey to understand how landowner preferences for participation in a gopher tortoise conservation program are related to program structure, delivery, and perceived efficacy. Further, we were interested in exploring the inherent trade-off between maximizing participation and maximizing the conservation benefits of a single agreement when designing a conservation incentive program. Using a stated preference choice experiment, we mailed surveys to over a thousand landowners who resided in counties with known gopher tortoise populations. Landowners were randomly selected from mailing lists from the American Tree Farm System and the Longleaf Alliance. They were given a brief description of the gopher tortoise and the proposed program that included a voluntary conservation agreement. We then asked the landowners to respond to a series of scenarios in which they would maintain or restore gopher tortoise habitat on their land and sell the credits generated. To examine preferences for individual components of a conservation agreement, we constructed hypothetical scenarios in which landowners compared programs that randomly varied in the level of individual components (table 16.1). For each scenario, landowners had the option to choose between two alternative programs or to opt out and choose neither program.

The response rate of the survey approached 50 percent, and the results revealed important insights with respect to program design (Sorice et al. 2013). Approximately 50 percent of landowners expressed no interest in opting in to a conservation program focused on the gopher tortoise. Those who expressed interest were most sensitive to programs that are highly controlling, require permanent conservation easements, and put landowners at risk for future regulation. Programs designed with greater levels of compensation and that support landowner autonomy to make land management decisions not only increased a landowner's probability of opting in to a program but also increased a landowner's acceptance of program components that were generally unfavorable, like long-term contracts and permanent easements. Our survey results not only helped inform the current and future design of PLC incentive programs; it also allowed us to develop a quantitative and cost-effective exploratory tool to assess inherent trade-offs of program components by predicting participation rates in programs that differ in certain attributes (see Sorice et al. 2013 for more detail).

Ultimately, a PLC program is more likely to maximize uptake by landowners if it does not require permanent conservation easements. However, as we discuss below, permanence is a centerpiece of the current iteration of the gopher tortoise program to ensure conservation benefit. It is yet to be determined whether this feature will be problematic for supply-side participation.

TRANSACTIONAL INFRASTRUCTURE

"Transactional infrastructure" refers to the mechanisms and stakeholder roles that allow a market-based program to function. Key components include a broker to streamline supply; a market administrator to manage third-party validation, monitoring, and verification of credits; and a

TABLE 16.1 PROGRAM ATTRIBUTES USED IN CONSTRUCTING SCENARIOS FOR HYPOTHETICAL CONSERVATION AGREEMENTS WITH PRIVATE LANDOWNERS FOCUSED ON INCENTIVIZING IMPROVED MANAGEMENT OF GOPHER TORTOISE HABITAT

Attribute	Description	Levels
Conservation Easement	A legally enforceable agreement between a landowner and a qualified land protection organization for the purposes of permanently restricting real estate development uses on a property. Landowner individually negotiates the terms with the organization. The land remains as private property.	• No easement • Permanent donated easement • Permanent sold easement
Contract Length	The number of years a landowner agrees to perform the necessary land management practices to preserve and restore gopher tortoise habitat.	• 10 years • 40 years • 70 years • 100 years
Profit Margin	Amount of profit landowners receive when a credit is sold. This amount is in addition to the costs of management activities, which are covered by the program.	• $100 per credit • $200 per credit • $400 per credit • $800 per credit • $1,600 per credit
Payment Structure	The way landowners would receive profit payments from the sale of the credits.	• 25% Year 1, 75% Year 5 • 50% Year 1, 50% Year 5 • 75% Year 1, 25% Year 1 • 100% Year 1
Structure	Level of control the program administrators have over creation of the land management plan required in the conservation agreements and implementation of the practices outlined in the management plan.	• Program staff makes almost all land management decisions • Landowner shares management decision making with program staff • Landowner has complete responsibility for land management decisions

Obligation	Responsibility the landowner has for maintaining gopher tortoise habitat once the conservation agreements ends and if it becomes listed as an endangered species under the Endangered Species Act.	• No obligation • Baseline obligation • Full obligation
Effectiveness	The expected increase of gopher tortoises in the county as a result of landowners opting in to the program and improving habitat on their land.	• No increase (0%) • Low increase (5%) • Moderate increase (10%) • High increase (15%)

science-based methodology to quantify conservation measures for gopher tortoises into a currency (i.e., credit) that can be bought and sold.

Brokers can be critical to achieve transactions at scale (Donlan et al. this volume). They can recruit and negotiate agreements with disparate and dispersed landowners, absorb financial risk associated with generating and selling credits, provide upfront financing, and in some cases act as expert implementers, directly performing the conservation measures on credit sellers' land. The broker's role is critical in streamlining the supply side of the market, thereby reducing transaction costs and helping the market scale. Brokers are particularly crucial given that regulatory bodies are unlikely to perform this role.

Similarly, a PLC program administrator can provide some key services that are unlikely to be performed by the regulatory body. An administrator can validate plans to generate credits and provide accreditation to third parties that conduct monitoring and verification of credits. The administrator also handles registration of credits to ensure transparency and avoid double counting, and can serve as a liaison to all stakeholders, including the regulatory body. While we identified the need for a broker and a program administrator for the gopher tortoise program, we have not yet identified specific entities or the exact roles they would play. The same entity could play the roles of broker and program administrator.

The crediting methodology is the centerpiece of the program. Biodiversity metrics is an area of active research, with some currencies focused on habitat quality and others focused on population abundance and dynamics of the target species (Parkes et al. 2003; Doherty et al. 2010; Pascoe et al. 2011). There are advantages and disadvantages to both approaches. For the gopher tortoise program, we were charged with developing a crediting methodology using the best science available while also striving to make the methodology cost-effective. We did so collaboratively and adaptively: multiple stakeholders were involved, and the methodology evolved over time, which is discussed later in the chapter. Specifically, we developed a preliminary protocol for landowners and project developers on the creation of PLC credits that included (1) eligibility requirements for the creation and selling of credits and (2) a methodology for the quantification of those credits. The methodology combines population- and habitat-based approaches and provides a framework for quantifying gopher tortoise conservation benefits through a repeatable science-based evaluation and monitoring protocol. The program produces gopher tortoise credits that are actively managed and audited over the length of a contract. Eligibility requirements and the crediting methodology are consistent with guidelines developed by the USFWS for Candidate Conservation Agreements in the eastern range of the gopher tortoise and conservation banks operating in the ESA-listed range (USFWS 2009a, 2009b).

A private landowner must successfully undertake three steps in order to create and sell gopher tortoise credits. First, there are eligibility requirements. Those requirements may be met at an initial land assessment, or after certain land management practices are undertaken following the initial assessment. Second, the potential land parcel is assessed for baseline conditions and scored for credits. We developed a hybrid approach for our credit methodology that takes into account species abundance and habitat quality. Two surveys are to be conducted to establish a baseline: a gopher tortoise population survey and a habitat quality survey. Certified third-party evaluators will conduct both surveys. We envision a program administrator and an advisory board that will ultimately approve and set standards for third-party evaluators and credit verification. And third, if credits are sold or in order to maintain eligibility for credit sales, gopher tortoise populations must be resurveyed every five years following the baseline survey. Likewise, habitat must be resurveyed at least every three years, and results must be integrated into the required management plan. The habitat survey provides regular feedback to the credit seller, as well as assurances to the buyer or broker that the land parcel attached to the credits is being properly managed. Properly managed land parcels may produce additional credits for sale when the population is resurveyed five years after the initial survey. The costs of the surveys, along with meeting the eligibility requirements, are the responsibility of the credit seller. However, financial and technical assistance may be provided up front by a broker or the credit buyer (Donlan et al. this volume).

Eligibility Requirements

There are eleven biological and management requirements of the land parcel for eligibility (table 16.2). These requirements help ensure conservation benefits for the gopher tortoise. For example, soil type is an especially important attribute for gopher tortoises and their burrowing behavior. Priority or suitable soils, which are well studied and classified, must be present on the land parcel (Ashton and Ashton 2007; USFWS

TABLE 16.2 REQUIREMENTS THAT MUST BE MET FOR THE LANDOWNER AND LAND PARCEL THAT IS PRODUCING AND SELLING GOPHER TORTOISE CREDITS

Requirement	Description
Land Parcel Eligibility Requirements	
Service Area	A property must be located within the designated service area. The current service area includes all counties with appropriate soil types, extant gopher tortoise populations, and where the species is not currently listed under the ESA. Service areas could be more restrictive for the sale of PLC credits that include regulatory predictability.
Habitat Type	Within eligible counties, land parcels must be designated as one of the following habitat types as defined in the USFWS Gopher Tortoise Candidate Conservation Agreement: Sandhill, Upland Pine Forest, or Oldfield Pinelands.
Available Habitat Property Size	Land parcel must be a minimum of 200 contiguous acres (80 hectares). This requirement is consistent with the USFWS Guidelines for the Establishment, Management, and Operation of Gopher Tortoise Conservation Banks in the listed range of the species.
Soil Type	Land parcel must have priority or suitable soils for gopher tortoises. See text.
Fragmentation	Major barriers to tortoise movement, such as paved roads, railroad beds, impenetrable fences, dense pine plantations, lakes, and perennial streams or rivers, must not fragment the land parcel creating credits. If these barriers exist, preventing connectivity of habitat for gopher tortoises, the property has to be treated as two separate land parcels for credit generation. Road density must be less than 1 km of roads/km^2 and verified with documentation (e.g., land parcel maps).
Landscape Conditions	Properties that are adjacent (within 1 mi) from major urban or suburban developments (500 people per sq. mi.) with extensive road networks and infrastructure are ineligible. Properties greater than 1,000 acres are exempt from this eligibility requirement. Conditions must be verified with documentation.
Invasive Ants and Predators	Imported red fire ants (*Solenopsis invicta*) and other predators (e.g., coyotes, feral dogs, and feral hogs) are a significant threat to gopher tortoises, as they prey on juveniles and eggs. If invasive fire ants or other predators are present on the land parcel, a predator management plan must be in place that is consistent with the USFWS Guidelines for the Establishment, Management, and Operation of Gopher Tortoise Conservation Banks.

Invasive Plants	The land parcel should have less than 10% coverage of non-native, invasive plants. Consistent with the USFWS Guidelines for the Establishment, Management, and Operation of Gopher Tortoise Conservation Banks, an invasive plant management plan must be in place if invasive plant coverage is 10%.
Management Requirements	
Legal Agreement and Management Plan	A legal agreement and management plan signed by all parties. Parties include the private landowner, the USFWS, and possibly a broker. By the time credits are sold, the credit buyer must also be a signatory to the agreement.
Conservation Easement	A conservation easement in place and held by a third party.
Financial Assurances	Financial assurances to cover annual management costs in perpetuity must be in place no later than 1 year after credit sale. Financial assurances can be directly covered by the landowner or through a broker.

NOTE: Some of these requirements are further assessed in the habitat survey of the land parcel. A land parcel may not necessarily include an entire property.

2009a). Roads and traffic have been demonstrated to be a significant barrier and mortality factor for gopher tortoises (Gibbs and Shriver 2002). Thus a land parcel must have a minimum number of barriers to avoid potential fragmentation and mortality. Eligibility also requires that a management plan and legal contract be in place, along with financial assurances sufficient to provide for management and monitoring activities over the life of the contract. Prescribed burning and invasive plant control programs are required as critical aspects of the management plan for maintaining and improving gopher tortoise habitat. The costs of these two key, required activities, along with monitoring, are incorporated into the price of the credits (Donlan et al. this volume). For the initial pilot design, a conservation easement was also required. A qualified third-party evaluator verifies whether a landowner has met the eligibility requirements.

Population Survey Methodology

Population survey methods follow those outlined in the *Gopher Tortoise Survey Handbook* published by the US Army Corp of Engineers, which is freely accessible (Smith et al. 2009b). Based on thoroughly field-tested best practices (Smith et al. 2009a), the handbook presents a detailed methodology using line transect distance sampling to estimate population size and density and to detect trends to assess the effects of habitat management (Buckland et al. 2001).

The goal of an initial population survey is twofold:

- Estimate the size of the gopher tortoise population on the land parcel, along with the variance of the point estimate (i.e., coefficient of variation <20%).
- Establish a baseline from which to measure trends in the population size over a 20+ year time frame by resurveying the land parcel every five years.

The population survey consists of five basic steps:

1. Define the sampling area (i.e., land parcel).
2. Conduct a pilot survey to estimate an encounter rate for tortoises on the land parcel.
3. Using the encounter rate, design the survey and allocate effort needed to produce a point estimate with coefficient of variation <20%.

FIGURE 16.3. A burrow cam can be used to verify gopher tortoise presence in burrows when conducting population surveys.

4. Conduct the survey.
5. Analyze the data using the publicly available software DISTANCE (Thomas et al. 2010).

A three-person field team conducts the survey, using a burrow camera to confirm tortoise presence (figure 16.3). Results from the baseline survey serve as the basis for estimating the number of gopher tortoise credits eligible for sale. Results also serve as the baseline to compare with additional surveys every five years to audit the performance of the management plan. Results of the five-year survey influence the release of credits. A landowner is initially required to retain 10 percent of the generated credits as a risk deposit to protect against issues such as improper implementation or "acts of god." The conditions under which risk deposit credits may be released, if any, have not yet been determined. In addition, initial conversations included the possibility of additional credit allocations if population and habitat resurveys indicate an increase in credit score (see Worked Example below). Details for survey methodology and analysis can be found in the *Gopher Tortoise Survey Handbook* (Smith et al. 2009a, 2009b).

Habitat Survey Methodology

An initial habitat survey is also conducted on the land parcel (figure 16.4). Habitat surveys, which are less cost-prohibitive than population surveys, are then conducted at least every three years. The effects of any recent prescribed burning events should be considered when determining the timing of habitat surveys.

The goal of the habitat survey is twofold:

- Provide a cost-effective and complementary measure of gopher tortoise habitat that allows sellers, landowners, and other stakeholders to assess the latent potential gopher tortoise benefits of a land parcel, as well as potential risk of credit degradation.
- Provide timely feedback to the private landowner and other stakeholders on the performance and outcomes from the management plan. The habitat surveys will facilitate adaptive management of the land parcel over the medium and long term. This is particularly useful for long-lived and slowly reproducing species like the gopher tortoise (Lindemayer 1999).

The habitat survey includes ten criteria: four single measurements at the parcel scale and six measurements that are replicated at the plot scale across the land parcel using a systematic sample technique (table 16.3). For the latter, the land parcel is sampled with a grid of points and a sampling frequency of 25 sample plots per 100 acres (based on a sample plot every 66 feet [i.e., chain] per 100 acres). Each plot is scored on the six criteria.

For each of the six plot-level criteria, a global mean score is calculated. Mean scores, along with the four single measurements, are then combined into a single habitat score. Criteria are combined via taking the geometric mean: each criterion is weighted by raising it to the power of each relative weighting (e.g., 50^{X}) and then combined by multiplying all criteria together to arrive at a single habitat score (table 16.4). A geometric, multiplicative approach ensures that the complete compensation for a reduction in one criterion requires a much larger increase in another criterion. Such an approach, as opposed to adding the scores, implies that different habitat criteria are not perfectly substitutable (Parkes et al.

FIGURE 16.4. Foresters conduct a habitat survey on a private longleaf pine (*Pinus palustris*) forest. The developed methodology measures ten different criteria, which in aggregate provide an index for habitat quality, particularly for the gopher tortoise (*Gopherus polyphemus*). See text for details.

2003). Based on feedback from our advisory committee (see below), we concluded that soil type, canopy closure, and herbaceous plant cover are of greatest importance to gopher tortoises. Thus these criteria are weighted twice as heavily in their contribution to the total habitat score compared to the remaining seven criteria. Soil type, canopy closure, and herbaceous plant cover each contribute 15 percent to the habitat score; the remaining criteria each contribute 8 percent. The habitat score is then scaled between 0 and 1; possible scores can range from 0.05 to 1.0.

Gopher Tortoise Credit: Combining Population and Habitat Scores

Credits for sale are calculated by scaling the point estimate of gopher tortoises from the population survey with the habitat score (see table 16.4). In our current approach, we use the conservative point estimate of the lower 95% confidence interval. For example, if the above land parcel

TABLE 16.3 CRITERIA AND SCORING FOR HABITAT SURVEY METHODOLOGY

Criteria	Description	Scoring
Single Measurements at Land Parcel Scale		
Property Size	Minimum area is 200 acres.	• 200–499 acres: 25 points • 500–749 acres: 50 points • 750–999 acres: 75 points • Greater than 1,000 acres: 100 points
Fragmentation	Properties with limited fragmentation are a priority, since this will maximize potential gopher tortoise movement. Minor Fragmentation is defined as minor road infrastructure, transportation infrastructure, fences, and/or other barriers such as non-crossable waterways. No Fragmentation is defined as no barriers to tortoise movement.	• Minor Fragmentation: 50 points • No Fragmentation: 100 points
Adjacent Lands	Properties directly adjacent to existing high- quality gopher tortoise habitat are a priority, since large, viable tortoise populations are more likely to persist. The land parcel is scored based on the state of the majority (50%) of the adjacent land, defined as land sharing a property boundary and without a major barrier to tortoise movement. This criterion should be scored with the aid of maps and, ideally, existing GIS data.	• Adjacent to agricultural lands: 25 points • Adjacent to pine habitat that is not protected from development: 50 points • Adjacent to land that is protected from development but is not pine habitat: 75 points • Adjacent to pine habitat that is protected from development: 100 points
Landscape Conditions	Properties with surrounding landscapes that provide gopher tortoise habitat are a priority, to facilitate natural dispersal and species persistence. This criterion should be scored with the aid of maps, and ideally existing GIS data.	• Rural with some road infrastructure but with at least 25% of wooded or open space: 33 points • Greater than 50% of surrounding landscape is forested: 66 points • Greater than 75% of surrounding landscape is forested: 100 points

Replicated Measurements at Plot Scale		
Soil Type	The program provides eligible soil types and categories.	• Suitable Soils: 50 points • Priority Soils: 100 points
Canopy Closure	Open canopy with grasses, forbs, and other tortoise forage plants in the understory is desirable. An open canopy is necessary for understory plant recruitment and for tortoise basking and incubation. Measured at 1/10-acre radius (37m). Cover is estimated to the nearest 5%.	• <10% or 65% canopy cover: 1 point • 41–65% canopy cover: 50 points • 10–40% canopy cover: 100 points
Midstory Woody Vegetation	Little or no midstory is preferred due to the impact on understory plant recruitment and the ability to conduct prescribed burns. Midstory is defined as 5–20 feet aboveground. Measured at 1/100-acre radius (12 m). Cover is estimated to the nearest 5%.	• 30%: 1 point • 15–30%: 50 points • <15%: 100 points
Overstory Vegetation	In general, the property should have at least 25% of the area wooded, of which at least 75% should be pine. The overall wooded requirement can be determined using aerial photography. Longleaf pine (*Pinus palustris*) is the preferable overstory species because it is more fire tolerant and has fewer economic and silvicultural conflicts with tortoise management. Loblolly (*P. taeda*) or slash (*P. elliottii*) pine in existing stands, at the time of the Agreement, is acceptable when stocked according to the canopy cover requirements. Loblolly or slash pine stands thinned to suitable coverage should be converted to longleaf pine when regenerated, either naturally or artificially, whether management is even or uneven aged, and at a rate that will provide suitable habitat cover and forage for tortoises. Measured at 1/10-acre radius (37 m).	• Hardwoods (50% of wooded area): 1 point • Loblolly or slash pine (50% of wooded area) with remaining percentage fire tolerant hardwoods: 25 points • Loblolly or slash pine (75% of wooded area) with remaining percentage fire-tolerant hardwoods: 50 points • Longleaf pine (75% of wooded area) with remaining percentage fire- tolerant hardwoods: 75 points • Longleaf pine (75% of wooded area) with remaining percentage mixed pine: 100 points

TABLE 16.3 *(continued)*

Criteria	Description	Scoring
Herbaceous Plants	Gopher tortoises prefer patchy understory with some bare ground. Measured using a 1/1000-acre (1m^2) sampling plot replicated four times at each sample plot (sampled haphazardly) and averaged.	• <25% cover: 1 point • 25–49% cover: 33 points • 50–74% cover: 66 points • 75% with some bare ground present: 100 points
Invasive Plants	Invasive plants include, but are not limited to, Cogongrass (*Imperata cylindrica*), Glossy and Chinese Privet (*Ligustrum* sp.), Japanese Climbing Fern (*Lygodium japonicum*), Chinese Tallow Tree (*Triadica sebifera*), Shrub Lespedeza (*Lespedeza bicolor*), Tung Oil Tree (*Aleurites fordii*), and Kudzu (*Pueraria lobata*). Future invasive plant issues are addressed in the required management plan. Measured at 1/10-acre radius (37m). Cover is estimated to the nearest 5%.	• 10%: 1 point • 5–10% invasive plant coverage: 50 points • <5% invasive plant coverage: 100 points

NOTE: See table 16.4 and text for credit calculation and integration with the population survey.

TABLE 16.4 AN EXAMPLE OF GOPHER TORTOISE CREDIT CALCULATION BASED ON A 200-ACRE LONGLEAF PINE LAND PARCEL IN CHATTAHOOCHEE COUNTY, GEORGIA

Habitat Survey	Score (Mean [95% CI])	Points
Fragmentation	Minor	50
Adjacent Lands	Adjacent to pine habitat that is not under any formal protection from development	50
Landscape Conditions	Greater than 75% of the surrounding landscape is forested	100
Soil Type	Priority	100
Property Size	200	25
Canopy Closure	35 [4.6]	100
Midstory Woody Vegetation Coverage	22 [4.4]	50
Overstory Vegetation	87 [8.4]	100
Herbaceous Plant Cover	32 [6.7]	33
Invasive Plants	0	100
Habitat Score Calculation	$[(50^{0.08}) \times (50^{0.08}) \times (100^{0.15}) \times (100^{0.08}) \times (25^{0.08}) \times (100^{0.15}) \times (50^{0.08}) \times (100^{0.08}) \times (33^{0.15}) \times (100^{0.08}] \div 100$	
Habitat Score	0.65	
Population Survey		
Estimated Population Size	105	
Lower 95% CI	75	
Upper 95% CI	147	
Total Credits	0.65 x 75 = 49	

NOTE: The habitat and population surveys are combined into gopher tortoise credits. See text for details. Each criterion for the habitat survey receives a score (mean, 95% confidence interval (CI)), which is translated into points (see table 16.3). The habitat score is then used to scale the lower 95% CI point estimate to arrive at the total number of credits eligible for sale.

example had an estimated lower 95% confidence interval of 120 tortoises (with a CV <20%) and a habitat score of 0.73, the total number of gopher tortoise credits would be 120 × 0.73 = 89. Ten percent of the total credits (i.e., 8.9) are risk deposit credits and cannot be sold until the five-year gopher tortoise survey is conducted. Scaling the credit score by habitat quality awards high-quality habitat and helps mitigate for the higher risk of credit default (i.e., tortoise decline due to marginal habitat).

A Worked Example and Exploring Survey Costs

We provide a worked example from a land parcel in Chattahoochee County, Georgia. A nonprofit organization owns 791 acres of pine forest that are managed for biodiversity conservation. The parcel is dominated by longleaf pine plantation (404 acres), along with some sand pine (*Pinus clausa*), loblolly pine (*P. taeda*), and hardwood forests. Fort Benning, where the US Army maintains active military training, is nearby, which does result in some negative impacts on gopher tortoises. A forest management plan is in place, and one of the primary goals is to improve habitat for Red-Cockaded Woodpeckers (*Picoides borealis*) and gopher tortoises (Mellette Forestry Group 2011). In 2011, scientists from the Joseph W. Jones Ecological Research Center surveyed a section of the property (~200 acres of longleaf pine forest) for gopher tortoises using the described methodology (L. Smith, pers. com.; Smith et al. 2009b). In 2011, we also conducted a habitat survey. Based on our pilot credit methodology, the organization would be eligible to sell 49 credits (see table 16.4).

The costs of the methodologies to initially assess a land parcel for credits, as well as the ongoing monitoring, are a critical aspect of a PLC program if it is going to be widely applicable and scalable. We explored this question by interviewing academic and consulting biologists who regularly use these methodologies. The leading scientist who developed the *Gopher Tortoise Survey Handbook* estimates that the maximum cost in equipment is $11,730, and 26 total person-days are needed to conduct and analyze a population survey for a <500-acre parcel. The main equipment costs are for a burrow camera, which ranges between $2,500 and $7,500, and a GPS and other field electronics, estimated at $4,000 (L. Smith, personal communication). Assuming an average rate of $50 per hour, labor costs would be around $10,600. A leading gopher tortoise consulting biologist provided an estimate of $9,000 to initially assess a land parcel to determine its tortoise population using the *Gopher Tortoise Survey Handbook* methodology for the land parcel described above (M. Bailey, personal communication). The habitat survey is less fieldwork-intensive, in terms of both person-days and specialized equipment. Based on our experience, we estimate it would take 4 to 5 person-days with skilled technicians to sample a 200- to 500-acre parcel ($1,600–$2,000, with an average rate of $50 per hour). Thus we estimate that initial baseline surveys for a 200- to 500-acre parcel would cost between $10,000 and $15,000 (~$50 per acre). Cost per acre is likely to decrease with increasing parcel size. We incorporated these costs, along with ongoing monitoring costs, into our estimate of the minimum cost of a gopher tortoise credit (see Donlan et al. this volume).

PUTTING IT TOGETHER: IMPLEMENTING A PLC PROGRAM

The pilot development process included extensive stakeholder engagement with private landowners, local conservation NGOs, academics, and state and federal government agencies. Without overarching policy guidance from the USFWS on PLC programs, we engaged in program development efforts while simultaneously seeking feedback and approval from the USFWS, both at a regional and a national level. We briefly discuss those efforts below, along with a discussion of achieving a net conservation benefit within our proposed PLC program.

Stakeholder Engagement

To ensure the quality of our program design and to facilitate adoption, we focused much of our early efforts on consultations with experts and stakeholders to guide the development of key program elements like metrics and eligibility requirements. The centerpiece of the stakeholder engagement process was the establishment of an advisory committee. The committee included representatives from the USFWS, the USDA Natural Resources Conservation Service, national and local conservation NGOs, state resource agencies (Georgia, Florida, and Alabama), academia, private consultants, land trusts, forest industry, family woodland owners, market infrastructure providers, and the Department of Defense.

In early 2009, gopher tortoise experts were convened with a broader array of stakeholders in a two-day meeting to reach consensus on the priority ecological attributes for a market-based PLC framework. The working group agreed that preserving and improving management on high-quality habitat parcels is the most important conservation measure for the gopher tortoise. In collaboration with experts and stakeholders, we then turned our attention to the development of credit methodology and program rules that would create necessary incentives and achieve a net conservation benefit within a mitigation framework. This process resulted in identifying a suite of habitat-based measures (e.g., soil type, canopy closure, species composition, understory composition, etc.) to inform the credit assessment methodology. Along with the requirement of gopher tortoise presence and some broader landscape attributes, we developed an initial scoring process to assess gopher tortoise habitat quality. Our initial efforts also explored important programmatic framework elements, such as whether habitat restoration and preservation should be eligible for credit creation and how mitigation ratios might be integrated into a program. Since many factors, including the latter, will be ultimately decided by the USFWS, we then began to focus our efforts on working with local and national USFWS offices to identify and resolve issues and concerns.

Once the working group had advised on an initial version of the pilot program, including a habitat-based crediting methodology, we met with regional USFWS staff to present the program and solicit interest and feedback. The USFWS expressed concerns about the program's focus on habitat as opposed to populations, which was more consistent with existing USFWS programs for the gopher tortoise. The USFWS provided detailed, critical feedback on the program. In collaboration with the advisory committee, we revised our initial credit methodology to include a population component. We also modified the methodology to be more consistent with existing programs, such as Georgia's State Wildlife Action Plan, the USFWS's Guidance for Conservation Banking and Candidate Conservation Agreements for the gopher tortoise, and the Range-Wide Conservation Plan for Longleaf Pine (Georgia Department of Natural Resources 2005; Regional Working Group for America's Longleaf 2009; USFWS 2009a, 2009b). Over the entire process, we field-tested the credit methodology multiple times, often with members of the advisory committee.

Last, we paid close attention to how the pilot program would interact with state-level policy. In addition to the ESA, many states have their own regulations, assurances, and protections associated with the gopher tortoise. A PLC program focused on advance mitigation will be attractive to buyers and sellers only if regulatory predictability is aligned at the federal and state levels. In locations where the gopher tortoise is not listed under the ESA, it is either listed as threatened under state law (e.g. Florida and Georgia) or protected as nongame wildlife (Alabama). We coordinated with state wildlife agencies to ensure consistency with state regulations, identify potential areas of contradiction or concern, and share lessons learned.

While stakeholder engagement was time-intensive, our inclusive, iterative, and adaptive approach was valuable. Addressing and incorporating different concerns, liabilities, and perspectives helped build support for the program. It also helped identify the pivotal challenges that must be addressed for success. One of those challenges is regulatory approval and the need for clear regulatory predictability for participants of a PLC program.

Obtaining Regulatory Approval and Buyer Commitment

Concurrent with the iterative revision process for the crediting methodology, we worked closely with the Department of Defense to secure buyer commitment and with the USFWS to obtain its support for the core parameters of the program. While we had conversations directly with decision makers at local military installations, most of our collaboration and dialogue occurred with Department of Defense staff at the national level. Installation decision makers—ultimately those who need to say yes—hesitated to engage before the program had the full backing of the USFWS on a national level.

Once we had a preliminary version of the program, the USFWS regional office assigned a staff person to work through major science and policy issues with the project team. Having a designated representative was critical to moving forward and would have been beneficial from the outset of design efforts. It soon became clear, however, that the champions within the agency who have the ability to move the program forward—once engaged—were likely to need support from national-level policy guidance to experiment with an incentive-based PLC approach, particularly one that would provide some level of regulatory predictability to participants.

Arriving at an apparent impasse between the needs of buyers and commitment from the USFWS, we turned our efforts to obtaining policy guidance at the national level. In March 2012, the Department of Interior issued an Advance Notice of Proposed Rulemaking on the incentive-based PLC approach (USFWS 2012a). This notice offered the opportunity for high-level dialogue among major stakeholders and the USFWS. As part of this dialogue, a USFWS Region 4 Coordinator for Regional Candidate and Ecosystem Conservation indicated that the USFWS is committed to a candidate conservation credit program (pers. com., February 6, 2013).

Achieving Net Conservation Benefit

The program's ultimate objective is to mobilize conservation efforts for the gopher tortoise upstream of regulation within a science-based framework that will ensure a net conservation benefit for the species, even when credits are used as mitigation for species impacts. This objective fundamentally hinges on the requirements and metrics used in a PLC program and how these factors are implemented to reduce the risk of not achieving a net conservation benefit. The metrics used to determine credit allocations, monitor progress, and inform adaptive management set the incentives for landowners. Program design, including credit metrics, should capture key ecological and biological elements like habitat conditions and population dynamics and weight those elements according to their importance for species recovery based on best available science.

In the pilot design, we began with a consensus from leading gopher tortoise experts that preservation and active management of remaining high-quality habitat should be a top priority for conservation efforts, given the disappearance of longleaf pine stands across the southern United States. Accordingly, early iterations of the crediting methodology focused on habitat-related metrics that were most important for gopher tortoise viability. Then, as described earlier, we integrated a population component into the crediting methodology. This approach focused on creating an incentive to conserve and manage large, high-quality habitat land parcels for the gopher tortoise.

However, over the course of the pilot development process, we struggled to reconcile the consensus recommendation from leading experts with a mitigation framework in which individual tortoises might be killed due to activities at an impact site. The primary mechanism for dealing with this issue in the listed range is translocation. However, most experts and stakeholders we consulted felt that translocation on its own, without a mechanism to address continued habitat degradation and lack of active management, would not be sufficient to ensure a net conservation benefit. Translocation could remain an option (or requirement) within a PLC program, which would further ensure a net conservation benefit but would increase costs and potentially negatively affect the scalability of the program.

The biology of the gopher tortoise further complicates the goal of achieving a net conservation benefit and the issues of focusing on preservation, restoration, and translocation. Because it evolved with the fire-dependent longleaf pine ecosystem, the gopher tortoise is reliant on active management of its habitat (i.e., prescribed burning), without which the habitat is likely to continue to degrade along with the gopher tortoise population (Diemer 1986; McCoy et al. 2006; Mushinsky et al. 2006; Ashton and Ashton 2007). In other words, the default projected baseline for a gopher tortoise population on a land parcel declines over time in the absence of active management. This is especially the case since private landowners are not obligated under the ESA to take proactive steps for species protection. Consequently, both preservation and habitat restoration through active habitat management for the gopher tortoise may provide the additionality needed for a net conservation benefit relative to projected baseline conditions. Tailoring the design of our program to the specific biology of the gopher tortoise, the program permits preservation and restoration to generate credits. This is because active habitat management is required, which will result in either habitat restoration or the preservation of high-quality habitat; the latter would be in a period of degradation in terms of viable habitat for gopher tortoises in the absence of active management. Preservation, however, should be carefully considered in future PLC efforts, on a case-by-case, species-by-species basis.

CONCLUSION

Throughout our efforts to establish the pilot program for the gopher tortoise, a number of key lessons emerged. We believe these issues provide value for the successful design and implementation of any PLC program.

Regulatory predictability is key. At the onset of our project, we assumed some level of demand for habitat credits was present based on early conversations with the Office of the Deputy Under-Secretary of Defense. From our subsequent work and conversations with the Department of Defense and US Army over the past two years, however, it became clear that regulatory predictability is the key to generating demand for PLC programs. Demand from the Department of Defense will clearly be driven by predictability under the ESA (Li and Male this volume). We believe this is likely to be the case for nonfederal project developers as well. In our dialogue with the US Army, they consistently made the case that they need to be able to quantify the return on investment in order to justify participation in a PLC program (Orndoff this volume). Robust demand for PLC programs will materialize only if the USFWS explicitly offers some reasonable level of predictability that credits can be used toward future regulatory requirements (e.g., compensatory mitigation) if and when a candidate species is later listed under the ESA.

A "chicken-and-egg dilemma" between buyers, sellers, and regulators can stall efforts. A PLC market needs active participation from buyers, sellers, and regulators to function. We found that securing commitment from one party was difficult without having firm commitment from other parties. Demand is the fundamental driver and the logical place to start. In the case of the gopher tortoise, securing buy-in from the US Army would be a powerful motivator for other stakeholders to move forward with the program. However, the US Army has not committed to the program without a clear sense of the regulatory predictability that the USFWS is willing to offer. In turn, the USFWS, in the absence of national policy guidance, has not yet outlined that regulatory predictability.

National policy guidance may grease the wheels at the regional level. Clear policy guidance from the USFWS at the national level—particularly on the matter of regulatory predictability—may provide the support and encouragement regional offices need to experiment with incentive-based PLC approaches.

Programs must be precise enough to ensure conservation benefits but practical enough to work at a meaningful scale. To be successful, incentive-based PLC programs must be based on the best available science. However, some metrics can serve as a barrier to adoption at meaningful scale by introducing prohibitive transaction costs. Other complex metrics end up promoting a "wait until we have more science" attitude, which can result in inaction. Thus PLC programs must balance scientific precision with on-the-ground practicality. We grappled with this issue when considering population and habitat metrics for the gopher tortoise, as well as the roles of preservation, restoration, and translocation in a PLC program. At a minimum, crediting metrics must be able to measure on-the-ground conservation actions precisely, accurately, and cost-effectively. Ultimately, crediting metrics must be designed both to incentivize and to quantify the most effective conservation actions while also remaining feasible and tangible for landowners and associated stakeholders. Program participants must be able to understand how PLC programs work and to incorporate them into how they manage their land.

Don't let the perfect be the enemy of the good; adaptively manage instead. We found a temptation among the project team and stakeholders to get mired in the details of program design and its implications for net conservation benefit. Doing so had the effect of discouraging or slowing the implementation of a pilot program. While critical review and an iterative revision process are essential to give the program a solid chance of success from the outset, the incentive-based PLC approach is new and at some point needs to be tested on the ground. Pilot implementation will provide the best data for an adaptive approach to ensure that a net conservation benefit is being achieved. If program performance is carefully monitored, experimental pilot efforts can generate valuable insight into optimal program design. Stakeholders and the USFWS can then incorporate those insights adaptively into ongoing programs.

Buyers and sellers can have different preferences. Landowner survey results indicate a strong preference for short-term arrangements and flexibility (Sorice et al. 2013). Buyers, on the other hand, are likely to prefer long-term and fairly rigid arrangements in order to meet their needs and qualify for regulatory predictability. This was especially true for the US Army, which is interested in not only offsetting potential ESA liability but also securing compatible land use around its installations. Mapping buyer and seller preferences and perceptions, using social science techniques, is a rapid and effective means of optimizing program design for both participation and conservation effectiveness (Sorice et al. 2013; Sorice and Abel this volume)

PLC programs should integrate with the ESA listing process. A major point in feedback from the USFWS was that a PLC program and its metrics should clearly relate to the ESA listing process by addressing the specific threats to the species with respect to the USFWS's five factor analysis (USFWS 2006):

1. Damage to, or destruction of, a species' habitat.
2. Overuse of the species for commercial, recreational, scientific, or educational purposes.
3. Disease or predation.
4. The inadequacy of existing protection.
5. Other natural or human-related threats to the species' survival.

Integrating and addressing these factors into PLC programs may help to facilitate adoption, and also to generate the data that the USFWS uses in its listing decisions. While the major goal of advance mitigation is to recover candidate and other at-risk species, the species benefits of advance mitigation are unlikely to be incorporated into listing decisions if they cannot be tracked in a way that is relevant for the USFWS.

A variety of roles are needed for program development and operations to be successful. We initially underestimated the specialized roles that are needed for a successful PLC program. We assumed that core project partners could head metric and protocol development while also integrating program components for implementation. However, specialization in these roles is clearly necessary for success. A PLC program administrator, one with a local on-the-ground presence and regional credibility, would have facilitated pilot development efforts by serving as a connector to local politics. Further, a program administrator and a broker will be essential in order to provide validation and verification, conduct third-party monitoring and assessments, liaise with the USFWS, and aggregate sellers.

Getting those who need to say yes to the table at the outset is critical. The US Army and USFWS decision makers, whose buy-in is critical to progress, were not sufficiently engaged from the beginning of our PLC program development and pilot implementation efforts. While staff at the national level were supportive and lent credibility to our efforts, ultimately it is often the decision makers at the regional level who can move a program forward. Securing this engagement may be facilitated in the future by national-level encouragement and policy guidance.

CHAPTER 17

The Future of Pre-Listing Conservation Programs for Wildlife Conservation

TIMOTHY MALE AND C. JOSH DONLAN

ABSTRACT

Focusing on at-risk species that have yet to be listed under the US Endangered Species Act, pre-listing conservation is a strategy that falls under a portfolio of proactive policies. Pre-listing conservation programs have the potential to deliver value to all participating stakeholders in the form of regulatory predictability or financial compensation in exchange for early investment in species conservation actions. Addressing several factors and approaches will be critical for the success of pre-listing conservation programs, including demand generation, human-centered design, net conservation benefit, and additionality. Despite some limitations and challenges, pre-listing conservation has the potential to expand to the scale necessary to deliver landscape-scale benefits. It also provides a foundation and learning platform for designing programs in settings where incentives for conservation action from regulation are weak or nonexistent. Instead of relying on regulation to generate demand for conservation behaviors, pre-listing conservation programs rely on the risk of potential regulation and the opportunity to mitigate that risk in advance to generate demand. The frameworks and approaches connected to pre-listing conservation can spark new wildlife conservation strategies both in the United States and abroad.

INTRODUCTION

Around the world, success in environmental conservation depends in some part on actions in two overlapping spheres of policy: policies that prevent further environmental damage from occurring and those that promote proactive measures to improve environmental conditions. Laws like the US Endangered Species Act (ESA) are strongest at preventing additional harm from occurring. In contrast, the ESA and most other biodiversity laws around the globe offer few mandates that incentivize stewardship investments. This policy gap is important and will likely gain greater importance in the coming decades, for several reasons. First, today many of the world's species are conservation-reliant: the threats they face cannot be entirely eliminated; rather, threats must be constantly managed and minimized (Scott et al. 2010; Goble et al. 2012). Second, privately held land makes up the majority of land tenure in many countries, including the United States where the proportion of private land has increased over the past decade to 72 percent (Gorte et al. 2012). A high percentage of at-risk species and their habitats are found on these private lands (Groves et al. 2000; Shogren 2005). Third, demand for goods and services (e.g., energy, military readiness, food production, and recreation) on both private and public land is increasing. Thus policies that provide strong incentives, financial or otherwise, to take proactive actions to cost-effectively provide net conservation benefits for at-risk species are sorely needed to complement existing policies. Focusing on at-risk species that have yet to be listed under the ESA, pre-listing conservation (PLC) is but one strategy that falls into this new portfolio of proactive policies.

DESIGNING SUCCESSFUL PLC PROGRAMS

To encourage investment by the public and private sectors in species conservation, programs must offer some type of incentive that provides present or future value to investors—that is, any participant in a PLC program. That value could take the form of technical assistance, financial benefit, risk reduction, or regulatory predictability. In exchange, to be biologically successful, programs should deliver an overall benefit to the species that is the program target. For PLC programs to work in practice, however, they must balance the value delivered to investors and the value delivered to species conservation while providing sufficient benefit to both (Sorice and Abel this volume). This volume describes how value can be delivered to stakeholders on both sides of a PLC program: regulatory predictability or financial compensation for stakeholders whose actions affect species in exchange for investment in species conservation actions. Yet success is by no means a predetermined outcome of a PLC program. What issues must be considered and built into a program for it to work successfully? We briefly discuss what we believe are critical criteria when designing a PLC program.

Demand Generation. Incentive- and market-based solutions hold great promise for biodiversity conservation. In particular, these approaches are intriguing because they create incentives for managing resources sustainably, thereby aligning economic and conservation objectives rather than imposing regulations and restrictions. For example, there is increasing evidence that eco-labeled seafood products do capture an economic premium (Roheim et al. 2011). Yet research has also demonstrated that market differentiation with certification schemes is not successful using a "cookie cutter" approach (Loureiro and Umberger 2003). Rather, understanding the perceptions, preferences, and needs of consumers is critical to designing a program with sufficient demand (Loureiro and Umberger 2003; Karipidis and Sartzetakis 2013). This important aspect is all too often ignored in the design of market-based programs focused on biodiversity conservation. Customer-driven research should be conducted in parallel with other aspects of PLC program design in order to create a program that will have sufficient demand to finance and scale it.

For many scenarios, providing regulatory predictability and streamlining environmental compliance will generate demand for PLC programs. Kiernan (this volume) describes how difficult it is for solar companies to secure and retain financing during the long and uncertain period of navigating environmental compliance. Similarly, the Department of Defense has legal obligations to protect endangered species, and it seeks to reduce the regulatory risk that those obligations will affect military readiness (Orndoff this volume). Similar regulatory risk for at-risk species (i.e., potential ESA listing) is present in the private sector. Renewable energy, oil and gas development, and energy infrastructure all have impacts on at-risk species, which can result in lengthy compliance at best and project termination at worst (Donlan et al. 2013). Creating opportunities to mitigate environmental risk surrounding unlisted at-risk species in exchange for streamlined compliance and increased regulatory predictability would generate demand for PLC from project developers. Li and Male (this volume) outline the procedural steps under existing policy that could be used to make that outcome possible.

Human-Centered Design. Like the need for robust demand, sufficient supply—in the form of landowner participation—is needed for PLC programs to be successful. Program designers need to pay careful attention not only to how program structure influences potential conservation benefits but also to how it influences landowners and their potential to participate (Sorice et al. 2013). There will always be an inherent trade-off between maximizing conservation benefits within a single contract or agreement and the widespread participation needed for landscape-level benefits. The importance of understanding and integrating the preferences and needs of landowners is an important theme throughout this volume (Gartner et al.; Johnson and Snieckus; Fankhauser). In particular, Sorice and Abel in their chapter in this volume analyze how a landowner-centered approach to program design and incentives built into program structure and delivery can influence participation. As reported elsewhere (Sorice and Conner 2010; Wolfe et al. 2012), Gartner et al. in their chapter observe that program attributes that are commonly desirable from a conservation perspective, like easements in perpetuity, are generally unfavorable to landowners and thus are likely to decrease participation.

As important, Gartner et al. (this volume) demonstrate, with a landowner survey, that approximately 50 percent of potential forest landowners in the southeastern United Stated showed no interest in participating in a PLC program, even though multiple hypothetical programs were presented to them (also see Sorice et al. 2013). This possible limit on participation is a barrier to the potential landscape-level impact of PLC programs. That challenge calls for the use of "design thinking" in PLC programs. Originally developed in the private sector for new product innovation, design thinking is now being applied to a variety of social issues (Brown 2009; Brown and Wyatt 2010). Design thinking is human-centered, options-focused, possibility driven, and iterative. With this approach, any biodiversity conservation incentive program is more likely to be structured and delivered in a way that supports participants' basic needs for competence and autonomy. Although this approach has become an integral part of product and service innovation in the design, engineering, and business fields, it is glaringly absent across the biodiversity conservation sector. Human-centered design provides a framework to design better biodiversity conservation incentive programs that will garner the participation necessary to deliver landscape-scale benefits.

Net Conservation Benefit. What is the goal of PLC programs? Numerous authors in this volume describe the need to establish a net conservation benefit standard for species that are the subject of PLC programs. By definition, candidate species already meet the definition of threatened or endangered under the ESA, and thus they will likely require improvement in demographic rates and reduction in threats to change their status. For many candidate species, no decline is permissible: the species are in fact as endangered as those already listed, and permitting land use activities that allow net decline will further endanger them. However, another subset of candidate species may be able to tolerate further demographic decline as long as threats are managed sufficiently to stop the decline from going beyond a specified state. We feel the establishment of a net conservation benefit standard for PLC programs is important because it is one of the easiest standards to interpret by agencies and third parties, and it would ensure that PLC programs are explicitly designed to contribute to species conservation. However, net benefit should be considered a floor, not a ceiling, as many projects should seek greater contributions to conservation depending on the level of value provided to investors (i.e., program participants) in return.

Additionality. Additionality is an important and underappreciated feature that must be considered to confirm that a particular project or program has achieved its conservation objective. While additionality can be difficult to define and even harder to measure, it can be easily summarized as "what would have happened otherwise?" In the context of PLC programs, credits and any value that comes with those credits should only be calculated for species benefits that would not have happened in the absence of the program. Many carbon offset programs adopt a financial additionality criterion: that is, the project outcomes would not have happened without the financial incentive created by the program (Raymond 2010). Other offset programs focus on regulatory or technological additionality.

Defining and measuring additionality is difficult. First, in practical terms, additionality requires a reasonably accurate ability to predict a counterfactual: what would have resulted from a potential source of conservation actions for an at-risk species without the PLC program? Second, additionality metrics can lead to perverse incentives. By offering incentives for conservation benefits that "would not have happened otherwise," additionality rules could discourage voluntary action and may incentivize delay of specific actions for fear of forgoing an opportunity for future compensation for those actions.

Additionality per se is not a program objective but a means to achieve an objective (Trexler et al. 2006). Assuming that the policy objective of PLC is a net conservation benefit, the first task to determine whether a PLC program is meeting a net conservation benefit objective is to measure the losses at one site and the gains at another. This can be done by using appropriate proxies and methodologies dependent on the program's target species (Cochran and Maness this volume; Gartner et al. this volume). The second step involves an assessment of whether all or some portion of the losses and gains would have occurred in the absence of the development and project. Precise quantification of such counterfactuals may be difficult, but a well-designed PLC program will at least go through the procedural step of considering the issue of additionality and whether it can be measured.

LIMITS TO PLC APPROACHES

PLC will not achieve desired regulatory and time-sensitive conservation outcomes in many situations. Often species are too close to the brink of extinction or their management needs are too uncertain to provide regulators with enough certainty about species benefits to give assurances or other value to program participants. Early engagement would give programs a better chance of succeeding. Ideally, state and federal agencies would design PLC programs for declining at-risk species long before they are ESA candidate species. However, three challenges hamper such early investment. First, there is a "chicken and egg" problem. The US Fish and Wildlife Service (USFWS) needs to provide program participants with clear commitments that they will honor credits produced under such an early program, but the USFWS is unlikely to spend the time to do so if the species is not a candidate that is a priority for listing. Second, it will often be difficult for many potential participants to see sufficient benefits of early action when a regulatory driver appears remote (Ginger et al. this volume). For example, the Lesser Prairie-Chicken (*Tympanuchus pallidicinctus*) remained on the candidate list for more than a decade before meaningful conservation work began. A state-level regulatory driver could help overcome the absence of a federal one. Finally, PLC efforts are hampered by a lack of dedicated funding and staffing. Conservationists reasonably want to focus resources on those species that are closest to the brink of extinction rather than place investments in declining but more secure species. If these three challenges can be overcome in ways suggested by authors in this volume, it will be possible to expand PLC programs to the scale they are needed.

SCALING PRE-LISTING CONSERVATION

Individual projects for declining species already occur with some frequency but generally on a retail scale. Dedicated individuals work, often above and beyond their defined job descriptions, to navigate the difficult processes required to finalize a PLC project. Occasionally, bureaucracies have vertically integrated support for such projects, such as the Working Lands for Wildlife Initiative run by the US Department of Agriculture Natural Resource Conservation Service. Yet real success in PLC will come when more programs like the Working Lands for Wildlife Initiative operate at a wholesale scale. To get there, we believe federal agencies need stronger incentives to engage. Pre-listing conservation needs to be a higher priority for government and state agencies so that program participants know they can count on consistent agency support throughout the life cycle of a program.

We ask the provocative question, do conservation agreements and programs really need to be so hard to negotiate? We do not believe so. Agreements are hard to finalize because the USFWS currently approaches each one as a single negotiation rather than developing objective policy that would allow widespread use of templates to quickly structure potential agreements. Habitat Conservation Plans, Section 7 consultations, and PLC programs are commonly stalled because project proponents are asked to deliver new science instead of using the best available science. As described by Gartner and colleagues in this volume, the perfect often becomes the enemy of the good. In particular, Habitat Conservation Plans are in dire need of reform (Madsen this volume). The process can take a decade and costs millions of dollars; consequently, companies actively seek to establish a federal nexus with their project so they can receive incidental take coverage under Section 7 of the ESA. Ironically, this is easier and faster to negotiate and often provides a less beneficial species outcome than Habitat Conservation Plans. As Kiernan (this volume) describes for renewable solar projects, "From a practical standpoint, a utility-scale PV project that demands Section 10 permitting will have a very low likelihood of being built. The risk is simply too great." Simpler administrative processes are needed so that it is possible to negotiate agreements more quickly (Wolfe et al. 2012; Donlan et al. 2013). The USFWS and state wildlife agencies would also benefit by having more staff with legal and business training in regional positions to serve in project support (not solicitor) roles. Expertise in negotiation is an essential skill in order to achieve the potential conservation outcomes of PLC programs.

Federal agencies are among the most desirable participants in PLC programs, in both a supply and a demand role. However, federal agencies have lacked clear assurances that provide them with adequate predictability about the future regulatory benefits of early investments in species conservation. As a result, agencies like the US Marine Corps and the US Army, as described by Orndorff and Gartner et al. in this volume, are reluctant to participate. When the USFWS developed its conservation banking guidance for listed species, the agency indicated that the policy did not cover federal agencies but that future policy would do so (USFWS 2003b). Eleven years later, the USFWS has a clear opportunity to describe the form and degree of predictability they are willing to provide to federal agencies. One of the most beneficial commitments the USFWS could make is to allow federal agencies to use credits created before ESA listing to offset adverse effects of agency action after listing. By providing a contractual guarantee for this rollover assurance, the USFWS could provide a meaningful assurance of future regulation that may affect other federal agencies (Li and Male this volume). The USFWS should commit to a process for review and approval of crediting and debiting methodologies and give assurances that the methodology will not substantively change without sufficient opportunities for input by other agencies.

CONCLUSION

With a few important exceptions, most demand for market-based biodiversity conservation programs is generated by regulation. Wetland banking is a result of regulatory arbitrage: the US Clean Water Act creates business opportunities for private wetland mitigation firms (Robertson 2006). Likewise, demand for conservation easements in the United States is driven at least in part by tax arbitrage opportunities: landowners receive tax relief in exchange for placing an easement on their land (Ernst and Wallace 2008; Farmer et al. 2011). These arbitrage opportunities are only possible in settings where relatively strong environmental regulation or tax incentives are in place. Thus easements and wetland banking (and other biodiversity offset programs) are only common in countries like the United States, Australia, and parts of Europe (Madsen et al. 2010). Yet there is growing interest in market-based approaches in many countries that currently lack strong environmental laws or tax incentives.

We argue that proactive strategies for protecting species and PLC approaches are relevant to designing market-based and incentive programs outside of the United States. Why? Because they provide a foundation and learning platform for designing programs in settings where incentives for conservation action from regulation are weak or nonexistent. Instead of relying on regulation to generate demand for conservation behaviors, PLC programs rely on the *risk* of potential regulation and the *opportunity* to mitigate that risk in advance to generate demand. Thus PLC approaches are a step toward designing biodiversity incentive programs in settings where there are weaker regulatory incentives. Such settings are far more common around the globe than in the United States and other developed countries.

The chapters in this volume offer an important message to designers: be wary of one-sided solutions when it comes to building conservation programs. Program and project structure focused only on the needs of a species will result in programs with low participation on the supply side or no willing buyers on the demand side (Donlan et al. 2013; Sorice et al. 2013; Gartner et al. this volume; Sorice and Abel this volume). Programs should be custom-designed to reflect not only species' needs but also the needs of stakeholders whose desired behavior changes will result in the conservation benefits. Borrowing methodologies from human-centered design will result in landowner-centered programs that have strong support and high opt-in rates from local stakeholders. Program designers should pay close attention to potential demand drivers when designing a program's supply and transactional infrastructure. They must spend the time and resources to understand potential demand and design the products and services accordingly. Conservationists are getting better at designing products and services with biodiversity benefits. However, we are not yet very good at generating demand for those products and services. This will have to change if biodiversity conservation is going to access substantial capital from private consumers and investors (Huwyler et al. 2014).

During the final development of this volume, the USFWS announced a decision to list the Lesser Prairie-Chicken (figure 17.1). In many ways,

FIGURE 17.1. After over a decade on the candidate list, the Lesser Prairie-Chicken (*Tympanuchus pallidicinctus*) was listed as threatened under the Endangered Species Act in 2014. The listing includes an unprecedented special rule that establishes partnerships with states to provide regulatory certainty for landowners and businesses in exchange for conservation actions. © L. Lansa.

this species is a harbinger of the opportunity for PLC programs to benefit species and landowners. Significant population declines combined with a continued regional drought made listing almost inevitable. The listing, however, was accompanied by a special rule under section 4(d) of the ESA that creates just the kind of regulatory predictability described in this volume's chapters: landowners who participate in an approved crediting-debiting program operating in five states are rewarded with clear and minimal restrictions on their activities under the ESA (USFWS 2014b).

In response to comments from the Advance Notice of Proposed Rulemaking "Expanding Incentives for Voluntary Conservation Actions under the Endangered Species Act," the USFWS has announced that it expects to release a policy statement on PLC in the summer of 2014 (USFWS 2012a). To maximize its success, this policy needs to create explicit structures for future PLC programs, whether they are implemented by states or the USFWS. We hope this volume and its recommendations will inform and be considered in future PLC programs. The chapters in *Proactive Strategies for Protecting Species* are full of research, expert opinion, pilot project descriptions, and narrative stories of dedicated people working together to try to create conservation programs that reverse species decline in ways that work for the stakeholders involved. Such efforts must succeed if we are to get ahead of the growing challenge of conserving wildlife diversity in a rapidly changing world.

References

John Adams, "Discourses on Davila," in Charles Francis Adams, ed., The Works of John Adams, vol. 6 (1851), 280.

Adams, J., and C.F. Adams. 1850–56. The works of John Adams, second president of the United States: with a life of the author, notes and illustrations. 10 vols. Little, Brown, and Company, Boston, MA.

Adamus, P., J. Morlan, and K. Verble. 2010. Manual for the Oregon rapid wetland assessment protocol (ORWAP). Version 2.0.2. Oregon Department of State Lands, Salem.

Adler, J. 2011. Rebuilding the ark: new perspectives on Endangered Species Act reform. AEI Press, New York.

Aldridge, C.L., and M.S. Boyce. 2007. Linking occurrence and fitness to persistence: habitat-based approach for endangered Greater Sage-Grouse. Ecological Applications 17:508–526.

Andersen, M.C., J.M. Watts, J.E. Freilich, S.R. Yool, G.I. Wakefield, J.F. McCauley, and P.B. Fahnestock. 2000. Regression-tree modeling of desert tortoise habitat in the central Mojave Desert. Ecological Applications 10:890–900.

Anderson, D.R., K.P. Burnham, B.C. Lubow, L. Thomas, P.S. Corn, P.A. Medica, and R.W. Marlow. 2001. Field trials of line transect methods applied to estimation of desert tortoise abundance. Journal of Wildlife Management 65:583–597.

Anonymous. 2012a. Cattlemen land trust protects Saguache Creek Ranch. December 6, Valley Courier, http://www.alamosanews.com/v2_news_articles.php?heading=0&page=75&story_id=27497.

Ardour Capital Investments. 2010. Solar power plants on US public land. Legislative update. Ardour Capital Investments, New York.

Ashton, R.E., and P.A. Ashton. 2007. The natural history and management of the gopher tortoise *Gopherus polyphemus*. Krieger, New York.

Associated Press. 2010. Solar showdown in tortoises' home. Activists like renewable power, but not on that Mojave spot. January 1, NBC News.com, http://www.msnbc.msn.com/id/34659369/ns/us_news-environment/t/solar-showdown-tortoises-home/.

Auwahi Wind Energy. 2011. Draft Auwahi wind farm project Habitat Conservation Plan. TetraTech, http://hawaii.gov/dlnr/dofaw/hcp/Draft_HCP_Text_and_Appendices_Auwahi.pdf/

Averill-Murray, R.C., C.R. Darst, K.J. Field, and L.J. Allison. 2012. A new approach to conservation of the Mojave Desert tortoise. BioScience 62: 893–899.

Baron, J.S., N.L. Poff, P.L. Angermeier, C.N. Dahm, P.H. Gleick, N.G. Hairston, R.B. Jackson, C.A. Johnston, B.D. Richter, and A.D. Steinman. 2002. Meeting ecological and societal needs for freshwater. Ecological Applications 12:1247–1260.

Bean, M.J. 1998. The Endangered Species Act and private land: four lessons learned from the past quarter century. Environmental Law Reporter 28:10701–10710.

———. 2005. Second-generation approaches. Pages 274–285 in D. Goble, J.M. Scott, and F.W. Davis (editors). The Endangered Species Act at thirty: renewing the conservation promise. Island Press, Washington, DC.

Bean, M.J., J.P. Jenny, and B. van Eerden. 2001. Safe harbor agreements: carving out a new role for NGOs. Conservation in Practice 2:8–15.

Bedford, B.L. 1996. The need to define hydrologic equivalence at the landscape scale for freshwater wetland mitigation. Ecological Applications 6:57–68.

Beechie, T.J., D.A. Sear, J.D. Olden, G.R. Pess, J.M. Buffington, H. Moir, P. Roni, and M.M. Pollock. 2010. Process-based principles for restoring river ecosystems. BioScience 60:209–222.

BenDor, T. 2009. A dynamic analysis of the wetland mitigation process and its effects on no net loss policy. Landscape and Urban Planning 89:17–27.

BenDor, T., and N. Brozović. 2007. Determinants of spatial and temporal patterns in compensatory wetland mitigation. Environmental Management 40:349–364.

BenDor, T.K., J.A. Riggsbee, and M. Doyle. 2011. Risk and markets for ecosystem services. Environmental Science & Technology 45:10322–10330.

Benton, N., J.D. Ripley, and F. Powledge (editors). 2008. Conserving biodiversity on military lands: a guide for natural resource managers. NatureServe, Arlington, VA.

Bergmann, S.A., and J.C. Bliss. 2004. Foundations of cross-boundary cooperation: resource management at the public-private interface. Society & Natural Resources 17:377–393.

Bernhardt, E.S., and M.A. Palmer. 2011. River restoration: the fuzzy logic of repairing reaches to reverse catchment scale degradation. Ecological Applications 21:1926–1931.

Bernhardt, E.S., M.A. Palmer, J.D. Allan, G. Alexander, K. Barnas, S. Brooks, J. Carr, S. Clayton, C. Dahm, J. Follstad-Shah, D. Galat, S. Gloss, P. Goodwin, D. Hart, B. Hassett, R. Jenkinson, S. Katz, G.M. Kondolf, P.S. Lake, R. Lave, J.L. Meyer, T.K. O'Donnell, L. Pagano, B. Powell, and E. Sudduth. 2005. Synthesizing US river restoration efforts. Science 308:636–637.

Bernhardt, E.S., E.B. Sudduth, M.A. Palmer, J.D. Allan, J.L. Meyer, G. Alexander, J. Follastad-Shah, B. Hassett, R. Jenkinson, R. Lave, J. Rumps, and L. Pagano. 2007. Restoring rivers one reach at a time: results from a survey of U.S. river restoration practitioners. Restoration Ecology 15:482–493.

Berry, K.H. 1986. Desert tortoise (*Gopherus agassizii*) relocation: implications of social behavior and movements. Herpetologica 42:113–125.

Best, C. 2002. America's private forests: challenges for conservation. Journal of Forestry 100:14–17.

Bliss, J.C., and A.J. Martin. 1989. Identifying NIPF management motivations with qualitative methods. Forest Science 35:601–622.

BLM (Bureau of Land Management). 2011a. BLM national Greater Sage-Grouse land use planning strategy. Attachment to Instruction Memorandum no. 2012–044. US Bureau of Land Management, Washington, DC.

———. 2011b. A report of national Greater Sage-Grouse conservation measures. US Bureau of Land Management Sage-Grouse National Technical Team, http://www.blm.gov/pgdata/etc/medialib/blm/co/programs/wildlife.Par.73607.File.dat/GrSG Tech Team Report.pdf.

———. 2012. The BLM's balancing act: managing the needs of people and Sage Grouse on public lands. US Bureau of Land Management, http://www.blm.gov/wo/st/en/prog/more/fish__wildlife_and/sage-grouse-conservation/energy.print.html.

BLM (Bureau of Land Management) and DOE (Department of Energy). 2012. Final programmatic environmental impact statement (PEIS) for solar energy development in six southwestern states. US Bureau of Land Management and US Department of Energy, Washington, DC.

Boarman, W.I., and K.H. Berry. 1995. Common ravens in the southwestern United States, 1968–92. Pages 73–75 in E.L. LaRue, G.S. Farris, and C.E. Puckett (editors). Our living resources. National Biological Service, US Department of the Interior, Washington, DC.

Bødker, S., and O.S. Iversen. 2002. Staging a professional participatory design practice: moving participatory design beyond the initial fascination of user involvement. Pages 11–18 in Proceedings of the second Nordic conference on human-computer interaction (Aarhus, Denmark, October 19–23, 2002). ACM Press, New York.

Bonnie, R. 1997. Safe harbor for the Red-Cockaded Woodpecker. Journal of Forestry 95:17–22.

Bonnie, R., and D.S. Wilcox. 2008. Ecological considerations. Pages 53–67 in N. Carroll, J. Fox, and R. Bayon (editors). Conservation and biodiversity banking: a guide to setting up and running biodiversity credit trading systems. Earthscan, London.

Brenkman, S.J., J.J. Duda, C.E. Torgersen, E. Welty, G.R. Pess, R. Peters, and M.L. McHenry. 2012. A riverscape perspective of Pacific salmonids and aquatic habitats prior to large-scale dam removal in the Elwha River, Washington, USA. Fisheries Management and Ecology 19:36–53.

Brightsource Energy. 2012. The Ivanpah Solar Project: getting the facts straight. Brightsource Energy, http://ivanpahsolar.com/the-ivanpah-solar-project-getting-the-facts-straight.

Brook, A., M. Zint, and R. De Young. 2003. Landowners responses to an Endangered Species Act listing and implications for encouraging conservation. Conservation Biology 17:1638–1649.

Brosi, B.J., and E.G.N. Biber. 2012. Citizen involvement in the US Endangered Species Act. Science 337:802–803.

Brown, T. 2008. Design thinking. Harvard Business Review 86:84–82.

———. 2009. Change by design. HarperCollins, New York.

Brown, T., and J. Wyatt. 2010. Design thinking for social innovation. Stanford Social Innovation Review 8:30–35.

Bruggeman, D., M. Jones, F. Lupi, and K. Scribner. 2005. Landscape equivalency analysis: methodology for estimating spatially explicit biodiversity credits. Environmental Management 36:518–534.

Buckland, S.T., D.R. Anderson, K.P. Burnham, J.L. Laake, D.L. Borchers, and L. Thomas 2001. Introduction to distance sampling: estimating abundance of biological populations. Oxford University Press, Oxford.

Bull, J.W., K.B. Suttle, A. Gordon, N.J. Singh, and E.J. Milner-Gulland. 2013. Biodiversity offsets in theory and practice. Oryx 47:369–380.

Burgin, S. 2008. Biobanking: an environmental scientist's view of the role of biodiversity banking offsets in conservation. Biodiversity and Conservation 17:807–816.

Burkhead, N.M. 2012. Extinction rates in North American freshwater fishes, 1900–2010. BioScience 62:798–808.

Busch, D.E., and J.C. Trexler 2003. Monitoring ecosystems: interdisciplinary approaches for evaluating ecoregional initiatives. Island Press, Washington, DC.

Butler, B. 2008. Family forest owners of the United States, 2006. General technical report NRS-27. US Forest Service Northern Research Station, US Department of Agriculture, Newtown Square, PA.

Cain, Z., and S. Lovejoy. 2004. History and outlook for farm bill conservation programs. Choices 19:37–42.

Cannon, T., and H. Brown. 2008. Fish banking. Pages 159–170 in N. Carroll, J. Fox, and R. Bayon (editors). Conservation and biodiversity banking: a guide to setting up and running biodiversity credit trading systems. Earthscan, London.

Carpenter, S.R., E.H. Stanley, and M.J. Vander Zanden. 2011. State of the world's freshwater ecosystems: physical, chemical, and biological changes. Annual Review of Environment and Resources 36:75–99.

Carroll, N., J. Fox, and R. Bayon, editors. 2008. Conservation and biodiversity banking: A guide to setting up and running biodiversity credit trading systems. Earthscan, London.

Cart, J. 2012. Saving desert tortoises is a costly hurdle for solar projects. March 4. Los Angeles Times, http://articles.latimes.com/2012/mar/04/local/la-me-solar-tortoise-20120304.

CBD (Center for Biological Diversity). 2009. Petition to list 42 species of great basin springsnails from Nevada, Utah, and California as threatened or endangered under the Endangered Species Act. Center for Biological Diversity, http://www.biologicaldiversity.org/species/invertebrates/Great_Basin_spring_snails/pdfs/Great-Basin-Springsnail-Petition.pdf.

Cearly-Sanders, J. 2005. Relationships among landowner and land ownership characteristics and participation in conservation programs in central Texas. Master's thesis, Texas A&M University, College Station.

CEC (California Energy Commission). 2011. Ivanpah Solar Electric Generating System Compliance Submittals. http://www.energy.ca.gov/sitingcases/ivanpah/compliance/submittals/.

Center for Biological Diversity versus US Fish and Wildlife Service. 2002. 202 F.Supp.2d 594. US District Court, Western District of Texas.

Clark County and USFWS (US Fish and Wildlife Service). 2000. Clark County multiple species Habitat Conservation Plan and Environmental Impact Statement for issuance of a permit to allow incidental take of 79 species in Clark County, Nevada. Clark County Department of Comprehensive Planning and US Fish and Wildlife Service, http://www.clarkcountynv.gov/Depts/dcp/Pages/CurrentHCP.aspxw.

Clark, T.W. 1997. Averting extinction: reconstructing endangered species recovery. Yale University Press, New Haven, CT.

Clarke, C. 2012. Brightsource seeks changes in Ivanpah Tortoise Plan. November 29. KCET.org, http://www.kcet.org/news/rewire/solar/concentrating-solar/brightsource-seeks-changes-in-ivanpah-tortoise-plan.html.

COGCC (Colorado Oil and Gas Conservation Commission). 2009. 1200 series rules: protection of wildlife resources. Colorado Oil and Gas Conservation Commission, http://cogcc.state.co.us/rr_docs_new/rules/1200.htm.

Cole, S.G. 2011. Wind power compensation is not for the birds: an opinion from an environmental economist. Restoration Ecology 19: 147–153.

Connelly, J.W., H.W. Browers, and R.J. Gates. 1988. Seasonal movements of Sage Grouse in southeastern Idaho. Journal of Wildlife Management 52:116–122.

Connelly, J.W., S.T. Knick, C.E. Braun, W.L. Baker, E.A. Beever, T.H. Christiansen, K.E. Doherty, E.O. Garton, S.E. Hanser, D.H. Johnson, M. Leu, R.F. Miller, D.E. Naugle, S.J. Oyler-McCance, D.A. Pyke, K.P. Reese, M.A. Schroeder, S.J. Stiver, B.L. Walker, and M.J. Wisdom. 2011a. Conservation of Greater Sage-Grouse. Pages 549–563 in S.T. Knick, and J.W. Connelly (editors). Greater Sage-Grouse: ecology and conservation of a landscape species and its habitats. Studies in avian biology (vol. 38). University of California Press, Berkeley, California.

Connelly, J.W., E.T. Rinkes, and C.E. Braun. 2011b. Characteristics of Greater Sage-Grouse habitats: a landscape species at micro and macro scales. Pages 69–83 in S.T. Knick, and J.W. Connelly (editors). Greater Sage-Grouse: ecology and conservation of a landscape species and its habitats. Studies in Avian Biology (vol. 38). University of California Press, Berkeley.

Conner, R., D.C. Rudolph, and J.R. Walters 2010. The Red-Cockaded Woodpecker: surviving in a fire-maintained ecosystem. University of Texas Press, Austin.

Copeland, H.E., K.E. Doherty, D.E. Naugle, A. Pocewicz, and J.M. Kiesecker. 2009. Mapping oil and gas development potential in the US intermountain West and estimating impacts to species. PLoS ONE 4:e7400.

Copeland, H.E., A. Pocewicz, D.E. Naugle, T. Griffiths, D. Keinath, J. Evans, and J. Platt. 2013. Measuring the effectiveness of conservation: a novel framework to quantify the benefits of Sage-Grouse conservation policy and easements in Wyoming. PLoS ONE 8:e67261.

Dalke, P.D., D.B. Pyrah, D.C. Stanton, J.E. Crawford, and E. Schlatterer. 1963. Ecology, productivity, and management of Sage Grouse in Idaho. Journal of Wildlife Management 27:811–841.

Danelski, D., and B. Goad 2011. White House bashes desert tortoise website. June 15. Press-Enterprise, http://www.pe.com/local-news/local-news-headlines/20110616-white-house-bashes-desert-tortoise-website.ece.

Defenders of Wildlife. 2012. Sagebrush/Sage Grouse habitat metric: calculator and user's guide. Version March 2012. Defenders of Wildlife, http://marketplace.conservationregistry.org/about/habitat_metrics_guides—sage_brush_grouse.

Demirjian, K. 2013. One strange bird could pave way for more fire prevention funds. August 5. Las Vegas Sun, http://www.lasvegassun.com/news/2013/aug/05/one-strange-bird-could-pave-way-more-fire-preventi/.

Diemer, J.E. 1986. The ecology and management of the gopher tortoise in the southeastern United States. Herptologica 42:125–133.

Doak, D.F., K. Gross, and W.F. Morris. 2005. Understanding and predicting the effects of sparse data on demographic analyses. Ecology 86:1154–1163.

DOD (Department of Defense). 2013. Report to congress on sustainable ranges. Undersecretary of Defense Personnel and Readiness, Secretary of Defense, http://www.denix.osd.mil/sri/Policy/Reports.cfm.

DOD (Department of Defense) and EPA (Environmental Protection Agency). 2008. Compensatory mitigation for losses of aquatic resources. Federal Register 70:19593–19705.

DOD (Department of Defense), Environmental Protection Agency, Department of Agriculture, Department of Interior, and Department of Commerce. 1995. Federal guidance for the establishment, use and operation of mitigation banks. Federal Register 60:58605–58614.

Dodd Jr., C.K., and R.A. Seigel. 1991. Relocation, repatriation, and translocation of amphibians and reptiles: are they conservation strategies that work? Herpetologica 47:336–350.

DOE (Department of Energy). 2008. 20 percent wind energy by 2030—increasing wind energy's contribution to US electricity supply. Report DOE/GO-102008–2567. US Department of Energy, Washington, DC.

Doherty, K.E., D.E. Naugle, H.E. Copeland, A. Pocewicz, and J.M. Kiesecker. 2011. Energy development and Greater Sage Grouse. Pages 505–516 in S.T. Knick and J.W. Connelly (editors). Greater Sage-Grouse: ecology and conservation of a landscape species and its habitats. Studies in avian biology (vol. 38). University of California Press, Berkeley.

Doherty K.E., D.E. Naugle, and J.S. Evans. 2010. A currency for offsetting energy development impacts: horse-trading Sage Grouse on the open market. PLoS ONE 5: e10339.

Doherty, K.E., D.E. Naugle, B.L. Walker, and J.M. Graham. 2008. Greater Sage-Grouse winter habitat selection and energy development. Journal of Wildlife Management 72:187–195.

Donlan, C.J., T. Gartner, T. Male, and Y.W. Li. 2013. Species conservation incentives. Environmental Policy and Law 43:162–166.

Doyle, M.W., and T. BenDor. 2011. Evolving law and policy for freshwater ecosystem service markets. William & Mary Environmental Law and Policy Review 36:153–191.

Doyle, M.W., and F. D. Shields. 2012. Compensatory mitigation for streams under the Clean Water Act: reassessing science and redirecting policy. JAWRA: Journal of the American Water Resources Association 48:494–509.

DSE (Department of Sustainability and Environment). 2004. Vegetation quality assessment manual—guidelines for applying the habitat hectares scoring method. Version 1.3. Department of Environmental and Primary Industries, Victorian Government, Melbourne, Australia.

Dunford, R.W., T.C. Ginn, and W.H. Desvousges. 2004. The use of habitat equivalency analysis in natural resource damage assessments. Ecological Economics 48:49–70.

Dyckman, C.S., and K. Paulsen. 2012. Not in my watershed! Will increased federal supervision really bring better coordination between land use and water planning? Journal of Planning Education and Research 32:91–106.

East Contra Costa County. 2006. The final East Contra Costa County Habitat Conservation Plan/ Natural Community Conservation Plan. East Contra Costa County, California, http://www.co.contra-costa.ca.us/depart/cd/water/hcp/documents/HCP_NCCP/ECCC_HCP-NCCP_Informational_Booklet.pdf.

EDF (Environmental Defense Fund). 1999. Mitigation banking as an endangered species conservation tool. Environmental Defense Fund, http://moderncms.ecosystemmarketplace.com/repository/moderncms_documents/146_mb.pdf.

EIA (Energy Information Administration). 2011. International energy outlook 2011. Report number DOE/EIA-04842011. US Energy Information Administration, Washington, DC.

———. 2012. Annual energy outlook 2012 early release overview. Report number DOE/EIA-0383ER2012. US Energy Information Administration, Washington, DC.

———. 2013. State energy profiles, Oregon. US Energy Information Administration, http://tonto.eia.doe.gov/stat/.

Elkington, J. 2010. The transparent economy. Volans Report, London.

Ely, J.W., Jr. 2008. The guardian of every other right: a constitutional history of property rights. Oxford University Press, New York.

Environment Bank. 2012. Environment bank and mission markets launch online conservation credit platform. Press release, http://www.environment-bank.com.

Environment News Service. 2011. Court approves endangered species workplan for nearly 900 species. September 9. http://ens-newswire.com/2011/09/10/court-approves-endangered-species-workplan-for-nearly-900-species/.

Ernst, T., and G.N. Wallace. 2008. Characteristics, motivations, and management actions of landowners engaged in private land conservation in Larimer County, Colorado. Natural Areas Journal 28:109–120.

Esque, T.C., K.E. Nussear, K.K. Drake, A.D. Walde, K.H. Berry, R.C. Averill-Murray, A.P. Woodman, W.I. Boarman, P.A. Medica, and J. Mack. 2010. Effects of subsidized predators, resource variability, and human population density on desert tortoise populations in the Mojave Desert, USA. Endangered Species Research 12:167–177.

FAO (Food and Agriculture Organization). 2009. How to feed the world in 2050. Food and Agriculture Organization of the United Nations, Rome.

Farm Bureau News. 2013. Western states work on Sage Grouse conservation plans. Farm Bureau News, http://fbnews.fb.org/Templates/Article.aspx?id = 37264–sthash.VCxuqvKj.dpuf.

Ferraro, P.J., and S.H. Pattanayak. 2006. Money for nothing? A call for empirical evaluation of biodiversity conservation investments. PLoS Biology 4:e105.

Field, K.J., C.R. Tracy, P.A. Medica, R.W. Marlow, and P.S. Corn. 2007. Return to the wild: translocation as a tool in conservation of the desert tortoise (*Gopherus agassizii*). Biological Conservation 136:232–245.

Finch, B., B. Maynor Young, R. Johnson, and J.C. Hall. 2012. Longleaf, far as the eye can see: a new vision of North America's richest forest. University of North Carolina Press, Chapel Hill.

Fox, J., and A. Nino-Murcia. 2005. Status of species conservation banking in the United States. Conservation Biology 19:96–1007.

Farmer, J.R., D. Knapp, V.J. Dmeretsky, C. Chancellor, and B.C. Fischer. 2011. Motivations influencing the adoption of conservation easements. Conservation Biology 25:827–834.

Freilich, J.E., R.J. Camp, J.J. Duda, and A.E. Karl. 2005. Problems with sampling desert tortoises: a simulation analysis based on field data. Journal of Wildlife Management 69:45–56.

GAO (General Accountability Office). 2002. Endangered species: research strategy and long-term monitoring needed for the Mojave Desert tortoise recovery program. GAO-03–23. US General Accountability Office, Washington, DC.

———. 2005. Endangered species. Fish and Wildlife Service generally focuses recovery funding on high-priority species, but needs to periodically assess its funding decisions. US Government Accountability Office, Washington, DC.

Gardner, R. 2011. Lawyers, swamps, and money: U.S. wetland law, policy, and politics. Island Press, Washington, DC.

Gartner, T., and C.J. Donlan. 2011. Insights from the field: forests for biodiversity. World Resources Institute, http://www.wri.org/publication/insights-field-forests-species-and-habitat.

Georgia Department of Natural Resources. 2005. Georgia Wildlife Action Plan. Georgia Wildlife Resources Division, http://www.georgiawildlife.com/conservation/wildlife-action-plan.

GfK. 2009. Report on working forest conservation easement focus groups. GfK Roper, Nuernberg, Germany.

Gibbons, P., and D. Freudenberger. 2006. An overview of methods used to assess vegetation condition at the scale of the site. Ecological Management & Restoration 7:S10–S17.

Gibbs, J., and W. Shriver. 2002. Estimating the effects of road mortality on turtle populations. Conservation Biology 16:1647–1652.

Gilliland, C., and M. Mays. 2003. Endangered Species Act: a landowner's guide. Texas A&M University Technical Report. Texas A&M University, http://recenter.tamu.edu/pdf/1648.pdf

Goble, D.D., J.A. Wiens, J.M. Scott, T.D. Male, and J.A. Hall. 2012. Conservation-reliant species. BioScience 62:869–873.

Gorte, R.W., C.H. Vincenty, L.A. Hanson, and M.R. Rosenblum. 2012. Federal land ownership: overview and data. Congressional Research Service, Washington, DC.

Gosnell, H., and J. Abrams. 2009. Amenity migration: diverse conceptualizations of drivers, socioeconomic dimensions, and emerging challenges. GeoJournal 76:303–332.

Government of the United Kingdom. 2011. The natural choice: securing the value of nature. Presented to Parliament by the Secretary of State for Environment, Food and Rural Affairs by Command of Her Majesty, http://www.official-documents.gov.uk/document/cm80/8082/8082.pdf.

Grabowski, T.B., and J.J. Isely. 2006. Seasonal and diel movements and habitat use of robust redhorses in the lower Savannah River, Georgia and South Carolina. Transactions of the American Fisheries Society 135:1145–1155.

Grabowski, T.B., and C.A. Jennings. 2009. Post-release movements and habitat use of robust redhorse transplanted to the Ocmulgee River, Georgia. Aquatic Conservation: Marine and Freshwater Ecosystems 19:170–177.

Groves, C., L.S. Kutner, D.M. Stoms, M.P. Murray, J.M. Scott, M. Schafale, A.S. Weakley, and R.L. Pressey. 2000. Owning up to our responsibilities: who owns lands important for biodiversity? Pages 275–300 in B.A. Stein, L.S. Kutner, and J.S. Adams (editors). Precious heritage: the status of biodiversity in the United States. Oxford University Press, New York.

Hagen, C.A. 2011a. Greater Sage-Grouse conservation assessment and strategy for Oregon: a plan to maintain and enhance populations and habitat. Oregon Department of Fish and Wildlife, Salem.

———. 2011b. Implementing habitat mitigation for Greater Sage-Grouse under the core area approach. Oregon Department of Fish and Wildlife, Salem, Oregon

Harris, J.B.C., J.L. Reid, B.R. Scheffers, T.C. Wanger, N.S. Sodhi, D.A. Fordham, and B.W. Brook. 2011. Conserving imperiled species: a comparison of the IUCN Red List and U.S. Endangered Species Act. Conservation Letters 5: 64–72.

Harrison III, J.R., and S.I. Guttman. 2003. A new species of *Eurycea* (Caudata: Plethodontidae) from North and South Carolina. Southeastern Naturalist 2:159–178.

Harwell, M.A., V. Myers, T. Young, A. Bartuska, N. Gassman, J.H. Gentile, C.C. Harwell, S. Appelbaum, J. Barko, B. Causey, C. Johnson, A. McLean,

R. Smola, P. Templet, and S. Tosini. 1999. A framework for an ecosystem integrity report card. BioScience 49:453–556.

Hastings, D. 2012. Millions of taxpayer dollars spent on Endangered Species Act litigation and attorney fees. June 19, US Committee on Natural Resources, http://naturalresources.house.gov/news/documentsingle.aspx?DocumentID=299899.

Hawkins, C.P., J.R. Olson, and R.A. Hill. 2010. The reference condition: predicting benchmarks for ecological and water-quality assessments. Journal of the North American Benthological Society 29:312–343.

Heaton, J., K. Nussear, T. Esque, R. Inman, F. Davenport, T. Leuteritz, P. Medica, N. Strout, P. Burgess, and L. Benvenuti. 2008. Spatially explicit decision support for selecting translocation areas for Mojave Desert tortoises. Biodiversity and Conservation 17:575–590.

Heimdal, C., E. Dimantchev, H. Chai, E. Mazzacurati, A. Nordeng, I. Sørhus, N. Yakymenko, and E. Zelljadt. 2012. Carbon 2012. Thomas Reuters Point Carbon Report, Oslo.

Henifin, K. 2013. National Conservation Easement Database (NCED), Phase III July 2013. Data basin, http://databasin.org/articles/57bfc8a46f714bbd826e862cf7f4f67f.

Herbert, M.E., P.B. McIntyre, P.J. Doran, J.D. Allan, and R. Abell. 2010. Terrestrial reserve networks do not adequately represent aquatic ecosystems. Conservation Biology 24:1002–1011.

Hershler, R. 1998. A systematic review of the hydrobiid snails (Gastropoda: Rissooidea) of the Great Basin, western United States. Part 1. Genus *Pyrgulopsis*. The Veliger 41:1–132.

Hill, T., E. Kulz, B. Munoz, and J. Dorney. 2010. Compensatory stream and wetland mitigation in North Carolina: An evaluation of regulatory success. North Carolina Department of Environment and Natural Resources, Raleigh.

Hoctor, T., and S. Beyeler. 2010. Regional gopher tortoise potential habitat model report. Final report to US Fish and Wildlife Service. University of Florida, http://share3.myfwc.com/GTCCA/Shared Documents/GT Regional Habitat Mapping/Regional Gopher Tortoise Potential Habitat Model Report.pdf.

Holloran, M.J., R.C. Kaiser, and W.A. Hubert. 2009. Yearling Greater Sage-Grouse response to energy development in Wyoming. Journal of Wildlife Management 74:65–72.

Hough, P., and M. Robertson. 2009. Mitigation under section 404 of the Clean Water Act: where it comes from, what it means. Wetlands Ecology and Management 17:15–33.

Huwlyer, F., J. Kappeli, K. Serafimova, E. Swanson, and J. Tobin. 2014. Conservation finance: moving beyond donor funding toward an investor-driven approach. WWF, Credit Suisse Group, and McKinsey & Company, Zurich.

IDEO. 2011. Human centered design toolkit. IDEO, http://www.ideo.com/by-ideo/human-centered-design-toolkit.

Inman, R.D., K.E. Nussear, and C.R. Tracy. 2009. Detecting trends in desert tortoise population growth: elusive behavior inflates variance in estimates of population density. Endangered Species Research 10:295–304.

Jack, B.K., C. Kousky, and K.R.E. Sims. 2008. Designing payments for ecosystem services: lessons from previous experience with incentive-based mechanisms. Proceedings of the National Academy of Sciences 105:9465–9470.

Jackson, D.R., and E.R. Milstrey. 1989. The fauna of gopher tortoise burrows. Pages 86–98 in J.E. Dimer, D.R. Jackson, J.L. Landers, J.N. Layne, and D.A. Wood (editors). Proceedings of the gopher tortoise relocation symposium. Florida Game and Fresh Water Commission, Tallahassee.

Jacobson, M.Z., and M.A. Delucchi. 2011. Providing all global energy with wind, water, and solar power, part I: technologies, energy resources, quantities and areas of infrastructure, and materials. Energy Policy 39:1154–1169.

Jenkins, M., S. Scherr, and M. Inbar. 2009. Markets for biodiversity services: potential roles and challenges. Environment 46:32–42.

Johnson, D.J., M.J. Holloran, J.W. Connelly, S.E. Hanser, C.L. Amundson, and S.T. Knick. 2011. Influences of environmental and anthropogenic features on Greater Sage-Grouse populations, 1997–2007. Pages 407–450 in S.T. Knick, and J.W. Connelly (editors). Greater Sage-Grouse: ecology and conservation of a landscape species and its habitats. Studies in Avian Biology (vol. 38). University of California Press, Berkeley.

Joseph, L.N., R.F. Maloney, and H.P. Possingham. 2009. Optimal allocation of resources among threatened species: a project prioritization protocol. Conservation Biology 23:328–338.

Kaczor, S.A., and D.C. Hartnett. 1990. Gopher tortoise (*Gopherus polyphemus*) effects on soils and vegetation in a Florida USA sandhill community. American Midland Naturalist 123:100–111.

Karipidis, P., and E. Sartzetakis. 2013. Firm's decisions based on consumers' choices in ecocertified food markets. Economics Research International 2013:1–10.

Kellert, S.R. 1994. A sociological perspective: valuational, socioeconomic, and organizational factors. Pages 371–389 in T.W. Clark, R.P. Reading, and A.L. Clarke (editors). Endangered species recovery: finding the lessons, improving the process. Island Press, Washington, DC.

Kiesecker, J.M., H.E. Copeland, B.A. McKenney, A. Pocewicz, and K.E. Doherty. 2011. Energy by design: making mitigation work for conservation and development. Pages 159–181 in D.E. Naugle (editor). Energy development and wildlife conservation in western North America. Island Press, Washington, DC.

Knick, S.T. 2011. Historical development, principal federal legislation, and current management of sagebrush habitats: implications for conservation. Pages 13–31 in S.T. Knick and J.W. Connelly (editors). Greater Sage-Grouse: ecology and conservation of a landscape species and its habitats. Studies in Avian Biology (vol. 38). University of California Press, Berkeley.

Knick, S.T., and J.W. Connelly. 2011. Greater Sage-Grouse and sagebrush: an introduction to the landscape. Pages 1–9 in S.T. Knick and J.W. Connelly (editors). Greater Sage-Grouse: ecology and conservation of a landscape species and its habitats. Studies in Avian Biology (vol. 38). University of California Press, Berkeley.

Knick, S.T., D.S. Dobkin, J.T. Rotenberry, M.A. Schroeder, W.M. Vander Haegen, and C. van Riper. 2003. Teetering on the edge or too late? Conservation and research issues for avifauna of sagebrush habitats. Condor 105: 611–634.

Knick, S.T., S.E. Hanser, R.F. Miller, D.A. Pyke, M.J. Wisdom, S.P. Finn, E.T. Rinkes, and C.J. Henry. 2011. Ecological influence and pathways of land use in sagebrush. Pages 203–251 in S.T. Knick and J.W. Connelly (editors). Greater Sage-Grouse: ecology and conservation of a landscape species and its habitats. Studies in Avian Biology (vol. 38). University of California Press, Berkeley.

Knick, S.T., and S.E. Hasner. 2011. Connecting pattern and process in Greater Sage-Grouse populations and sagebrush landscapes. Pages 383–405 in S.T. Knick and J.W. Connelly (editors). Greater Sage-Grouse: ecology and conservation of a landscape species and its habitats. Studies in Avian Biology (vol. 38). University of California Press, Berkeley.

Knick, S.T., S.E. Hanser, and K.L. Preston. 2013. Modeling ecological minimum requirements for distribution of Greater Sage-Grouse leks: implications for population connectivity across their western range, USA. Ecology and Evolution 3:1539–1551.

Knight, R.L., and C. White, editors. 2009. Conservation for a new generation. Island Press, Washington, DC.

Knobloch, F., and R.M. Cawley. 2005. Endangered species protection and ways of life: beyond economy and ecology. Pages 131–146 in J.F. Shogren (editor). Species at risk: using economic incentives to shelter endangered species on private lands. University of Texas Press, Austin.

Kofinas, G.P., and F.S.I. Chapin. 2009. Sustaining livelihoods and human well-being during social-ecological change. Pages 55–75 in F.S.I. Chapin, G.P. Kofinas, and C. Folke (editors). Principles of ecosystem stewardship. Springer, New York.

Konrad, C.P., J.D. Olden, D.A. Lytle, T.S. Melis, J.C. Schmidt, E.N. Bray, M.C. Freeman, K.B. Gido, N.P. Hemphill, M.J. Kennard, L.E. McMullen, M.C. Mims, M. Pyron, C.T. Robinson, and J.G. Williams. 2011. Large-scale flow experiments for managing river systems. BioScience 61:948–959.

Koontz, T.M. 2001. Money talks? But to whom? Financial versus nonmonetary motivations in land use decisions. Society & Natural Resources 14:51–65.

Kreuter, U.P., M.V. Nair, D. Jackson-Smith, J.R. Conner, and J.E. Johnston. 2006. Property rights orientations and rangeland management objectives: Texas, Utah, and Colorado. Rangeland Ecology & Management 59:632–639.

Kuby, M.J., W.F. Fagan, C.S. ReVelle, and W.L. Graf. 2005. A multi-objective optimization model for dam removal: an example trading off salmon passage with hydropower and water storage in the Willamette basin. Advances in Water Resources 28:845–855.

Langpap, C. 2004. Conservation incentives programs for endangered species: an analysis of landowner participation. Land Economics 80:375–388.

———. 2006. Conservation of endangered species: can incentives work for private landowners? Ecological Economics 57:558–572.

Langpap, C., and J. Kerkvliet. 2010. Allocating conservation resources under the Endangered Species Act. American Journal of Agricultural Economics 92:110–124.

Lave, R., M. M. Robertson, and M. W. Doyle. 2008. Why you should pay attention to stream mitigation banking. Ecological Restoration 26:287–289.

Lawrence, D. J., E. R. Larson, C. A. R. Liermann, M. C. Mims, T. K. Pool, and J. D. Olden. 2011. National parks as protected areas for US freshwater fish diversity. Conservation Letters 4:364–371.

Legg, C. J., and L. Nagy. 2006. Why most conservation monitoring is, but need not be, a waste of time. Journal of Environmental Management 78:194–199.

Leonard, K. M., K. P. Reese, and J. W. Connelly. 2000. Distribution, movements and habitats of Sage Grouse *Centrocercus urophasianus* on the upper Snake River plain of Idaho: changes from the 1950s to the 1990s. Wildlife Biology 6:265–270.

Lindemayer, D. B. 1999. Future directions for biodiversity conservation in managed forests: indicator species, impact studies and monitoring programs. Forest Ecology and Management 115:277–287.

Loomis, B. 2012. Sage Grouse is becoming Utah's Spotted Owl. April 30, Salt Lake Tribune, http://www.sltrib.com/sltrib/politics/53969425–90/grouse-sage-wyoming-utah.html.csp.

Loureiro, M. L., and W. J. Umberger. 2003. Estimating consumer willingness to pay for country-of-origin labeling. Journal of Agricultural and Resource Economics 28:287–301.

Lovich, J. E., and J. R. Ennen. 2011. Wildlife conservation and solar energy development in the desert Southwest, United States. Bioscience 61:982–992.

———. 2013. A quantitative analysis of the state of knowledge of turtles of the United States and Canada. Amphibia-Reptilia 34:11–23.

Lowe, W. H., G. E. Likens, and M. E. Power. 2006. Linking scales in stream ecology. BioScience 56:591–597.

Lubowski, R. N., M. Vesterby, S. Bucholtz, A. Baez, and M. J. Roberts. 2006. Major uses of land in the United States, 2002. Economic Information Bulletin 14, US Department of Agriculture, Washington, DC.

Lueck, D., and J. A. Michael. 2003. Preemptive habitat destruction under the Endangered Species Act. Journal of Law and Economics 46:27–60.

Madsen, B., N. Carroll, D. Kandy, and G. Bennett 2011. 2011 update: state of biodiversity markets. Forest Trends, http://www.ecosystemmarketplace.com.

Madsen, B., N. Carroll, and K. Moore Brands 2010. State of biodiversity markets report: offset and compensation programs worldwide. Forest Trends, http://www.ecosystemmarketplace.com.

Male, T. D. 2014a. A green olive branch on endangered species. June 16, Wall Street Journal, http://online.wsj.com/news/articles/SB10001424052702303933104579302941981656818.

———. 2014b. U.S. is overspending to save salmon. March 17, Seattle Times, http://seattletimes.com/html/opinion/2023155976_timothymaleopedendangeredspecies18xml.html.

Male, T. D., and M. J. Bean. 2005. Measuring progress in US endangered species conservation. Ecology Letters 8:986–992.

Mann, R., and J. Goldman-Carter. 2008. Avoidance: still the best solution to the compensatory mitigation challenge. National Wetlands Newsletter 30:8–10.

Marsh, L. L., D. R. Porter, and D. A. Salvesen, editors. 1996. Mitigation banking: theory and practice. Island Press, Washington, DC.

McCoy, E. D., H. R. Mushinsky, and J. Lindzey. 2006. Declines of the gopher tortoise on protected lands. Biological Conservation 128:120–127.

McDonald-Madden, E., P. W. J. Baxter, R. A. Fuller, T. G. Martin, E. T. Game, J. Montambault, and H. P. Possingham. 2010. Monitoring does not always count. Trends in Ecology & Evolution 25:547–550.

Mead, D. L. 2008. History and theory: the origin and evolution of conservation banking. Pages 9–31 in N. Carroll, J. Fox, and R. Bayon (editors). Conservation and biodiversity banking: a guide to setting up and running biodiversity credit trading systems. Earthscan, London.

Mehmood, S. R., and D. Zhang. 2005. Determinants of forest landowner participation in the Endangered Species Act Safe Harbor Program. Human Dimensions of Wildlife 10:249—257.

Mellette Forestry Group. 2011. Forest management plan for the Blackjack Crossing tract. Nature Conservancy, Columbus, Georgia.

MFWP (Montana Fish, Wildlife and Parks). 2010. 2010 annual report—Candidate Conservation Agreement with Assurances for fluvial arctic grayling in the upper Big Hole River. Montana Fish, Wildlife and Parks, Helena, Montana.

MFWP (Montana Fish, Wildlife and Parks) and USFWS (US Fish and Wildlife Service). 2005. Candidate Conservation Agreement with Assurances for fluvial arctic grayling in the upper big hole river: between Montana Department of Fish, Wildlife and Parks and US Fish and Wildlife Service in cooperation with Montana Department of Natural Resources and Conservation and USDA Natural Resources Conservation Service. Montana Fish, Wildlife, and Parks, Helena, Montana.

Miller, R. F., S. T. Knick, D. A. Pyke, C. W. Meinke, S. E. Hanser, M. J. Wisdom, and A. L. Hild. 2011. Characteristics of sagebrush habitats and limitations to long-term conservation. Pages 145–184 in S. T. Knick and J. W. Connelly (editors). Greater Sage-Grouse: Ecology and conservation of a landscape species and its habitats. Studies in Avian Biology (vol. 38). University of California Press, Berkeley.

Milne, S., and E. Niestan. 2009. Direct payments for biodiversity for conservation in developing countries: practical insights for design and implementation. Oryx 43:530–541.

Moilanen, A., A. J. A. Van Teeffelen, Y. Ben-Haim, and S. Ferrier. 2009. How much compensation is enough? A framework for incorporating uncertainty and time discounting when calculating offset ratios for impacted habitat. Restoration Ecology 17:470–478.

Morris, W. F., and D. F. Doak 2002. Quantitative conservation biology. Theory and practice of population viability analysis. Sinauer, Sunderland, MA.

Murchison, K. M. 2007. The snail darter case: TVA versus the Endangered Species Act. University Press of Kansas, Lawrence.

Murphy, J., J. Goldman-Carter, and J. Sibbing. 2009. Avoidance avoided: how the new rule fails to adequately promote avoidance and places difficult-to-replace systems at risk. National Wetlands Newsletter 31:14.

Mushinsky, H.R., E.D. McCoy, J.D. Berish, R.E. Ashton, and D.S. Wilson. 2006. *Gopherus polyphemus*—gopher tortoise. Pages 350–375 in P.A. Meylan (editor). Biology and conservation of Florida turtles. Chelonian Research Monographs 3. Chelonian Research Foundation, Lunenberg, MA.

NAS (National Academy of Sciences). 2008. Environmental impacts of wind-energy projects. National Academy of Sciences, Washington, DC.

Naugle, D.E., K.E. Doherty, B.L. Walker, J. Holloran, and H.E. Copeland. 2011. Energy development and Greater Sage-Grouse. Pages 489–503 in S.T. Knick and J.W. Connelly (editors). Greater Sage-Grouse: ecology and conservation of a landscape species and its habitats. Studies in Avian Biology (vol. 38). University of California Press, Berkeley.

NDOW (Nevada Department of Wildlife). 2013. Greater Sage-Grouse habitat categorization: revised white paper. Nevada Department of Wildlife, Reno.

Nichols, M. 2003. Conservation strategy for the robust redhorse (*Moxostoma robustum*). Robust Redhorse Conservation Committee, http://www.robustredhorse.com/f/ConservStrategyMay62003.pdf.

Nicholson, J. 2013. ND working to import Sage Grouse from Montana. July 20. Bismarck Tribune. http://bismarcktribune.com/bakken/nd-working-to-import-sage-grouse-from-montana/article_adf0b268-f107–11e2-bae4–001a4bcf887a.html.

Nidumolu, R., C.K. Prahalad, and M.R. Rangaswami. 2009. Why sustainability is now the key driver of innovation. Harvard Business Review September:1–10.

Norris, S. 2004. Only 30: a portrait of the Endangered Species Act as a young law. Bioscience 54:288–294.

Norton, D.A. 2000. Conservation biology and private land: shifting the focus. Conservation Biology 14:1221–1223.

NRC (National Research Council). 2001. Compensating for wetland losses under the Clean Water Act. National Academy Press, Washington, DC.

Nussear, K.E., T.C. Esque, R.D. Inman, L. Gass, K.A. Thomas, C.S.A. Wallace, J.B. Blainey, D.M. Miller, and R.H. Webb. 2009. Modeling habitat of the desert tortoise (*Gopherus agassizii*) in the Mojave and parts of the Sonoran Deserts of California, Nevada, Utah, and Arizona. US Geological Survey Open-File Report 1102:1–18.

Nussear, K.E., C.R. Tracy, P.A. Medica, D.S. Wilson, R.W. Marlow, and P.S. Corn. 2012. Translocation as a conservation tool for Agassiz's desert tortoises: survivorship, reproduction, and movements. Journal of Wildlife Management 76:1341–1353.

Oregon Biodiversity Project. 1998. Oregon's living landscape: strategies and opportunities to conserve biodiversity. Oregon State University Press, Corvallis.

Page, R.W., and L.S. Wilcher. 1990. Memorandum of agreement between the Environmental Protection Agency and the Department of the Army concerning the determination of mitigation under the Clean Water Act Section 404(b)(1) guidelines. US Environmental Protection Agency, http://water.epa.gov/lawsregs/guidance/wetlands/mitigate.cfm.

Palmer, M.A., E.S. Bernhardt, J.D. Allan, P.S. Lake, G. Alexander, S. Brooks, J. Carr, S. Clayton, C.N. Dahm, J. Follstad Shah, D.L. Galat, S.G. Loss, P.

Goodwin, D.D. Hart, B. Hassett, R. Jenkinson, G.M. Kondolf, R. Lave, J.L. Meyer, T.K. O'Donnell, L. Pagano, and E. Sudduth. 2005. Standards for ecologically successful river restoration. Journal of Applied Ecology 42: 208–217.

Parkes, D., G. Newell, and D. Cheal. 2003. Assessing the quality of native vegetation: the habitat hectares approach. Ecological Management & Restoration 4:29–38.

Pascoe, S., C. Wilcox, and C.J. Donlan. 2011. Biodiversity offsets: a cost-effective interim solution to bycatch in fisheries. PLoS One 6:e25762.

Pennsylvania Infrastructure Investment Authority. 2013. Pennvest. State of Pennsylvania, http://www.pennvest.state.pa.us/portal/server.pt/community/nutrient_credit_trading/19518.

Peters-Stanley, P., K. Hamilton, T. Marcello, and M. Sjardin. 2011. Back to the future: state of the voluntary carbon markets 2011. Bloomberg New Energy Finance and Ecosystem Marketplace, Washington, DC.

Peterson, M.N., T.R. Peterson, M.J. Peterson, R.R. Lopez, and N.J. Silvy. 2002. Cultural conflict and the endangered Florida key deer. Wildlife Management 66:921–942.

Peterson, T.R., and C.C. Horton. 1995. Rooted in the soil: how understanding the perspectives of landowners can enhance the management of environmental disputes. Quarterly Journal of Speech 81:139–166.

Poff, N.L., B.D. Richter, A.H. Arthington, S.E. Bunn, R.J. Naiman, E. Kendy, M. Acreman, C. Apse, B.P. Bledsoe, M.C. Freeman, J. Henriksen, R.B. Jacobson, J.G. Kennen, D.M. Merritt, J.H. O'Keeffe, J.D. Olden, K. Rogers, R.E. Tharme, and A. Warner. 2010. The ecological limits of hydrologic alteration (ELOHA): a new framework for developing regional environmental flow standards. Freshwater Biology 55:147–170.

Ravenscroft, C., R.M. Scheller, D.J. Mladenoff, and M.A. White. 2010. Forest restoration in a mixed-ownership landscape under climate change. Ecological Applications 20:327–346.

Raymond, L. 2010. Beyond additionality in cap-and-trade offset policy. Governance Studies July:1–9.

Raymond, L., and A. Olive. 2008. Landowner beliefs regarding biodiversity protection on private property: an Indiana case study. Society & Natural Resources 21:483–497.

RECON Environmental. 1995. Clark County desert conservation plan: Final draft. RECON Regional Environmental Consultants, http://www.clarkcountynv.gov/Depts/dcp/Documents/Library/Guiding Docs/previous/2971_DesertConservationPlanAugust_1995.pdf.

Reed, J.M., N. Fefferman, and R.C. Averill-Murray. 2009. Vital rate sensitivity analysis as a tool for assessing management actions for the desert tortoise. Biological Conservation 142:2710–2717.

Regional Working Group for America's Longleaf. 2009. Range-wide conservation plan for longleaf pine. Regional Working Group for America's Longleaf. http://www.sref.info/resources/publications/range-wide-conservation-plan-for-longleaf-pine/?searchterm=br.

Ribaudo, M., L. Hansen, D. Hellerstein, and C. Greene. 2008. The use of markets to increase private investment in environmental stewardship. Economic Research Service, Washington, DC.

Ricciardi, A., and J.B. Rasmussen. 1999. Extinction rates of North American freshwater fauna. Conservation Biology 13:1220–1222.

Richter, B.D., D.P. Braun, M.A. Mendelson, and L.L. Master. 1997. Threats to imperiled freshwater fauna. Conservation Biology 11:1081–1093.

Richter, B.D., M.M. Davis, C. Apse, and C. Konrad. 2012. A presumptive standard for environmental flow protection. River Research and Applications 28:1312–1321.

Richter, B.D., and G.A. Thomas. 2007. Restoring environmental flows by modifying dam operations. Ecology and Society 12:12.

Rissman, A.R., L. Lozier, T. Comendant, P. Kareiva, J.M. Kiesecker, M.R. Shaw, and A.M. Merenlender. 2007. Conservation easements: biodiversity protection and private use. Conservation Biology 21:709–718.

Riverside County. 2004. Western Riverside County multiple species Habitat Conservation Plan: Nexus report. Riverside County, California, http://www.rctlma.org/mshcp/nexusreport/nexus.html.

Robertson, M.M. 2006. Emerging ecosystem service markets: trends in a decade of entrepreneurial wetland banking. Frontiers in Ecology and the Environment 4:297–302

Robertson, M., and M. Mikota. 2007. Water quality trading and wetland mitigation banking: different problems, different paths? National Wetlands Newsletter 29:1.

Robertson, S., and H.B. Rinker 2010. Third party evaluation of the recovery credit system proof of concept. Robertson Consulting Group Inc., http://rcs.tamu.edu/media/277203/final_rcs_eval_report_march_2010.pdf.

Robles, M.D., C.H. Flather, S.M. Stein, M.D. Nelson, and A. Cutko. 2008. The geography of private forests that support at-risk species in the conterminous United States. Frontiers in Ecology and the Environment 6:301–307.

Roheim, C.A., F. Asche, and J.I. Santos. 2011. The elusive price premium for ecolabelled products: evidence from seafood in the UK market. Journal of Agricultural Economics 62:655–668.

RRCC (Robust Redhorse Conservation Committee). 2011. Report of the Robust Redhorse Conservation Committee annual meeting. Morrow Mountain State Park, Albemarle, North Carolina. October 3–5, 2011. Robust Redhorse Conservation Committee, http://www.robustredhorse.com/f/2011 RRCC Annual Meeting Report.pdf.

Ruhl, J.B., A. Glen, and D. Hartman. 2005. A practical guide to habitat conservation banking law and policy Natural Resources and the Environment 20:26–32.

Ruhl, J.B., S.E. Kraft, and C. L. Lant. 2007. The law and policy of ecosystem services. Island Press, Washington, DC.

Salzman, J., and J.B. Ruhl. 2000. Currencies and the commodification of environmental law. Stanford Law Review 53:607–694.

Schamberger, M.L., and L.J. O'Neil. 1986. Concepts and constraints of habitat-model testing. Pages 177–182 in J. Verner, M.L. Morrison, and C.J. Ralph (editors). Wildlife 2000. University of Wisconsin Press, Madison.

Scheerer, P.D., and T.A. O'Neill. 2010. A species crediting methodology that supports conservation banking for an endangered floodplain minnow. Fisheries 35:280–291.

Schenk, A., M. Hunziker, and F. Kienast. 2007. Factors influencing the acceptance of nature conservation measures-a qualitative study in Switzerland. Journal of Environmental Management 83:66–79.

Schroeder, M.A., C.L. Aldridge, A.D. Apa, J.R. Bohne, C.E. Braun, S.D. Bunnell, J.W. Connelly, P.A. Deibert, S.C. Gardner, M.A. Hilliard, G.D. Kobriger, S.M. McAdam, C.W. McCarthy, J.J. McCarthy, D.L. Mitchell, E.V. Rickerson, and S.J. Stiver. 2004. Distribution of Sage-Grouse in North America. The Condor 106:363–376.

Schroeder, M.A., J.R. Young, and C.E. Braun. 1999. Sage Grouse (*Centrocercus urophasianus*). Pages 1–25 in A. Poole, and F. Gill (editors). The birds of North America. The Birds of North America, Inc., Philadelphia, PA.

Schwartz, M.W. 1999. Choosing the appropriate scale of reserves for conservation. Annual Review of Ecology and Systematics 30:83–108.

———. 2008. The performance of the Endangered Species Act. Annual Review of Ecology, Evolution, and Systematics 39:279–299.

Scott, J.M., D.D. Goble, F.W. Davis. 2006. The Endangered Species Act at thirty Volume 2: Ccnserving biodiversity in human-dominated landscapes. Island Press, Washington, DC.

Scott, J.M., D.D. Goble, A.M. Haines, J.A. Wiens, and M.C. Neel. 2010. Conservation-reliant species and the future of conservation. Conservation Letters 3:91–97.

Scott, J.M., D.D. Goble, J.A. Wiens, D.S. Wilcove, M. Bean, and T. Male. 2005. Recovery of imperiled species under the Endangered Species Act: the need for a new approach. Frontiers in Ecology and the Environment 3:383–389.

SEIA (Solar Energy Industries Association). 2012a. Report: US solar installations continue to surge in Q1 2012, but domestic manufacturing woes continue. Solar Energy Industries Association, http://www.seia.org/news/report-us-solar-installations-continue-surge-q1–2012-domestic-manufacturing-woes-continue.

———. 2012b. Utility-scale solar projects in the United States operating, under construction, or under development. Solar Energy Industries Association, http://www.seia.org/research-resources/major-solar-projects-list.

Sempra. 2012. Auwahi wind project summary. Sempra, San Diego, California, http://www.semprausgp.com/energy-solutions/wind-auwahi-wind.html.

SGI (Sage Grouse Initiative). 2013. Tracking success. Sage Grouse Initiative, http://static.sagegrouseinitiative.com/sites/default/files/sgi-tracking_success-final_low_res-020613.pdf.

Sheridan, T.E. 2007. Embattled ranchers, endangered species, and urban sprawl: the political ecology of the new American west. Annual Review of Anthropology 36:121–138.

Shogren, J.F., editor. 2005. Species at risk: using economic incentives to shelter endangered species on private lands. University of Texas Press, Austin.

Smith, L.L., J.M. Linehan, J.M. Stober, M.J. Elliot, and J.B. Jensen. 2009a. An evaluation of distance sampling for large-scale gopher tortoises in Georgia, USA. Applied Herpetology 6:355–368.

Smith, L.L., J.M. Stober, H.E. Balbach, and W.D. Meyer 2009b. Gopher tortoise survey handbook ERDC/CERL TR-09–7. US Army Corps of Engineers, http://www.dtic.mil/cgi-bin/GetTRDoc?AD = ADA522655.

Sorice, M., C. Oh, T. Gartner, M. Sniekus, R. Johnson, and C.J. Donlan. 2013. Increasing participation in incentive programs for biodiversity conservation. Ecological Applications 12:1146–1155.

Sorice, M.G. 2012. Retooling the traditional approach to studying the belief–attitude relationship: Explaining landowner buy-in to incentive programs. Society & Natural Resources 25:499–512.

Sorice, M.G., and J.R. Conner. 2010. Predicting private landowner intentions to enroll in an incentive program to protect endangered species. Human Dimensions of Wildlife 15:77–89.

Sorice, M.G., J.R. Conner, U.P. Kreuter, and R.N. Wilkins. 2012. Centrality of ranching lifestyle and attitudes toward a voluntary incentive program to protect endangered species. Rangeland Ecology and Management 65:144–152.

Sorice, M.G., W. Haider, J.R. Conner, and R.B. Ditton. 2011. Incentive structure of and private landowner participation in an endangered species conservation program. Conservation Biology 25:587–596.

Sprankling, J.G. 1996. The antiwilderness bias in American property law. University of Chicago Law Review 63:519–590.

State of Nevada. 2010. Nevada energy and infrastructure development standards to conserve Greater Sage Grouse populations and their habitats. Nevada Governor's Sage-Grouse Conservation Team, Reno, Nevada.

State of Oregon. 2012a. 10-year energy action plan. State of Oregon, http://www.oregon.gov/energy/Ten_Year/Ten_Year_Energy_Action_Plan_Final.pdf.

———. 2012b. 10-year plan for Oregon project: healthy environment policy vision. State of Oregon, http://www.oregon.gov/COO/TEN/docs/Environment.pdf?ga = t.

———. 2013. State of Oregon 2013–2015 biennial energy plan. Oregon Department of Energy, Salem, Oregon.

State of Wyoming. 2011. Executive order 2011–5: Greater Sage Grouse core area protection. http://will.state.wy.us/sis/wydocs/execorders.html.

Stein, B.A., C. Scott, and N. Benton. 2008. Federal lands and endangered species: The role of military and other federal lands in sustaining biodiversity. BioScience 58:339–347.

Stein, S.M., M.A. Carr, R.E. McRoberts, L.G. Mahal, and S.J. Comas. 2010. Threats to at-risk species in America's private forests: a forests on the edge report. General Technical Report NRS-73. US Department of Agriculture, Forest Service, Northern Research Station, Newtown Square, Pennsylvania.

Stein, S.M., R.E. McRoberts, L.G. Mahal, M.A. Carr, R.J. Alig, S.J. Comas, D.M. Theobald, and A. Cundiff. 2009. Private forests, public benefits:

increased housing density and other pressures on private forest contributions. General Technical Report PNW-GTR-795. US Department of Agriculture, US Forest Service Pacific Northwest Research Station, Portland, Oregon.

Stephens, M. 2012. Auwahi wind farm breaks ground. May 10. Maui Weekly, http://www.mauiweekly.com/page/content.detail/id/509765/Auwahi-Wind-Farm-Breaks-Ground.html?nav = 13.

Stiver, S.J., E.T. Rinkes, and D.E. Naugle. 2010. Sage Grouse habitat assessment framework. Unpublished report. US Bureau of Land Management, Boise, Idaho.

Stokstad, E. 2005. What's wrong with the Endangered Species Act? Science 309:2150–2152.

Strayer, D.L., and D. Dudgeon. 2010. Freshwater biodiversity conservation: recent progress and future challenges. Journal of the North American Benthological Society 29:344–358.

Suring, L.H., M.M. Rowland, and M.J. Wisdom. 2005. Identifying species of conservation concern. Pages 150–162 in M.J. Wisdom, M.M. Rowland, and L.L. Suring (editors). Habitat threats in the sagebrush ecosystem: methods of regional assessment and applications in the Great Basin. Alliance Communications Group, Lawrence, Kansas.

Susskind, L.E., A.E. Camacho, and T. Schenk. 2010. Collaborative planning and adaptive management in Glen Canyon: a cautionary tale. Columbia Journal of Environmental Law 35:2–53.

Taylor, C.A., M.L. Warren, J.F. Fitzpatrick, H.H. Hobbs, R.F. Jezerinac, W.L. Pflieger, and H.W. Robison. 1996. Conservation status of crayfishes of the United States and Canada. Fisheries 21:25–38.

Templeton, S.R., C.F. Dumas, and W.T. Sessions 2008. Estimation and analysis of expenses of design-bid-build projects for stream mitigation in North Carolina (Research Report RR08–01). Clemson University Department of Applied Economics and Statistics, Clemson, South Carolina.

Ten Kate, K., J. Bishop, and R. Bayon 2004. Biodiversity offsets: views, experience, and the business case. IUCN and Insight Investment, Gland, Switzerland.

Theobald, D.M., T. Spies, J. Kline, B. Maxwell, N.T. Hobbs, and V.H. Dale. 2005. Ecological support for rural land-use planning. Ecological Applications 15:1906–1914.

Thomas, L., S.T. Buckland, E.A. Rexstad, J.L. Laake, S. Strindberg, S.L. Hedley, J.R.B. Bishop, T.A. Marques, and K.P. Burnham. 2010. Distance software: Design and analysis of distance sampling surveys for estimating population size. Journal of Applied Ecology 47:5–14.

Thuiller, W., C.H. Albert, A. Dubuis, C. Randin, and A. Guisan. 2010. Variation in habitat suitability does not always relate to variation in species' plant functional traits. Biology Letters 6:120–123.

Tracy, C.R. 2006. Translocation long-term monitoring, tortoise density evaluation, and establishment of new LSTSS. Clark County, Nevada, http://www.clarkcountynv.gov/Depts/dcp/Documents/Library/dcp reports/2006/Desert Tortoise Translocation Research UNR-289 Final Rpt 2006.pdf.

Tracy, C.R., R. Averill-Murray, W.I. Boarman, D. Delehanty, J. Heaton, E. McCoy, D. Morafka, K. Nussear, B. Hagerty, and P. Medica. 2004. Desert tortoise recovery plan assessment. US Fish and Wildlife Service, Reno, Nevada.

Trexler, M.C., D.J. Broekhoff, and L.H. Kosloff. 2006. A statistically driven approach to offset-based GHG additionality determinations: What can we learn? Sustainable Development Law & Policy 6:30–40

Turner, R.E., A.M. Redmond, and J.B. Zedler. 2001. Count it by acre or function: mitigation adds up to net loss of wetlands. National Wetlands Newsletter 23:5–6.

Urban, D.T., J.H. Ryan, and R. Mann. 1999. A lieu-lieu policy with serious shortcomings. National Wetlands Newsletter 21:9–11.

US Army 2009. Installation summaries from the FY2007 survey of threatened and endangered species on army lands. Army Environmental Division, Installation Services Directorate, Office of the Assistant Chief of Staff for Installation Management, Washington, DC.

US Army Environmental Command 2010. Army compatible use buffer program FY. US Army, http://aec.army.mil/usaec/acub/docs_acub/eoys-fy10.pdf.

USDA (US Department of Agriculture). 2008. Who owns America's forests? Forest ownership patterns and family forest highlights from the national woodland owner survey. Information Report NRS-INF-06–08. US Department of Agriculture, Northern Research Station, Newtown Square, Pennsylvania.

USFWS (US Fish and Wildlife Service). 1980a. Habitat evaluation procedure handbook. Division of Ecological Services, US Fish and Wildlife Service, US Department of the Interior, Washington, DC.

———. 1980b. Listing as threatened with critical habitat for the beaver dam slope population of the desert tortoise in Utah. Federal Register 45:55654–55666.

———. 1989. Endangered and threatened wildlife and plants; emergency determination of endangered status for the Mojave population of the desert tortoise. Federal Register 54:32326–32331.

———. 1990. Endangered and threatened wildlife and plants; determination of threatened status for the Mojave population of the desert tortoise Federal Register 55:12178–12191.

———. 2002. Candidate Conservation Agreement with Assurances for the robust redhorse, *Moxostoma robustum*, Ocmulgee River, Georgia. Agreement #1448–40181–01-K-005. US Fish and Wildlife Service, http://www.robustredhorse.com/f/ccaa2002.pdf.

———. 2003a. Draft handbook for Candidate Conservation Agreements with Assurances and enhancement of survival permit processing. Federal Register 68:51029–51030.

———. 2003b. Guidance for the establishment, use, and operation of conservation banks. Federal Register 68:24753.

———. 2004. The Endangered Species Act of 1973, as amended through the 108th Congress. US Fish and Wildlife Service, http://www.fws.gov/endangered/esa-library/pdf/ESAall.pdf.

———. 2006. ESA basics: 30 years of protecting endangered species. Department of Interior, http://www.fws.gov/wafwo/pdf/ESABASICS_050806.pdf.

———. 2008. Endangered and threatened wildlife and plants; recovery crediting guidance. Federal Register 73:44761.

———. 2009a. Candidate conservation agreement for the gopther tortoise (*Gopherus polyphemus*)—eastern population. http://www.fws.gov/southeast/candidateconservation/PDF/CCA_GopherTortoise.pdf.

———. 2009b. Guidelines for the establishment, management, and operation of gopher tortoise conservation banks. US Fish and Wildlife Service, http://www.fws.gov/mississippiES/pdf/USFWSGopherTortoiseBankGuidance_27Jan2009.pdf.

———. 2010a. Endangered and threatened wildlife and plants; 12-month finding for petitions to list the Greater Sage Grouse as threatened or endangered; proposed rule. Federal Register 75:13910–13958.

———. 2010b. Revised 12-month finding to list the upper Missouri River distinct population segment of Arctic grayling as endangered or threatened. Federal Register 75:54708–54753.

———. 2011a. Candidate species: Section 4 of the Endangered Species Act. US Fish and Wildlife Service, http://www.fws.gov/endangered/esa-library/pdf/candidate_species.pdf.

———. 2011b. Critical habitat: What is it? US Fish and Wildlife Service, http://www.fws.gov/endangered/esa-library/pdf/critical_habitat.pdf.

———. 2011c. Endangered and threatened wildlife and plants; 12-month finding on a petition to list the gopher tortoise as threatened in the eastern portion of its range. Federal Register 76:45130–45162.

———. 2011d. Improving ESA implementation. US Fish & Wildlife Service, http://www.fws.gov/endangered/improving_ESA/listing_workplan.html.

———. 2011e. Revised recovery plan for the Mojave population of the desert tortoise (*Gopherus agassizii*). US Fish and Wildlife Service, http://www.fws.gov/nevada/desert_tortoise/documents/recovery_plan/rrp for the mojave desert tortoise—may 2011.pdf.

———. 2011f. Texas conservation plan for the dunes sagebrush lizard (*Sceloporus arenicolus*). US Fish and Wildlife Service, http://www.fws.gov/southwest/es/documents/r2es/tx_cons_plan_dsl_20110927.pdf.

———. 2012a. Endangered and threatened wildlife and plants; expanding incentives for voluntary conservation actions under the Endangered Species Act. Federal Register 77:15352–15354.

———. 2012b. Notice of intent to sue regarding obey crayfish (*Cambarus obeyensis*). US Fish and Wildlife Service, http://www.fws.gov/southeast/candidateconservation/pdf/IntenttoSue_ObeyCrayfish.pdf.

———. 2012c. Species reports: listings and occurrences for California. US Fish and Wildlife Service, http://ecos.fws.gov/tess_public/pub/stateListingAndOccurrenceIndividual.jsp?state=CA.

———. 2012d. Who's on the lek: a guide to players. Primer #2. Greater Sage Grouse conservation primer series. US Fish and Wildlife Service, http://www.fws.gov/mountain-prairie/species/birds/sagegrouse/Primer2SGWhoOnTheLek.pdf.

———. 2013a. ESA basics: 40 years of conserving endangered species. US Fish and Wildlife Service, http://www.fws.gov/endangered/esa-library/pdf/ESA_basics.pdf.

———. 2013b. Greater Sage Grouse (*Centrocercus urophasianus*) conservation objectives: final report. US Fish and Wildlife Service, Denver, Colorado.

———. 2013c. Summary of listed species listed populations and recovery plans. US Fish and Wildlife Service, http://ecos.fws.gov/tess_public/pub/boxScore.jsp.

———. 2013d. US Fish and Wildlife Service Federal Register documents. US Fish and Wildlife Service, http://www.fws.gov/policy/frsystem/default.cfm.

———. 2014a. US Fish and Wildlife Service delisting report. http://ecos.fws.gov/tess_public/pub/delistingReport.jsp

———. 2014b. Endangered and threatened wildlife and plants; determination of threatened status for the Lesser Prairie-Chicken. Federal Register 79:19974–20071.

USFWS (US Fish and Wildlife Service), and NMFS (National Marine Fisheries Service). 1996. Habitat conservation planning and incidental take permit processing handbook. US Department of the Interior and US Department of Commerce, Washington, DC.

USFWS (US Fish and Wildlife Service), and NMFS (National Marine Fisheries Service). 1998. Section 7 consultation handbook: procedures for conducting consultation and conference activities under the Endangered Species Act (final). US Department of the Interior and US Department of Commerce, Washington, DC.

———. 1999. Announcement of final policy for Candidate Conservation Agreements with Assurances. Federal Register 64:32726.

USFWS (US Fish and Wildlife Service), USDA (US Department of Agriculture), USDOD (US Department of Defense), and BLM (Bureau of Land Management). 2008. Environmental assessment to implement a desert tortoise recovery plan task: reduce common raven predation on the desert tortoise. US Fish and Wildlife Service, US Department of Agriculture, US Department of Defense, and US Bureau of Land Management, Ventura, CA.

Verbeke, W. 2001. The emerging role of traceability and information in demand-oriented livestock production. Outlook on Agriculture 30:249–255.

Walker, B. L., D. E. Naugle, and K. E. Doherty. 2007. Greater Sage-Grouse population response to energy development and habitat loss. Journal of Wildlife Management 71:2644–2654.

WGA (Western Governors Association). 2011. Inventory of state and local government's conservation initiatives for Sage Grouse. Western Governor's Wildlife Council Report to Governors, http://www.westgov.org/reports.

WGFD (Wyoming Game and Fish Department). 2009. Recommendations for development of oil and gas resources within important wildlife habitats, version 2.0. Wyoming Game and Fish Department, Cheyenne, Wyoming.

Wilcox, C., and C. J. Donlan. 2007. Compensatory mitigation as a solution to fisheries bycatch-biodiversity conservation conflicts. Frontiers in Ecology and Environment 5:325–331.

Wilhere, G. 2009. Three paradoxes of Habitat Conservation Plans. Environmental Management 44:1089–1098.

Wilkinson, J. 2009. In-lieu fee mitigation: Coming into compliance with the new compensatory mitigation rule. Wetlands Ecology and Management 17:53–70.

Willamette Partnership 2011. Measuring up: synchronizing biodiversity measurement systems for markets and other incentive programs. Willamette Partnership, http://willamettepartnership.org/measuring-up/.

Williams, C.E., R.D. Bivens, and B.D. Carter 2006. A status survey of the obey crayfish (*Cambarus obeyensis*). Tennessee Wildlife Resources Agency, http://www.twra4streams.org/obeyensis_report_final.pdf.

Williams, J.D., M.L. Warren, K.S. Cummings, J.L. Harris, and R.J. Neves. 1993. Conservation status of freshwater mussels of the United States and Canada. Fisheries 18:6–22.

Wisdom, M.J., C.W. Meinke, S.T. Knick, and M.A. Schroeder. 2011. Factors associated with extirpation of Sage-Grouse. Pages 451–472 in S.T. Knick, and J.W. Connelly (editors). Greater Sage-Grouse: ecology and conservation of a landscape species and its habitats. Studies in Avian Biology (vol. 38). University of California Press, Berkeley.

Wohl, E. 2005. Compromised rivers: Understanding historical human impacts on rivers in the context of restoration. Ecology and Society 10:2.

Wolfe, D.W., K. Brian Hays, S.L. Farrell, and S. Baggett. 2012. Regional credit market for species conservation: Developing the Fort Hood recovery credit system. Wildlife Society Bulletin 36:423–431.

Womack, K. 2008. Factors affecting landowner participation in the candidate conservation agreements with assurances program. Master's thesis, Utah State University, Logan.

Womble, P., and J.K. Doyle. 2012. The geography of trading ecosystem services: a case study of wetland and stream compensatory mitigation markets. Harvard Environmental Law Review 36:229–296.

Woody, T. 2012. Sierra Club, NRDC sue Feds to stop big California solar power project. March 27, Forbes Magazine, http://www.forbes.com/sites/toddwoody/2012/03/27/sierra-club-nrdc-sue-feds-to-stop-big-california-solar-power-project/.

World Bank. 2011. State and trends of the carbon market 2011. World Bank, Washington, DC.

Wright, J.B., and A. Anella. 2007. Saving the ranch: fresh eyes on taxes, development, and conservation easements. Rangelands 29:13–20.

Young, T.F., and S. Sanzone, editors. 2002. A framework for assessing and reporting on ecological condition. Science Advisory Board report no. EPA-SAB-EPEC-02–009. US Environmental Protection Agency, Washington, DC.

Zhang, D., and S.R. Mehmood. 2002. Safe harbor for the Red-Cockaded Woodpecker: private forest landowners share their views. Journal of Forestry 100:24–29.

Zimmerman, L.C., M.P. O'Connor, S.J. Bulova, J.R. Spotila, S.J. Kemp, and C.J. Salice. 1994. Thermal ecology of desert tortoises in the eastern Mojave

Desert: seasonal patterns of operative and body temperatures, and microhabitat utilization. Herpetological Monographs 8:45–59.
Zylstra, E.R., R.J. Steidl, and D.E. Swann. 2010. Evaluating survey methods for monitoring a rare vertebrate, the Sonoran desert tortoise. Journal of Wildlife Management 74:1311–1318.

Index

abiotic conditions, 98–99
adaptive management, 77, 79, 95, 101, 161, 186, 198, 204, 212, 214, 216–217
additionality, 215, 219, 223–224
Advance Notice of Proposed Rulemaking, 8, 74, 213, 229
Alabama, 64, 190, 193, 211–212
American Forest Foundation, 188, 191
Arctic grayling *(Thymallus arcticus)*, 154–155, 160, 162, 165
Arizona, 19
Artemisia spp., 168
assessment methodologies
  Biobanking Assessment Methodology, 99
  Oregon Rapid Wetlands Assessment Protocol, 100
  Sage-Grouse Habitat Assessment Framework, 173
auctions, 11, 131, 135, 138–140
Australia, 12, 99, 227
avoidance, 14, 16, 19, 21–22, 39, 50, 79, 89–91, 93, 156, 167, 175, 178, 180–182, 185

Bald Eagle *(Haliaeetus leucocephalus)*, 27
baseline conditions, 100, 103, 107, 123, 125, 197, 199, 202–203, 210, 214–215
biodiversity offsets, 16, 87, 142, 145, 182–186; *see also* compensatory mitigation, 14–17, 19–21, 23, 25, 42, 79, 90–91, 155–156, 168, 175, 182, 215
Black-capped Vireo *(Vireo atricapilla)*, 108–109
Blackburn's sphinx moth *(Manduca blackburni)*, 15
Bobwhite Quail *(Colinus virginianus)*, 67
Brightsource Energy, 32–34
broker, 117, 119–120, 122–126, 128, 135, 144, 155, 191, 195, 198–199, 201, 218
Bureau of Indian Affairs, 173
Bureau of Land Management, 29, 31, 33–35, 38, 40, 42, 164, 172–174, 178, 180–181, 186
Bureau of Reclamation, 153

California, 18, 25, 29, 32–34, 37, 46, 156, 165
California gnatcatcher *(Polioptila californica)*, 18
Camp Lejeune, 45–46, 48
Camp Pendleton, 46, 48
Candidate Conservation Agreements
  Arctic Grayling CCAA, 154–155, 160, 165
Candidate Conservation Agreements with Assurances (CCAAs), 7, 75, 77–80, 89–90, 92–93, 151–155, 157, 159–162, 165
  Robust Redhorse CCAA, 152–153, 159, 162

Candidate Conservation Agreements with Assurances (CCAAs) *(continued)*
  Southern Idaho Ground Squirrel CCAA, 89
carbon markets, 119, 132, 142–143, 158, 223
categorical exclusion (Endangered Species Act), 20
Chamberlain's dwarf salamander *(Eurycea chamberlaini)*, 165
Chattahoochee County, 209
Clark County, 27–28, 31–32, 37–38
Colinus virginianus, 67
Colorado, 10, 52–55, 58–59, 106, 163, 176–177
Colorado Cattlemen's Association, 10, 52–53
Colorado Division of Wildlife, 59
compensatory mitigation, 14–17, 19–21, 23, 25, 42, 79, 90–91, 155–156, 168, 175, 182, 215; *see also* biodiversity offsets, 16, 87, 142, 145, 182–186
conservation banking, 12, 23–24, 77, 80, 82–84, 119, 129, 132, 134, 155–156, 158, 185, 188, 191–192, 212, 226
conservation easement, 15, 19, 22, 50, 53, 61, 64, 66, 68, 82, 84, 117, 119–120, 142, 174, 179, 195–196, 201–202, 222, 226–227
conservation-reliant species, 6, 74, 220
consultation (Endangered Species Act), 18–19, 39, 47–48, 76, 78, 85–88, 113, 151, 153, 177, 182, 211, 225
counterfactual, 223–224
coyotes *(Canis latrans)*, 200
currency (biodiversity credits), 117, 157, 184–185, 192, 198

Defenders of Wildlife, 11–12, 173, 187
delisting (Endangered Species Act), 4
demography, 63, 91, 101, 103, 108–109, 157, 186, 223
Department of Agriculture, 62, 67, 95, 173, 194, 211, 225
Department of Defense
  US Army, 16, 40, 132, 153, 156, 160, 162, 193, 202, 210, 215–218, 226
  US Army Corp of Engineers, 160, 162, 202
  US Marine Corps, 10, 43–44, 46, 48–50, 226
  US Navy, 47
Department of Energy, 35, 38, 42, 175
desert tortoise *(Gopherus agassizii)*, 6, 10, 26–35
disease, 66, 99, 164, 217
disincentives, 110, 191
Dunes Sagebrush Lizard *(Sceloporus arenicolus)*, 92

electricity generation, 33, 36–37
elk *(Cervus canadensis)*, 58
emissions (greenhouse gases), 40, 137, 158
encroachment, 45, 174
Endangered Species Act (ESA), 3–13, 15–18, 20–21, 28, 31, 37, 39–41, 44–51, 54–56, 74–75, 77–78, 80–81, 86, 88, 91, 93, 105–108, 116, 119, 121, 127, 129–130, 151, 154, 158–159, 163, 166, 168–170, 172–174, 177, 181, 183, 190–193, 199–200, 212, 214–215, 217, 220–221, 223–226, 228
endowment, 23, 64, 124, 126
energy development, 7, 10, 12, 15, 18, 26, 32–37, 39, 41–42, 92, 143, 152, 164, 167–168, 170, 172–173, 175–183, 185–186, 220–221
environmental compliance, 36, 38–42, 48, 57, 126, 133, 137–139, 143, 180, 221
ethics, 53, 60, 68, 111, 183
European Union Emissions Trading Scheme, 137
extinction, 3–4, 15, 28, 62, 149, 165, 224–225

farmers, 52, 54–56, 58, 60, 145, 170, 226
fisheries, 28, 144, 156
flathead catfish *(Pylodictis olivaris)*, 152
Florida, 64, 189–190, 193, 211–212
Food and Agricultural Organization (FAO), 58–59
forests, 45, 61–64, 66–69, 107, 118, 189–191, 194, 210
Fort Benning (US Army), 210
fungibility, 137–139

General Accountability Office, 4, 28, 45, 106
Geographic information Systems (GIS), 206
Georgia, 122, 127, 152, 190, 193, 209, 211–212
Golden-cheeked Warbler *(Dendroica chrysoparia)*, 108–109
gopher tortoise *(Gopherus polyphemus)*, 9, 11–13, 64–65, 67–68, 115–120, 122, 124, 126–130, 188–206, 209–217
Great Basin pyrgs, 164

Great Basin springsnails *(Pyrgulopsis spp.)*, 165
Greater Sage-Grouse *(Centrocercus urophasianus)*, 6, 9, 12–13, 55, 167–183, 185–187
guidance (Endangered Species Act), 8, 17, 23, 82–85, 89, 91, 100, 152, 158, 173–174, 176, 182, 211–213, 216, 218, 226

Habitat Conservation Plans (HCPs), 14–15, 18, 20–23, 25, 28, 31, 39, 75, 83, 92–93
habitat fragmentation, 99, 103, 143, 150, 161, 163, 167, 172, 176, 200, 202, 206, 209
hardwoods, 45, 207, 210
Hawaiian Goose *(Branta sandvicensis)*, 15
Hawaiian hoary bat *(Lasiurus cinereus semotus)*, 15
Hawaiian Petrel *(Pterodroma sandwichensis)*, 15
human-centered design, 11, 113, 219, 222, 227
hydroelectric, 17, 19, 152–153, 159

Idaho, 89
IDEO, 113
incentives, 3–9, 11, 13, 15, 36, 41–43, 47–54, 57, 61–63, 66–69, 74–75, 85, 94–97, 101, 104–107, 109–111, 114, 120, 127, 130, 139, 143, 149, 151, 158, 165, 169–170, 173, 177, 183, 185–187, 191, 194–196, 211, 213–214, 216–217, 219–225, 227, 229
Indiana, 106
Indiana bat *(Myotis sodalis)*, 18–19
innovation, 42, 55, 60, 113–114, 142, 193, 222
invasive species, 67, 92, 99, 117, 123, 128, 159, 168, 172, 175, 189, 194, 200–202, 208–209
Ivanpah Solar Electric Generating Station, 29, 32–34

landowner attitudes, 107, 109–110, 117, 216
landowner autonomy, 114, 195, 222
lawsuits, 4–5, 12–13, 36–37
leks, 170, 172, 176–178
Lesser Prairie-Chicken *(Tympanuchus pallidicinctus)*, 9, 89, 224, 227–228
liability, 5, 19, 57, 106, 142, 191, 212, 217
litigation, 4, 52, 54, 60, 119, 130, 168
livestock, 19, 53, 174
loblolly pine *(Pinus taeda)*, 64–65, 207, 210
Longleaf Alliance, 64, 67, 188, 191, 194
longleaf pine *(Pinus palustris)*, 64–65, 67, 112, 189–191, 194, 205, 207, 209–210, 212, 214
Louisiana, 190

market models
  demand, 9–10, 54, 59, 85, 119, 121, 126, 129, 132, 137, 143, 157–158, 161, 164–165, 182–183, 185–188, 191–193, 215–216, 219–222, 226–227
  supply, 9–10, 54, 59, 150, 175, 182–183, 185, 188, 191–192, 194–195, 198, 222, 226–227
  transactional infrastructure, 9, 11, 59, 182–184, 188, 191, 195, 227
Markit, 11, 123, 125, 138, 140
metrics, 56, 59, 90, 94–98, 101–103, 116, 173, 184–185, 198, 211, 213–214, 216–218, 223
military readiness, 7, 10, 43–51, 188, 193, 220–221
minimization, 14–17, 19, 21–23, 25, 79, 89–91, 93, 156, 167, 175, 178, 181, 185
Mission Markets, 11, 141, 143–144
Mississippi, 67, 175, 190
Missouri, 18
mitigation, 10–12, 14–23, 25–26, 30–32, 35, 39–40, 42, 58–59, 79, 83, 85, 89–93, 106, 108, 115–116, 119, 121, 127, 129–130, 132, 142, 149, 151, 155–158, 167–169, 172–175, 177, 180–187, 191–193, 209, 211–215, 217–219, 221, 226–227
mitigation hierarchy, 10, 14, 16–17, 58, 91, 168, 182, 185
mitigation ratio, 40, 91, 192
Mojave Desert, 10, 28, 30, 33–35, 42
Montana, 154, 176
Montana Fish, Wildlife and Parks, 154
Multiple Species Habitat Conservation Plans (MSHCPs), 31

National Environmental Policy Act (NEPA), 20, 183
National Marine Fisheries Service (NMFS), 4, 7, 14–17, 19–22, 25, 39–40, 44, 75, 78, 86–88, 92

Natural Resources Conservation Service (NRCS), 67, 154, 173–174, 181, 194, 211
Nature Conservancy, 160
net conservation benefit, 9, 13, 89, 116, 159, 168, 187, 192, 211, 213–217, 219, 223–224
net present value, 123–124, 126–128
Nevada, 27–28, 165, 177
New England cottontail rabbit *(Sylvilagus transitionalis)*, 92
New Zealand, 12
North Carolina, 45, 47
North Dakota, 176

Obey crayfish *(Cambarus obeyensis)*, 164–165
Ocmulgee River, 152
Oconee River, 152–153
Ohio, 19
oil and gas development, 7, 92, 175–178, 221
Oklahoma, 62
Oregon, 100, 174–175, 177, 179–182

Pennsylvania, 138
philanthropy, 119, 121, 192
platforms (electronic markets), 11, 116, 121, 131–132, 134–135, 137–140, 142–145, 162, 184, 219, 227
power purchase agreement (PPA), 38–39
prescribed burning, 19, 46, 64–65, 67, 98, 117, 123, 128, 202, 204, 207, 214

ranchers, 10, 52–56, 58, 60, 170
Recovery Crediting System (RCS), 82, 84–85, 91
red fire ant *(Solenopsis invicta)*, 200
Red-Cockaded Woodpecker *(Picoides borealis)*, 45–46, 49, 107, 210
registry, 11, 59, 123, 125, 131–140, 144
regulatory assurances, 7–8, 21, 49, 51, 56–57, 74–75, 77, 79–80, 83–84, 88–89, 106–107, 109–111, 116, 119–121, 151, 174, 185, 192, 199, 201–202, 212, 224, 226
regulatory predictability, 7, 9, 13, 43, 50–51, 73, 75, 78, 81, 86, 116, 119–121, 151, 165, 192–193, 200, 212–213, 215–217, 219–221, 228
renewable energy, 10, 26, 32, 35–37, 39, 41, 143, 175–176, 180–181, 183, 186, 221, 225
Rio Grande cutthroat trout *(Oncorhynchus clarkii virginalis)*, 163, 165
riparian areas, 62, 150, 156–157, 160, 162, 165
rivers, 151–152, 160, 190, 200
roads, 99, 176, 200, 202
robust redhorse *(Moxostoma robustum)*, 152–153, 159, 162

salmon, 12, 15, 28, 154
Section 7 (Endangered Species Act), 14, 16–19, 21–22, 39–40, 73, 77–80, 83–88, 151, 153, 225
Section 10 (Endangered Species Act), 14, 16, 18–23, 31, 39–40, 73, 78–79, 81, 89, 91–93, 225
slash pine *(Pinus elliottii)*, 64, 67, 207
solar power, 7, 10, 29, 32–42, 180, 221, 225
South Carolina, 18–19, 107, 152, 190
South Dakota, 176
steelhead trout *(Oncorhynchus mykiss)*, 12
stewardship, 4, 7, 9, 13, 52–55, 57, 59, 61–64, 66–68, 99, 122–123, 125–128, 163, 166, 185, 194, 220
SunEdison, 10

technology, 8, 11, 37, 132, 138, 141–142
Texas, 18–19, 45, 62, 92, 106, 108–109, 189
traceability, 121, 133–134
transaction platforms, 11, 121, 135, 137–139, 141–142
translocation (species), 21, 32–34, 214, 216

urbanization, 58, 172
Utah, 106, 165, 176

value transfer mechanism, 9
Virginia, 11, 19, 45, 189

Washington, 161, 172
Western Association of Fish and Wildlife Agencies, 173–174
wetlands, 16, 22–23, 97, 100–101, 132, 142, 149, 156–159, 182, 226–227
wildfire, 46, 66, 172
Willamette Partnership, 11, 95, 100, 123
wind power, 7, 10, 15, 18–19, 92, 99, 175–176, 178–180
World Resources Institute, 12, 188, 191
Wyoming, 176–179, 181–182, 187